Grammar Practice
for Intermediate Students

with key

Sheila Dignen and Brigit Viney
with Elaine Walker and
Steve Elsworth

with CD-ROM

PEARSON
Longman

Contents

GRAMMAR

Sentence and text structure

Statements and questions

-ing forms and infinitives

The passive

Reported speech

Relative clauses

Conditionals

Linking words and structures

VOCABULARY

Prepositions

Words that go together

Word formation

Nouns and determiners

1 Singular and plural nouns

- Nouns can be countable (*one book, two tables*) or uncountable (*some bread, some information*).
- Countable nouns can be singular or plural. To make a noun plural, we usually add *-s* or *-es*: *car* → *car**s**   *bus* → *bus**es***
- Some plural nouns are irregular: *child* → *children   foot* → *feet   man* → *men   mouse* → *mice   person* → *people   tooth* → *teeth   woman* → *women*
- These nouns have the same form in the singular and plural: *aircraft* → *aircraft   deer* → *deer   fish* → *fish   sheep* → *sheep*
- Some nouns end in *-s* in both the singular and plural: *crossroads* → *crossroads   means* → *means   series* → *series   species* → *species*
- Some nouns end in *-s*, but are singular/uncountable and take a singular verb: *athletics, gymnastics, maths, news, physics: Math**s is** my best subject.*
- Some nouns are always plural and take a plural verb: *belongings, clothes, goods, surroundings: Her **clothes are** always fashionable.*
- These nouns refer to one thing made of two similar parts and take a plural verb: *glasses, jeans, scissors, shorts, tights, trousers: These **trousers are** a bit tight.* To refer to a single item, we use *a pair of*: ***a pair of** jeans*
- These nouns refer to a group of people: *army, audience, class, family, government, group, public, staff, team.* We can use the singular form of the noun with a singular verb if we see them as a single unit, or with a plural verb to refer to members of the group: *My family **lives** (or **live**) in Prague.*

▶▶ **See Appendix 1: Spelling rules for plural nouns, page 169.**

PRACTICE

1a   Complete the sentences. Use the plural of the nouns in brackets.

0 Could you get the ....*knives*.......... and ....*forks*.......... , please? (knife, fork)

1 The first two .... of books were about famous ....
and the next two were about famous .... (series, woman, man)

2 .... in this region eat .... and ....
(wolf, deer, sheep)

3 Different .... prefer different .... of communication.
(person, means)

4 The largest of our .... is now very rare and many
other .... of butterfly are also becoming rarer. (butterfly, species)

5 That museum has a wonderful collection of .... and old
.... (photo, aircraft)

6 There are some nice .... for .... in this catalogue.
(toy, child)

1b **Write sentences. Use the present simple of *be*.**

o all her clothes / black   *All her clothes are black.* ....

1 my sunglasses / very good   ....

2 all her belongings / in that bag   ....

3 tonight's audience / very small   ....

4 this pair of jeans / my favourite   ....

5 the news / very worrying   ....

6 the electrical goods here / quite cheap   ....

7 biology / a fascinating subject   ....

8 these scissors / sharp?   ....

1c **Complete the sentences. Use the present simple of the verbs in brackets. There may be more than one possible answer.**

o My running group .... *trains* .... on Wednesdays. (train)

1 The staff at the sports centre .... very hard. (work)

2 The government .... to encourage more sport. (want)

3 Athletics .... very popular in Britain. (be)

4 My family .... a lot of sport. (do)

5 My brother's football team usually .... very well. (play)

6 Their colours are red and white. Their shirts are white and their shorts .... red. (be)

7 They're just a local team. The public .... to watch them. (not pay)

8 My class at college .... some excellent athletes. (have)

1d **Circle the correct answer.**

o The surroundings *was* / (*were*) beautiful and the food was delicious.

1 How much *does this* / *do these* pair of tights cost?

2 Are you looking for your black jeans? *It's* / *They're* on your bed.

3 I'm so tired! My feet *hurt* / *hurts*.

4 Physics *is* / *are* the scientific study of physical objects and substances, and natural forces such as light and heat.

5 I didn't like his glasses. *It was* / *They were* too big.

6 This programme's part of a series. Have you seen the others in *it* / *them*?

7 He hates Maths. He can't understand *it* / *them*.

8 I bought some nice clothes yesterday. *It wasn't* / *They weren't* expensive.

2 Countable and uncountable nouns

- Most common nouns are countable. They have a singular and plural form (e.g. *box → boxes*). We can use singular countable nouns with *a/an*: *a box*
- Uncountable nouns often refer to things we think of as a single mass, e.g. substances, liquids and gases, and abstract ideas. They don't have a plural form and we can't use them with *a/an*. They are followed by a singular verb: *I like **cheese**. I need **some information**.   **Accommodation is** expensive.*
- These are some common uncountable nouns: *accommodation, advice, furniture, homework, information, luggage, money, news, progress, traffic, travel, work.*
- We can use countable noun + *of* to count uncountable nouns: *a piece of chocolate/ cake/cheese   a piece of advice/information/evidence   a slice of bread   a sheet/ piece of paper   a bottle of water   a carton of juice   a can of cola   a cup of coffee   a litre of water   a kilo of sugar   500 grams of cheese   two metres of cable*
- Some nouns can be countable or uncountable, with a change in meaning. The countable noun usually refers to one particular object or amount. The uncountable noun usually refers to something in general.

Countable noun	Uncountable noun
a paper (= a newspaper)	paper (= the substance)
a glass (= for drinking from)	glass (= the substance)
a chicken (= the animal)	chicken (= the meat)
a coffee/a tea (= one cup of it)	coffee/tea (= the drink in general)
an ice cream (= an amount you buy)	ice cream (= in general)
a hair (= one single piece of it)	hair (= all the hair on your head)
a noise (= one particular noise)	noise (= in general)
a room (= one room in a building)	room (= space)

PRACTICE

2a Complete the table. Write *C* after the countable nouns and *U* after the uncountable nouns.

coin	*C*	bread		furniture	
money	*U*	electricity		cupboard	
suitcase		plastic		magazine	
luggage		machine		article	
advice		progress		news	
career		homework		weather	
office		college		accident	
information		project		storm	
piece		lecture		music	

2b **Complete the conversation. Use *a, an* or – .**

A: Can I help you?

B: Yes. I'm looking for (0) ....–..... accommodation in the centre of town. I'd like (1) .... quiet place. I don't like (2) .... noise. I'm staying in (3) .... guesthouse on (4) .... very noisy street at the moment. I hate (5) .... traffic, so I want to move.

A: You could try this guesthouse. It's on a very quiet road.

B: Oh, Russell House. I saw (6) .... advertisement for it in (7) .... brochure. It looks nice. Do they serve breakfast?

A: Yes. And you can make (8) .... tea and (9) .... coffee in your room. Would you like this brochure? It's got (10) .... information about all the guesthouses in the town.

B: Thank you very much.

2c **Complete the sentences. Use the words in the box.**

can carton cup grams kilos ~~litres~~ metres piece (x3) slices

0 We need three ....*litres*........ of paint for this room.

1 I'm going to have a .... of that chocolate cake.

2 There's a .... of milk in the fridge.

3 I usually have two .... of bread for breakfast.

4 Let me give you a .... of advice.

5 Could you get me a .... of cola from the shop?

6 I'd like 450 .... of cheese, please.

7 I've bought two .... of rice.

8 Would you like a .... of coffee?

9 How many .... of material do you need for your skirt?

10 She wrote something on a .... of paper.

2d **Circle the correct answer.**

A: What are you looking for?

B: (0) *A furniture /* (*Furniture*) for my room. I need a chair and a small table. There isn't (1) *a room / room* for a big one.

A: This one with the glass top is nice. I like (2) *a glass / glass* on tables.

A: Would you like (3) *an ice cream / ice cream* from the shop? They have some nice ones.

B: No, thanks. I don't like (4) *an ice cream / ice cream* very much. But could you get me (5) *a paper / paper*, please? I want to look at the job advertisements. I'm looking for a part-time job, you know. I need (6) *a money / money* for my trip.

A: I heard (7) *a strange / strange* noise next door. Did you hear it?

B: No. There's no one next door. It's just (8) *an empty / empty* room!

3 Quantifiers (*some, any,* etc.)

	+ uncountable noun	+ plural countable noun	+ plural countable/ uncountable noun
Affirmative sentences	(a) little, a bit of	(a) few, several	some, a lot/lots of, plenty of, enough, no
Negative sentences and questions	much	many	any, a lot/lots of, enough

- We use *some* in affirmative sentences and in requests or offers: *I've got **some** cheese.   Can I have **some** water, please?   Would you like **some** coffee?*

- We use *any* in negative sentences and questions: *I haven't got **any** money. Did you buy **any** apples?*

- We can use *no* instead of *not any*. We use *no* with an affirmative verb: *I **haven't got any** money. → I**'ve got no** money.   There **aren't any** chairs. → There **are no** chairs.*

- We use *much* and *many* in negative sentences and questions: *We haven't got **much** time.   How **many** people were there?*

- *A little* and *a few* have a positive meaning, like *some*: *Add **a little** salt and pepper. I've invited **a few** friends round for dinner.*

- *Little* and *few* have a negative meaning, like *not much* and *not many*: *We had very **little** time to get ready.   She's got very **few** friends.*

- *Plenty of* and *enough* mean 'as much as we need': *There's **plenty of** food.   Have we got **enough** sandwiches?*

- *Too much* and *too many* mean 'more than we need': *You added **too much** water. You bought **too many** eggs.*

P R A C T I C E

3a **Complete the conversation. Use *some, any* or *no*.**

A: Would you like a piece of cake or (0) .....*some*.... biscuits?

B: Oh – (1) .... cake, please.

A: And would you like (2) .... coffee or a glass of juice?

B: Could I have (3) .... orange juice, please?

A: Of course. Oh ... I'm sorry. We haven't got (4) .... juice, I'm afraid.

B: That's OK. Coffee will be fine. I meant to get a few cakes from the bakery, but they didn't have (5) .... nice ones. Sorry.

A: Don't worry! Oh ... there are (6) .... clean cups – they're all dirty! And I can't find (7) .... clean plates! I'll just wash (8) .... cups and plates and then we can sit in the living room. There's (9) .... room in the kitchen for us.

B: My hands are really dirty – I had to help a man in the street move his car. Have you got (10) .... soap?

A: Yes, by the sink. There's (11) .... nice soap in a yellow bottle, but I'm afraid there's (12) .... hot water. I used it all for my bath!

B: That's OK. Cold water's fine.

3b   Circle the correct answer.

    A: Have you got (0) (*much*)/ *many* work this week?

    B: Well, I've got (1) *a lot of* / *much* lectures, so I'm not going to make (2) *much* / *many* progress with my project.

    A: How (3) *much* / *many* time have you got for it?

    B: Two weeks.

    A: And how (4) *much* / *many* words do you have to write?

    B: Three thousand. I'm a bit worried because I can't find (5) *much* / *many* books about the European Union in the library.

    A: There are (6) *lots of* / *much* websites about it, aren't there?

    B: Yes, but I can't find (7) *much* / *many* information that is relevant.

    A: Why don't you ask George? He knows a lot about European politics. He helped my brother with his project last year. I know he borrowed (8) *a lot of* / *much* books from him.

    B: Really? That would be wonderful! Thanks!

3c   Complete the travel brochure. Use *few*, *a few*, *little* or *a little*.

Very (0) .... *few* .... people live on these small islands. In the summer, (1) .... tourists come to enjoy the peace and quiet, but very (2) .... people visit the islands in the winter. The islanders earn (3) .... money from tourism, but they earn more from farming and fishing.

Getting there is difficult: you have to go in a small plane and you can take very (4) .... luggage – just one small bag. But when you do you get there, it is an amazing experience. You are in a place which has (5) .... contact with the outside world: no televisions, Internet or mobile phones. There are no cars or buses – only (6) .... bikes. There are no cinemas or theatres, of course, but there are (7) .... cafés and restaurants.

3d   Circle the correct answer.

Our new house is in a small street, not far from the town centre. I haven't taken (0) *no* / (*any*) photos of the house yet, but I'll send you some soon. My room isn't very big, but there's (1) *enough* / *much* room for all my furniture.

Our part of town's lively, but there are (2) *too much* / *too many* cars. There's a nice park near us – it's got (3) *plenty of* / *too many* trees and a little lake. I spend (4) *several* / *a bit of* hours a week there. It's a beautiful place.

I'd love to come back and see you and everyone soon, but I haven't got (5) *too much* / *enough* money at the moment. With (6) *a bit of* / *much* luck and (7) *several* / *a lot of* hard work (!), I'll be there in December.

4 *all (of), most (of), some (of), no, none of*

People/Things in general	People/Things in a specific group
All plants need water.	**All/All of** her plants are healthy.
Most furniture is made in factories.	**Most of** my furniture is modern.
Some food is bad for you.	**Some of** the food we ate was nice.
No student likes failing exams.	**None of** the students in our college failed.

- We can use *all/most/some/none* + *of* + pronoun: ***Some of us*** *were hungry*.
- We can use *all* and *all of* to refer to people or things in a specific group. *All* is more common: ***All (of) these books*** *belong to me*.
- We can use *none of* + plural noun + singular or plural verb: ***None of the books is/are*** *expensive*.
- We can use *not* + *all*: ***Not all universities*** *teach medicine*.

PRACTICE

4a Circle the correct answer.

0 *Some* / *Some of* my friends go to my college.

1 He's busy *most* / *most of* the time.

2 I'm going to take *some* / *some of* my CDs with me.

3 *Most* / *Most of* families own a television.

4 I don't like these jackets. *No* / *None of* them fit me.

5 *Not all* / *None* sports centres have tennis courts.

6 *No* / *None of* team has ever broken their record.

4b Look at the information about students at a college and complete the sentences. Use *all*, *most of*, *some of* and *none of*.

0 ....*All*.... the students are aged 19–22.

1 .... the students come from Britain.

2 .... the students are married.

3 .... the students live at home.

4 .... the students work in the holidays.

5 .... the students are looking for part-time jobs.

6 .... them get money from their parents.

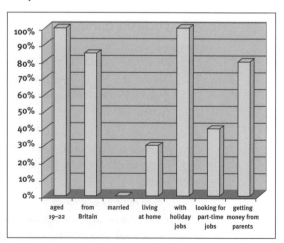

5 *each (of), every, each/every one (of)*

- We use *each* and *every* + singular noun to talk about the people or things in a group. They have similar meanings and often both are possible.
  - We prefer *each* when we think of the people or things in a group separately: *She read **each letter** carefully.*
  - We prefer *every* when we think of all the people or things in a group together: *I managed to answer **every question** in the exam.*
- We can use *each* (but not *every*) to talk about two people or things: *There were houses on **each** side of the river.* (Not ~~on every side~~)
- We can use *each of* + plural noun/pronoun: *She read **each of the letters** carefully. He gave a present to **each of us**.*
- We always use *every* + singular noun: *We go swimming **every day**.*
- We often use *each/every* + *one of* + plural noun/pronoun: *We lost **every one of our games** last season!   He gave a present to **each one of us**.*
- We can use *each* as a pronoun before a verb, after a verb and object, or after the verb *be*: *They **each got** a present.   They **got a present each**.   The paintings are **each** worth over £10,000.*

PRACTICE

5a **Complete the sentences. Use *each* or *every*. Sometimes both are possible.**

    0 I watch ....*every*....... series about crime that is on TV.

    1 I've watched .... episode in this series.

    2 .... episode is different.

    3 They .... tell a story about a crime.

    4 .... episode has some new characters in it.

    5 .... one of them is interesting and unusual.

5b **Circle the answer we prefer.**

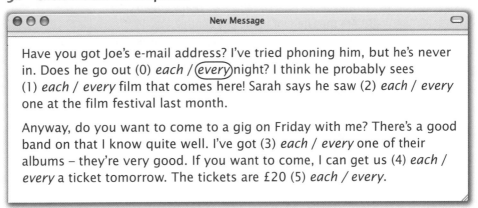

○ ○ ○   New Message   ▭

Have you got Joe's e-mail address? I've tried phoning him, but he's never in. Does he go out (0) *each / every* night? I think he probably sees (1) *each / every* film that comes here! Sarah says he saw (2) *each / every* one at the film festival last month.

Anyway, do you want to come to a gig on Friday with me? There's a good band on that I know quite well. I've got (3) *each / every* one of their albums – they're very good. If you want to come, I can get us (4) *each / every* a ticket tomorrow. The tickets are £20 (5) *each / every*.

6 *both (of), either (of), neither (of)*

- We use *both* + plural noun + plural verb and *either/neither* + singular noun + singular verb to talk about two people or things.
  - *Both* means 'one and the other': **Both films were** very good.
  - *Either* means 'one or the other': **Either jacket looks** nice with that skirt.
  - *Neither* means 'not one or the other': **Neither team was** happy with the result.
- We can say: **Both rooms/Both the rooms/Both of the rooms** are nice.
- Before a pronoun, we must use *both of*: **both of** them (Not ~~both them~~)
- We use *either/neither of* + plural noun/pronoun + singular or plural verb: **Neither of us has/have been** to America.
- We can use *both, either* and *neither* on their own: *I've got two watches, but **both** are broken.   They're **both** expensive.   I can't afford **either**.*

PRACTICE

6a **Complete the sentences. Use *both*, *either* or *neither*.**

0 ....*Both*........ leaders still hope to reach an agreement.

1 .... answer is correct, I'm afraid.

2 You can park on .... side of the street. There's plenty of space.

3 I called two hotels, but .... of them had any rooms.

4 The government received two reports, but they did not accept ....

5 .... the cars were badly damaged.

6 They're .... teachers. Jo teaches French and Tim teaches Biology.

7 You can use blue or green. .... colour is OK.

8 .... solution is perfect, but it's better than nothing.

6b **Complete the conversations. Use *both (of), either (of)* or *neither (of)*.**

A: Have you seen these two flats in the paper? They're (0) ....*both*........ really cheap.

B: Are they here or in the city centre?

A: (1) .... them is in the centre, but they're not far from it. You could live in (2) ....

B: Yes. I'll try to see (3) .... them today – then I can choose one of them.

A: You saw (4) .... those flats, didn't you? What did you think of them?

B: I did see them, but I didn't like (5) .... them. They were (6) .... on a noisy street and I hate noise. And (7) .... them got much light – the rooms were really depressing!

Check 1 Nouns and determiners

1 Circle the correct answer.

1 *Some / Some of* these buildings are really old.

2 Maths *has / have* always been an easy subject for me.

3 David didn't have many friends here, so *few / a few* people kept in touch with him when he moved to London.

4 The big black scissors *is / are* in the drawer on the left.

5 She always wears two or three rings on *each / every* hand.

6 He answered all the questions and he got *most / most of* them right.

7 Why don't you open the window and let in *a / some* fresh air?

8 Ask Tim or Simon. *Either / Neither* of them will help you. They know a lot about computers.

/ 8

2 Complete the conversations. Use the words in the boxes. You do not need all of them.

can a coffee coffee piece

A: Do you want to come with us? We're going to have (9) .... at the café down the road.

B: Yes, OK, thanks. I don't drink (10) .... , but I'll have a (11) .... of cakes. They have some lovely cakes there.

both either neither

A: Where do you want to sit? At the table at the back or by the window?

B: I don't mind. (12) .... table is fine.

A: Which cake are you going to have? The chocolate or the lemon?

B: I'm really hungry, so I'm going to have (13) .... of them!

/ 5

3 Complete the article. Use one word in each gap.

Have you ever thought of getting an aquarium and keeping fish? They are fascinating to watch and easy to look after.

You will need an aquarium which has plenty (14) .... space for the fish to swim freely in. It doesn't have to be very big, but it must have a large enough surface area of water for (15) .... of the fish to breathe.

It is a good idea to put a (16) .... water plants in the aquarium. They will produce oxygen. Put the aquarium in a place which has enough light so that the water plants will grow. Put some rocks in too so that the fish have places to hide. They live more happily when their surroundings (17) .... suitable.

Keep the water at the right temperature and change it regularly. Don't give the fish too (18) .... food. They only need (19) .... little.

Fish can get ill, like other animals. Check them (20) .... day and if you notice any signs of illness, take them to a vet.

/ 7

Total: / 20

Self-check

Wrong answers	Look again at	Try CD-ROM
2, 4, 17	Unit 1	Exercise 1
7, 9, 10, 11	Unit 2	Exercise 2
3, 14, 16, 18, 19	Unit 3	Exercise 3
1, 6, 15	Unit 4	Exercise 4
5, 20	Unit 5	Exercise 5
8, 12, 13	Unit 6	Exercise 6

Now do **Check 1**

Pronouns and possessives

7 Possessive 's, possessive *of*

- The possessive 's is normally used for people and animals, not for things.
- We add 's to singular nouns and plural nouns that don't end in -s: **Jane's** *phone* my **friend's** *house*   **Emma and Ben's** *mother*   the **children's** *clothes*
- We add an apostrophe (') to plural nouns that end in -s: *the* **boys'** *names*
- We can leave out the noun after 's when we are talking about where someone lives or works, or for the names of some shops: *We went back to* **Sam's**. (= Sam's house) *I'm going to the* **hairdresser's**.   *She's at the* **doctor's**.
- We use *of* for things and places: *a map* **of** *Britain*
- We always use *of* with these words: top, bottom, side, front, back, end, beginning: *the* **top of** *the hill*   *the* **beginning of** *the film*
- We sometimes use 's + *of* together: *a friend of* **Sarah's/my sister's**
- We can also use possessive pronouns with *of*: *a friend of* **mine/yours**
- We sometimes use noun + noun, especially with common nouns: *the* **door keys** *the* **kitchen window**   *a* **computer keyboard**

PRACTICE

7a **Complete the sentences. Use the words in brackets.**

0 ....*Some people's*....... hobbies are very expensive. (some people)

1 Is this .... bag or yours? (Fiona)

2 .... performance in the play was excellent. (Dan)

3 Did you see the .... basketball final? (men)

4 .... name is Indie. (the black horse)

5 .... clothes are much nicer than mine. (my sisters)

6 I love .... voice. (that singer)

7 Some of .... ideas are a bit old-fashioned. (my parents)

8 There are some great .... programmes on this channel. (children)

9 Did you like .... costumes? (the dancers)

10 Sometimes we can hear .... television through the wall. (our neighbours)

11 What's .... band called? (your friend)

12 .... food is in these packets. (the dogs)

7b **Complete the e-mail. Use the words in the box.**

> a very good baker   Emma   Matt and Luke   the butcher
> the chemist   the dentist   ~~the doctor~~

New Message

Sorry we didn't call you yesterday. We were really busy all day.
In the morning, Kate went to (0) ....*the doctor's*........... about her
stomach problems and I went to (1) ....
because one of my teeth was hurting. Kate had to go to
(2) .... to get some tablets. Then we had to do
some shopping for Matt and Luke's barbecue. We got some nice
sausages from (3) .... at the market and some
bread from (4) .... After that we went to
(5) .... to pick her up. Then we took the food
round to (6) .... and cooked it with them. We got
home very late.

7c **Re-write the sentences. Change the parts that are underlined.**

0 I saw <u>one of your friends</u> yesterday.   *I saw a friend of yours yesterday.*

1 I left <u>one of my T-shirts</u> at your house.   ....

2 I think he's <u>one of Nina's cousins</u>.   ....

3 It's <u>one of his ideas</u>.   ....

4 She's <u>one of Mark's friends</u>.   ....

5 We went to <u>one of their gigs</u>.   ....

6 I've read <u>one of his poems</u>.   ....

7d **Complete the sentences. Use the words in brackets and *of* if necessary.**

0 Last year I did a ....*computer course*............... at my local college.
   (computer / course)

1 There was a big computer centre at the ....
   (side / the main building)

2 At lunchtime, we used to eat together in the ....
   (college / cafeteria)

3 At the .... , we exchanged addresses.
   (end / the course)

4 I wrote them on the .... , but then I lost it.
   (back / an envelope)

5 Luckily, I had some people's .... (phone /
   numbers)

8 Reflexive pronouns

Object pronouns	me	you	him	her	it	us	them
Reflexive pronouns	myself	yourself yourselves	himself	herself	itself	ourselves	themselves

- We use reflexive pronouns for actions we do to ourselves, not to someone else. Compare: *I hurt **him**.* (= someone else)   *I hurt **myself**.* (Not *I hurt me.*)

- A reflexive pronoun can come after a verb or a preposition: *He cut **himself**. We introduced **ourselves**.   I bought a present for **myself**.*

- Some verbs are followed by a reflexive pronoun to form an idiom or expression: ***Help yourselves** to food.   **Behave yourself**!   Did you **enjoy yourself**?*

- We can use a reflexive pronoun to emphasise the noun before it: *We met the Queen **herself**!   Did you see the manager **himself**?*

- If the pronoun refers to the subject, it can come at the end of the sentence: *The President **himself** opened the conference.   The President opened the conference **himself**.*

⚠ Notice the difference between (*my*)*self* and *each other/one another*:
*Sam and Jess only care about **themselves**.* (= Sam → Sam, Jess → Jess)
*Sam and Jess care about **each other/one another**.* (= Sam → Jess, Jess → Sam)

P R A C T I C E

8a **Complete the sentences. Use reflexive pronouns.**

   0 How did you cut ....*yourself*........ ?

   1 Mr Blake introduced .... and then began the lecture.

   2 I felt very ashamed of ....

   3 Did you and Kate take all these photos .... ?

   4 The Queen .... planted this tree.

   5 I hope they'll behave .... at the restaurant.

   6 My mobile phone turns .... off after a few minutes.

8b **Circle the correct answer.**

Becky and I really enjoyed (0) *us* /(*ourselves*) at the party. There was some nice food that Kirsty had made (1) *her / herself*, but I didn't get much of it. Mel and Jenny ate most of it. They're so selfish! They only think about (2) *each other / themselves*! Adam and Scott were there, but they only talked to (3) *each other / themselves* all night. I talked to a nice girl called Tanya. I met (4) *her / herself* last year at another party. She told me a lot about (5) *her / herself*. I introduced her to Becky. I think they liked (6) *one another / themselves*.

9 (of/on) *my own, by myself*

- We use (*of*) *my own*, (*of*) *your own*, etc. to show that something belongs to someone and no one else: *Have you got **your own** phone?   I want a home **of my own**.*

- We can also use *my own, your own*, etc. to show that we do something ourselves: *They grow **their own** vegetables.* (= They grow them themselves.)   *I can find **my own** way home.*

- *On my own, on our own*, etc. and *by myself, by ourselves*, etc. mean 'alone, with no one else there, or no one else helping': *My grandmother lives **on her own/by herself**.   We spent two days there **on our own/by ourselves**.*

PRACTICE

9a **Complete the sentences. Use (*on*) *my own*, (*on*) *your own*, etc.**

  0 Did you design ....*your own*........ website?

  1 My sister and I make a lot of .... clothes.

  2 She's just moved into .... flat.

  3 Do you want to do it .... or do you want some help?

  4 One day, I'd like to have .... restaurant.

  5 My mother takes my brother to school because he isn't old enough to go ....

  6 Some people like living .... , but I'd hate it.

  7 I think she's unhappy because she spends too much time ....

  8 They've got .... car now.

  9 He has to cook .... meals.

  10 We walked home ....

9b **Complete the blog entry. Use *my/your own* or *by myself/yourself*, etc.**

For the first three nights, Jack and I camped (0) ....*by ourselves*........ . Jack's got (1) .... tent, but it isn't big enough for two people, so we had to borrow one from a friend.

On the first day, Jack went for a walk (2) .... and I went into town to do some shopping. I wanted to get some food and also get (3) .... torch. Jack had one, but it wasn't very good.

On Wednesday, we moved to a campsite. There were two other boys of (4) .... age there. They were travelling (5) .... too. In the evening, one of them played the guitar and sang for us. He and his friends have got (6) .... band in Glasgow and we're going to see them next month.

10 *something, anything,* etc.

People	somebody/ someone	anybody/ anyone	nobody/ no one	everybody/ everyone
Things	something	anything	nothing	everything
Places	somewhere	anywhere	nowhere	everywhere

- We use *somebody/someone, something* and *somewhere* in affirmative sentences and in requests or offers: ***Somebody** phoned earlier.   Can we go **somewhere** to talk?   Would you like **something** to eat?*

- We use *anybody/anyone, anything* and *anywhere* in negative sentences and questions: *Is **anyone** else here?   There isn't **anything** to eat.   I can't find the key **anywhere**.*

- We use *nobody/no one, nothing* and *nowhere* with affirmative verbs: ***No one** answered the door.   There's **nothing** interesting to do!   There was **nowhere** to park.*

- *Everybody/everyone, everything* and *everywhere* contain the meaning of *all* or *every*: *Where is **everyone**?   We'll do **everything** possible to help.   I've looked **everywhere** for my bag!*

 We use a singular verb after *somebody, everybody,* etc.: ***Everybody's** happy.* But if we refer back to *somebody, everybody,* etc., we use *they, them, their* or *themselves*: ***Everybody has** a favourite place where **they** like to go.   **Someone's** left **their** coat in my car.   **Everybody's** enjoying **themselves**.*

P R A C T I C E

10a Circle the correct answer.

  0 Did *somebody /* (*anybody*) notice that Luke wasn't at the meal?

  1 *No one / Anyone* asked about him.

  2 Nobody from our group *was / were* there.

  3 There *was / were* somebody from Tom's drama group.

  4 Tom told me *something / anything* about Hayley, but now I can't remember it.

  5 I haven't seen *nobody / anybody* today.

  6 Everyone *is / are* at home with *his / their* family.

  7 I'm very tired, so I don't want to go *somewhere / anywhere*.

  8 There *'s / isn't* nothing on television.

  9 Shall we do *something / anything* together tomorrow?

  10 I'd like to have a really good pizza, but *nowhere / anywhere* here has good pizzas!

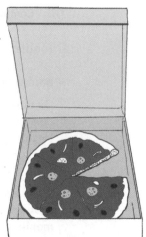

10b **Complete the conversations. Use *someone, something,* etc.**

A: Let's go (0) .....*somewhere*..... new next week.

B: (1) .... says that the Xscape Leisure Centre's really good.

A: OK. Let's go there. There's (2) .... to do here. It's really boring!

B: OK.

A: Would you like (3) .... to drink? Some water or juice?

B: Some juice, please.

A: Oh, there isn't any juice. (4) ....'s finished the last carton. I'm sorry.

A: Did you buy (5) .... in town?

B: Just some batteries. I wanted a DVD, but I couldn't find it (6) .... And I looked at some trainers in SuperSports, but they were too expensive.

A: (7) .... in that shop's expensive. I never buy (8) .... there.

10c **Circle the correct answer.**

I started my job at the café today. (0) (Everybody) / Anybody there was nice to me. (1) They were / He was very kind. I made a few mistakes, but (2) anybody / nobody complained about me. It's a busy place, so everyone (3) work / works hard. I didn't see (4) anybody / nobody that I knew.

At lunchtime, I went out because there was (5) anywhere / nowhere to sit in the café and I wanted to be (6) somewhere / anywhere quiet.

11 *one, ones, another, other*

- We can use *one* or *ones* to avoid repeating a noun: *I don't like this bag, but I like the brown **one**.   I don't like these shoes, but I like the black **ones**.*

- We use *another* + singular noun/*one* to mean 'one more' or 'a different one': *Would you like **another biscuit**?   She wants to get **another job**.   These biscuits are nice. Can I have **another one**?   This glass is dirty. Could you bring me **another one**, please?*

- We can use (*the/my/your,* etc.) *other* + singular or plural noun/*one*/*ones* to talk about different people and things that we've already mentioned: *We crossed to **the other side** of the road.   Where are **your other friends**?   I've found one shoe, but I can't find **the other one**.*

- We can use *another* and *other* without a noun: *We don't like our room. We're going to ask for **another**.   Here's one sock. Where's **the other**?*

- *The others* means 'the other people or things': *Shall we wait here for **the others**?* (= the other people)

P R A C T I C E

11a Complete the conversations. Use *one* or *ones*.

   0 A: Is there a café near here?   **B:** There's ......*one*...... at the end of this street.

   1 A: I love this song.   **B:** Do you? I prefer the last ....

   2 A: I need some new glasses.   **B:** What's the matter with your old .... ?

   3 A: Have you got a rucksack?   **B:** Yes, I've got a small ....

   4 A: Do you like these shorts?   **B:** No, I like those brown .... over there.

   5 A: These posters are great.   **B:** The .... in the other shop were nicer.

   6 A: There's a nice T-shirt here.   **B:** Yes. It's like that black .... I've got.

11b Circle the correct answer.

   0 I'm going to take my new CD player back and ask for (another)/ *other* one.

   1 If I can't find the box that it came in, I'll put it in *another* / *other*.

   2 The *another* / *other* things I bought from them were fine.

   3 My *another* / *other* CD player broke a few weeks ago.

   4 I chose this one because the *another* / *other* one was too expensive.

   5 One of the buttons works, but the *another* / *others* don't.

   6 The *another* / *other* problem is that the headphones don't fit.

   7 I'm not sure I want *another* / *other* one that's the same as this one.

   8 I might go to *another* / *other* shop to compare prices.

11c Complete the letter. Use *one, ones, other, others* or *another*.

I'm writing to express my objections to the plan for a car park near the river.

My first objection is that we have three car parks, so we do not need another (0) ......*one*...... . The (1) .... near the supermarket are often empty and the (2) .... one is never full.

My second objection is that this area is an important green space within the town. We don't have (3) .... place where we can walk by the river.

I would like to make two suggestions for this area. The first is to make it into a nature reserve. There are a lot of trees on this side of the river, and on the (4) .... side there is a field with rare orchids. The whole area is home to a lot of birds and (5) .... wildlife.

My second suggestion is to build a footbridge over the river near Ferry Path, about 500 metres away from the (6) .... at Mill Lane. If we had (7) .... footbridge, more people would walk into town and wouldn't use their cars. This would benefit the town and would mean that a fourth car park would not be necessary. The (8) .... would provide plenty of parking.

Check 2 Pronouns and possessives

1 Circle the correct answer.

1 If you don't like this DVD, let's get *another / other* one.

2 Don't worry about me. I can look after *me / myself*.

3 The *winner's / winners'* names are Joe and Kelly Sherman.

4 At the start of the lesson, everyone said a few things about *himself / themselves*.

5 Can you tell me where the *women's / womens'* magazines are?

6 Kate is an old friend of *me / mine*.

7 Lisa and Jessica have got *their own / on their own* apartment now.

/ 7

2 Complete the conversation. Use one word in each gap.

A: Are your exams this year really important?

B: Well, they're quite important, but the really important (8) .... are at the end (9) .... next year. And next year I've got to do a big project too.

A: Do they give you the topic or can you choose it (10) .... ?

B: I can choose it. I'm really looking forward to doing it. I like working (11) .... my own.

A: Do you? I don't like working (12) .... myself. I work better with other people.

/ 5

3 Circle the correct answer.

My brother Tom and I are twins and as children we did (13) .... together. We were in the same class at school, and at home we always played together. I had (14) .... friends, but (15) .... understood me as well as Tom.

When we got a bit older, we still spent a lot of time with (16) .... We did a lot of sport together and we went camping (17) .... a few times.

In our last year at school, we decided to go to different universities. Tom wanted to go to London, but I wanted to go (18) .... smaller. It's great here. I'm enjoying my course and I'm learning to do things for (19) .... – like shopping and cooking. At first, I couldn't cook (20) .... , but I'm quite good now!

13 A something   B anything   C nothing   D everything
14 A another one B one other   C another   D other
15 A somebody   B anybody   C nobody   D everybody
16 A another   B each other   C the other   D ourselves
17 A on ourselves B of ourselves C on our own D of our own
18 A somewhere   B anywhere   C nowhere   D everywhere
19 A myself   B by myself   C own   D my own
20 A something   B anything   C nothing   D everything

/ 8

Total: / 20

Self-check

Wrong answers	Look again at	Try CD-ROM
3, 5, 6, 9	Unit 7	Exercise 7
2, 4, 10, 16, 19	Unit 8	Exercise 8
7, 11, 12, 17	Unit 9	Exercise 9
13, 15, 18, 20	Unit 10	Exercise 10
1, 8, 14	Unit 11	Exercise 11

Now do **Check 2**

Articles

12 Definite and indefinite article

- We use *a/an* + singular countable noun when we talk about a thing or person, but we do not say which thing or person we mean: *Is there **a** supermarket near here?* *He's **a** doctor.* *She's **a** very nice girl.* *They have **a** lovely flat.* *My car's **a** Renault.*

- We use *the* to refer to something specific that we know about or is unique: *I went to **the** supermarket near my house.* *Look at **the** moon!* *Could you shut **the** door?* (There's only one door in this room.)

- We use *a/an* to refer to someone/something that has not been mentioned before: ***A** car stopped outside our house.* ***A** man got out and went into **a** shop.*

- We use *the* to refer to something that has been mentioned before. Compare: *I bought **a** T-shirt and **a** jacket.* ***The** T-shirt's blue and **the** jacket's black.*

 A/An means 'one' when we are not making a contrast with 'two', 'three', etc. If we are making a contrast, we use *one*. Compare these sentences: *We went to Spain for **a** week.* (no contrast) *Did you go for **one** week or two?* (contrast with 'two')

PRACTICE

12a **Complete the sentences. Use *a, an* or *the*.**

0 I haven't got ....*a*.... job at the moment.

1 I'm .... student.

2 I'd like to work in .... art gallery in London.

3 I'm working on .... project about Japanese art at the moment.

4 I spend a lot of time in .... library.

5 At lunchtime, I like having .... sandwich in the park.

6 I lie on .... ground and look up at .... sky.

7 I live in .... small village just outside Leeds.

8 There are some woods and .... lake near my village. My favourite place is .... lake.

12b **Circle the correct answer.**

0 How long does the course last? *A /* (*One*) day or two?

1 We had *a / one* wonderful evening at the theatre.

2 Would you like *a / one* biscuit?

3 You can only take *a / one* suitcase on the coach, not more.

4 Jamie scored *a / one* goal and Ryan scored two.

5 Lisa's sent me *a / one* postcard.

6 I've finished *an / one* essay, but I've got two more to do.

12C Complete the messages from a message board on the Internet. Use *a, the* or *one*.

Message 1: posted by <u>Martin</u>

I think it's (0) .....*a*..... good idea to exercise outdoors. It's good to be outside in (1) .... fresh air. I live quite near (2) .... sea, so it's quite easy for me to do my favourite sport – surfing. It's so exciting! There's only (3) .... surf club in my town – I joined it last year. I also went on holiday with some friends from (4) .... club – surfing, of course!

Message 2: posted by <u>SammyJ</u>

I go running with (5) .... friend. We plan our routes carefully because we enjoy running more if (6) .... route is interesting. We try and run in places that are nice. My favourite route takes us down (7) .... hill, along (8) .... river, back up (9) .... hill and past (10) .... small wood.

Message 3: posted by <u>Lisa202</u>

We only have (11) .... leisure centre in our town, but I've joined (12) .... girls' basketball team there and I really enjoy it. I go swimming too. There isn't (13) .... pool in (14) .... leisure centre, but when I go into Norwich, I go to (15) .... pool there.

13 Use of articles with general meaning

- When we refer to people and things in general, we don't use an article:
  - before plural nouns: **Doctors** *often work very long hours.*   **Cars** *are expensive.*
  - before uncountable nouns, e.g. nouns referring to substances or abstract ideas: **Rice** *is good for you.*   **Education** *is important.*   **Modern life** *is very stressful.* (Not ~~**The modern life** is very stressful.~~)
- We can also use *a* + singular noun to refer to people and things in general: **A doctor** *earns more money than* **a teacher**. (= all doctors, all teachers)
- We sometimes use *the* to refer to people, animals or things in general:
  - with plural nationality words: **the** *French*   **the** *Americans*
  - with adjectives: **the poor**   **the rich**   **the unemployed**
  - with types of animals (+ singular noun): **The whale** *is a mammal.*
  - with inventions (+ singular noun): *Who invented* **the computer**?
  - with musical instruments: *I play* **the piano**.

P R A C T I C E

13a Complete the extracts from newspaper articles. Use the words in brackets and *the* if necessary.

0 *Students* .... often leave university with large debts. (students)

1 .... **is making millions of people ill. (stress)**

2 The government has promised to improve the lives of . . . . (poor)

3 50% of British adults feel confused by .... (new technology)

4 .... buy more things on the Internet than other Europeans. (British)

5 .... can lower blood pressure, a study suggests. (dark chocolate)

13b Circle the correct answer.

0 We need to reduce *pollution* / *the pollution*.

1 I started playing *guitar* / *the guitar* when I was nine.

2 *King Cobra* / *The King Cobra* is the biggest poisonous snake in the world.

3 Wilbur and Orville Wright invented *aeroplane* / *the aeroplane*.

4 *Honesty* / *The honesty* is the most important thing to me.

5 Are you interested in *science* / *the science*?

6 Most people enjoy spending time in *nature* / *the nature*.

7 *A* / *The* journalist has to be able to write well.

8 *Children* / *The children* today are more independent.

13c Complete the article. Use *a, an, the* or – .

The Suzuki method is a way of teaching (0) ....– children to play (1) ....
music. It was invented by Dr Shinichi Suzuki, a Japanese violinist and music teacher
who taught himself to play (2) .... violin at the age of seventeen. He thought that
learning to play (3) .... instrument is like learning to speak (4) .... language
and that (5) .... very young can learn to play music if they hear a lot of music
around them. In his method, (6) .... pupils learn pieces of music by ear, repeat
them many times and often perform them in groups.

14 Special uses of articles

- We use *a/an*:
  - to mean 'one' with fractions and large numbers: *one and a half hours*
    a thousand people
  - to mean 'each' or 'per': *£2 a kilo   50 km an hour   twice a week*
  - with some illnesses, especially ones that aren't serious: *a cold   a headache*
- We use *the* with the names of:
  - countries that are plural or include the words *Kingdom, Republic,* etc:
    the Netherlands   the USA   the United Kingdom   the Czech Republic
  - seas, oceans, rivers, deserts, areas and groups of mountains: *the North Sea*
    the Pacific   the Thames   the Sahara   the North   the Andes
  - newspapers: *The Times   The Daily News*
  - some important buildings, hotels, theatres, cinemas and museums: *the White House   the Houses of Parliament   the Sheraton   the National Theatre the Odeon   the Science Museum*
- We also use *the*:
  - with surnames, when we are talking about more than one member of a family:
    Do you know the Smiths? (= the Smith family)
  - to refer to the media: *the theatre   the cinema   the radio* (but: *TV*, not *the TV*)
- We don't use an article with the names of:
  - people: *Is Tim coming with us?*
  - continents and most countries, cities, towns and states: *Africa   Europe   Japan India   London   Madrid   New York   California*
  - mountains and lakes: *Mount Everest   Lake Victoria*
  - streets, squares and parks: *Oxford Street* (but: *the High Street*)   *Central Square Hyde Park*
  - most shops and restaurants: *Harrods   McDonald's   Pizza Hut*
  - some magazines: *Time   Hello*
- We don't use an article with:
  - games, sports, school subjects and languages: *Do you play chess?   I like basketball.   I'm studying History.   Can you speak Spanish?*
  - meals: *Have you had lunch yet?*
  - some illnesses, especially serious ones: *She's got diabetes/cancer.*

▶▶ **See also: Unit 94 (preposition + noun, no article)**

PRACTICE

14a Circle the correct answer.

   0 I usually go out with my friends two or three times ⓐ/ *the* week.

   1 I didn't go out last week because I had *a* / *the* cold.

   2 We saw a great film at *an* / *the* Odeon on Saturday.

   3 Yesterday I played tennis for an hour and *a* / *the* half.

   4 Last month I went to *a* / *the* British Museum in London for the first time.

   5 We went to *a* / *the* Tower of London too.

   6 I spent more than *a* / *the* hundred pounds that day!

14b **Complete the sentences. Use the words in brackets and *the* if necessary.**

    0 .....*The Flatiron Building*..... was one of New York's first skyscrapers. (Flatiron Building)

    1 .... is the largest continent in the world. (Asia)

    2 .... is the richest state in .... (California, United States)

    3 .... is the highest mountain in .... (Mount Fuji, Japan)

    4 .... , the official language of .... , is the language with the largest number of speakers in the world. (Mandarin, China)

    5 .... kills more than 1.2 million people each year – mainly children in .... (malaria, Africa)

    6 .... covers a huge area of North Africa, from .... in the west to .... in the east. (Sahara, Atlantic, Nile)

    7 .... is the largest of the Great Lakes in .... (Lake Superior, North America)

    8 .... and .... are the national sports of .... (ice hockey, lacrosse, Canada)

    9 .... is the capital of .... (Edinburgh, Scotland)

    10 .... in .... is one of the most famous buildings of the twentieth century. (Sydney Opera House, Australia)

14c **Complete the conversation. Use *a*, *the* or – .**

A: Shall we have (0) ....–.... lunch now or later?

B: Let's have it now. Let's go to that café in (1) .... South Street – the one near (2) .... Pizza Express. My neighbours, (3) .... Armstrongs, often go there and they say it's very good.

A: All right. I went there with (4) .... Jamie once, a long time ago. It was quite nice.

B: OK. I just want to stop at a newsagent's. I want to get (5) .... *Times*. There's a good article in it about Costa Rica. It's an amazing place. They say that there are about (6) .... million different species of animals and plants there.

A: Really? That's a lot!

B: I saw a programme about it on (7) .... TV once and I was fascinated by it. I'd love to go there and see all the birds and animals.

A: Have you always been interested in (8) .... natural history?

B: Yes. I really love it.

Check 3 Articles

1 Choose and complete the sentences.

1 (motorbikes, the motorbikes)
I've always loved ...., so I'm really pleased to have one.

2 (United States, the United States)
My brother wants to do a degree in
....

3 (fashion, the fashion)
She's very interested in ....

4 (bronchitis, the bronchitis)
If you think you've got ...., go to the doctor.

5 (telephone, the telephone)
Who invented .... ?

/ 5

2 Complete the letter. Use the words in brackets and *the* if necessary.

Hello from (6) .... (Dublin)!

We're having a wonderful time! We're at a small hotel called (7) .... (West Court). We got here two days ago. Before that, we spent one night in Kilkenny and three in (8) .... (Cork).

We've been to two gigs and last night we went to (9) .... (theatre). We've met a lot of people. (10) .... (Irish) are great – really friendly.

We don't want to come home!

/ 5

3 Complete the article. Use one word in each gap.

Melting Ice Reveals Secrets

(11) .... group of scientists have been studying life in (12) .... Weddell Sea in Antarctica. Because of climate change, two ice shelves have melted and this has given scientists (13) .... rare opportunity to see what has been living below (14) .... ice.

The melting of (15) .... shelves in 1995 and 2002 opened up (16) .... large area of (17) .... sea floor, which had been covered for at least twelve thousand years.

Scientists spent ten weeks investigating (18) .... area. Using (19) .... remote camera, they found and collected about a thousand new species. They also found that other species of animals are now able to live in there because (20) .... water is warmer.

/ 10

Total: / 20

✓ Self-check

Wrong answers	Look again at	Try CD-ROM
11, 13, 14, 15, 16, 17, 18, 19, 20	Unit 12	Exercise 12
1, 3, 5, 10	Unit 13	Exercise 13
2, 4, 6, 7, 8, 9, 12	Unit 14	Exercise 14

Now do **Check 3**

Adjectives and adverbs

15 Position and order of adjectives

- Adjectives come before a noun or after the linking verb *be*: *She was wearing a **red dress**.   Her dress **was red**.*
- They can also come after these linking verbs: *become, feel, get, look, seem, smell, taste: He **became angry**.   The food **smelled delicious**.*
- These adjectives can only come before a noun: *former, indoor, main, only, outdoor, previous: the **main** road   the **former** president*
- These adjectives can only come after a linking verb: *afraid, alive, alone, ashamed, asleep, awake, glad, ill, pleased, sorry, sure: He **looked ill**.*
- After a linking verb, we use *and* to join adjectives. The order isn't important: *The car was **old and dirty/dirty and old**.   She was **tired, angry and upset**.*
- When there is more than one adjective before a noun, we use them in this order:

Opinion	Size	Other qualities	Age	Shape	Colour	Origin	Material	Type
pretty awful	big small	hot difficult	old new	round square	red green	British African	plastic wooden	electric digital

a beautiful old house   a big black cat   a new digital camcorder

 When there are two colour adjectives before a noun, we use *and*: *a blue **and** red tie*

PRACTICE

15a **Put the words in the correct order.**

0 is / place / amazing / this
This place is amazing.

1 seems / relaxed / everybody

....

2 nice / some / there / buildings / are

....

3 palace / is / enormous / former / the

....

4 fantastic / the / tastes / food

....

5 are / friendly / and / people / the / kind

....

6 and / streets / clean / are / the / quiet   ....

7 main / street / busy / is / the   ....

8 a / time / great / we're having   ....

15b **You want to sell these things on the Internet. Write a description of each one.**

o   A wooden bowl. It's large and brown.   *a large brown wooden bowl*

1   Some American comics. They're rare and old.   ....

2   A digital watch. It's black and plastic.   ....

3   A woollen coat. It's long and black.   ....

4   A nylon rucksack. It's practical and small.   ....

5   A lovely necklace. It's African and handmade.   ....

6   Two big rugs. They're Indian and colourful.   ....

15c **Complete the letter. Use the words in the box.**

| ~~awful~~   clean   crowded   good   only   outdoor   sick |

We had a(n) (0) ....*awful*........ journey here. It was really terrible! The
bus was very hot and (1) .... I felt (2) .... and I
had a headache.
The hotel is nice. Our room is (3) .... and comfortable. The
(4) .... problem is the shower, which doesn't work very well.
Lucy and I are doing lots of (5) .... activities – and we're
getting (6) .... at sailing.

16   Adjective or adverb?

- Adjectives describe a noun or pronoun: *They eat **healthy food**.   **He's happy**.*
- Adverbs describe verbs: *He **sat down quickly**.   She **opened** the box **carefully**.*
- To make most adverbs, we add *-ly* to an adjective: *quick → quickly   happy → happily   wonderful → wonderfully*

▶▶   **See Appendix 2: Spelling rules for adverbs, page 169.**

- These words can be both adjectives and adverbs: *fast, hard, long, far, early, late:*
  *Taking care of a baby is **hard** work.   They worked **hard**.*
- This adverb is irregular: *good → well: Did you sleep **well**?*
- These adjectives end in *-ly: friendly, lively, lovely, silly*. We can't make adverbs from
  them, so we say *in a friendly/silly*, etc. *way: He smiled **in a friendly way**.*
- Notice the difference between these pairs:
  – *hard/hardly: We worked **hard**.   You've **hardly** eaten anything today.*
  – *late/lately: They arrived **late**.   Have you seen Joe **lately**?*
  – *free/freely: We got into the museum **free**.   You can speak **freely**.*

⚠   We use an adjective after a linking verb (e.g *be, look, seem*, etc.): *The journey
  was quick.   He **seemed happy**.*
  But we use an adverb after other verbs: *We **drove quickly**.   He **smiled happily**.*

PRACTICE

16a Complete the story. Use adjectives or adverbs.

It had been a long day and I was (0) .... *tired* .... (tired), but I sat in the car and waited (1) .... (patient). After half an hour, he came out of the house and walked (2) .... (quick) towards the main street. I got out of the car and followed him. He was talking (3) .... (angry) to someone on his mobile phone. He looked (4) .... (worried).

I walked past him and was surprised when he asked me, 'Is there a bus to Gerrards Park from here?' 'I don't know. Sorry,' I replied (5) .... (polite). 'Oh, OK,' he said and turned away. He seemed (6) .... (nervous).

I guessed that he wanted to meet someone – the person on the phone, perhaps – in Gerrards Park. I walked on (7) .... (slow). After a minute or two, a bus arrived. He got on it, so I hurried back to the car. I wasn't (8) .... (confident) that I could follow him, but I had to try.

16b Complete the sentences. Use adverbs or *in a ... way*.

0 The sun shone .... *brightly* .... and the air was soft. (bright)

00 She teaches .... *in a lively way* .... (lively)

1 The film didn't last .... (long)

2 They celebrated New Year .... (lovely)

3 I swam .... , enjoying the cool, clear water. (lazy)

4 It was my fault. I answered a serious question .... (silly)

5 We had to run .... to catch the bus. (fast)

6 They smiled at me .... (friendly)

7 I woke up and looked at the clock .... (sleepy)

8 Mark listened to me .... (sympathetic)

16c Circle the correct answer.

0 She seems (nice)/ *nicely*, but she hasn't treated some of her friends *good* / (well).

1 Her ankle was swollen and *painful* / *painfully*. She could *hard* / *hardly* move it.

2 He got up *late* / *lately*, so he had his breakfast *quick* / *quickly* and left.

3 The tickets are *expensive* / *expensively*, but children under five can travel *free* / *freely*.

4 I haven't been swimming *late* / *lately* because I've been *busy* / *busily*.

5 I felt *happy* / *happily* because at last I could express myself *free* / *freely*.

6 He's worked *hard* / *hardly* for years and now he's become *famous* / *famously*.

7 I was *angry* / *angrily* with him because he hadn't been completely *honest* / *honestly* with me.

8 He cut my hair *bad* / *badly*, so now it looks *horrible* / *horribly*.

17 Position and order of adverbs

- Adverbs of frequency (e.g. *always, sometimes*) come after the verb *be* or before the main verb: *It's **often** hot.   She **always comes** by bus.   I've **never met** him.*
- Adverbs of manner (e.g. *quickly, slowly*) come after the main verb or after the object, if there is one: *She **smiled sweetly**.   He finished **his meal quickly**.*
- Adverbs of place (e.g. *there, in Spain*) and time (e.g. *today, tomorrow*) usually come at the end of a sentence: *Was Jon **there**?   I saw him **yesterday**.*
- If there is more than one adverb or adverbial phrase at the end of a sentence, the usual order is: manner, place, time: *She ran **quickly up the stairs**.   We went **to London last week**.   Come **here at once**!*
- But single-word adverbs often come before phrases: *I saw Sam **yesterday outside the cinema**.*
- Short phrases often come before long ones: *Let's meet **at six at our usual café**.*

PRACTICE

17a Put the words in the correct order.

   o often / tired / Kirsty / 's   *Kirsty's often tired.*

   1 hard / 's / working / she   ....

   2 start / our exams / on Monday   ....

   3 she / well / her time / organises   ....

   4 never / she / an exam / 's / failed   ....

   5 with / I / lunch / have /sometimes / her   ....

   6 yesterday / had / we / a nice chat   ....

   7 for / by the river / went / we / a walk   ....

   8 there / relaxing / was / it / very   ....

17b Re-write the sentences. Put the words in brackets in the correct place.

   o We don't go anywhere. (usually, at Christmas)
   We don't usually go anywhere at Christmas.
   ....

   1 Our relatives stay with us. (often, at New Year)
   ....

   2 I visit my grandparents. (sometimes, in the summer)
   ....

   3 I go camping. (occasionally, for a few days)
   ....

   4 I have a lovely time. (always, in Wales)
   ....

   5 I meet interesting people. (usually, there)
   ....

17C **Read the text and re-write the numbered sentences, putting the words in brackets in the correct place.**

(0) I arrived late and missed the bus. (at the bus stop) (1) I had arranged to meet my friends at the bowling alley. (at six) I tried to call them, but I couldn't find my phone. (2) I ran through the park. (quickly) (3) I got to the bowling alley. (at half past six) (4) My friends were waiting at the entrance. (patiently) (5) I played badly. (most of the evening) (6) I kept thinking about the things I had to do at home. (later that evening)

0 *I arrived late at the bus stop and missed the bus.*
....

1 ....

2 ....

3 ....

4 ....

5 ....

6 ....

18 Comparison of adjectives and adverbs

Type	Examples	Comparative	Superlative
One-syllable and some two-syllable adjectives	old, nice, happy	**+ -er**	**+ -est**
		older, nicer, happier	the oldest, the nicest, the happiest
Longer adjectives and other two-syllable adjectives	famous, expensive	***more, less***	***the most, the least***
		more famous, less expensive	the most famous, the least expensive
Irregular adjectives	good, bad, far	better, worse, farther/further	the best, the worst, the farthest/furthest
Adverbs	quickly carefully	***more, less***	***the most, the least***
		more quickly, less carefully	the most quickly, the least carefully
Irregular adverbs	well, badly, far	better, worse, farther/further	the best, the worst, the farthest/furthest

- We use *than* with comparatives: *I'm **older than** my brother.   This phone is **more expensive than** the others.   Tom drives **more slowly than** me/than I do.*
- We can use superlatives in these patterns:
  - (*one of*) *the* + superlative: *It's **the best** film I've seen.   He's **one of the best** singers of his generation.   It's **one of the most interesting** books she's written.*
  - *the second/third* + superlative: *It's **the second/third most expensive** hotel in the world.*

▶▶ *See Appendix 3: Spelling rules for comparative and superlative adjectives, page 169. For as … as, see Unit 22.*

P R A C T I C E

18a Look at the table showing the results of a survey of students in a class and complete the sentences. Use the comparative.

	go shopping	interested in clothes	like computer games	concerned with looks	using technology	saving money
Boys	•	•	••	•	••	•
Girls	••	••	•	••	•	••

0 Girls go shopping ....*more often*........... than boys. (often)

1 Boys are .... in clothes than girls. (interested)

2 Computer games are .... with boys than with girls. (popular)

3 Boys are .... with their appearance than girls. (concerned)

4 Boys learn to use technology .... than girls. (quickly)

5 Girls are .... at saving money than boys. (good)

18b Complete the sentences. Use the superlative.

0 It's a fantastic book! It's ....*the best*........... book I've read for ages! (good)

1 Football is the second .... sport for young people. Lots of people get injured playing it. (dangerous)

2 Helen, Rachel and I all speak Italian, but Helen speaks it .... She's very good at it. (fluently)

3 I had a horrible time. It was one of .... matches I've had this season. (enjoyable)

4 Of the three of us, Jack works .... He loves this job. (hard)

5 I knew she wasn't going to help me. When I asked people for help, she answered .... (enthusiastically)

18c Complete the second sentence so that it means the same as the first, using the word in bold. Use between two and five words.

0 Everyone in my group's older than me. **the**
   I'm ....*the youngest*............... in my group.

1 Everyone I know is more sporty than Jamie. **least**
   Jamie is .... person that I know.

2 She's a more careful driver than her sister. **carefully**
   She drives .... her sister.

3 Jo and Ted are the best at singing in the group, but Jo's better than Ted. **second**
   Ted's .... singer in the group.

4 Kelly reacts to problems less calmly than the rest of us. **the**
   Kelly reacts to problems .... of us all.

5 Kirsty is more cautious than me. **less**
   I'm .... Kirsty.

6 Everyone in our class behaves more maturely than Tim. **immaturely**
   Tim behaves .... in our class.

19 Modifying comparisons

● To express a big difference between two things, we can use:
  – *far/a lot/much* + comparative: *The second film's **far better than** the first one.
  Canoeing's **a lot more exciting than** swimming.   He drives **much more quickly
  than** I do.*
  – *by far/easily* + superlative: *She's **by far the most talented** player.   This **is easily
  the best** guidebook.*

● To express a small difference, we can use *a (little) bit/slightly* + comparative: *This
  restaurant's **a little bit more expensive than** the others.   Could you drive **a bit
  more slowly**?   I'm **slightly older than** the other students.*

▶▶   **For as ... as, see Unit 22.**

PRACTICE

19a Circle the correct answer.

  0 The train's (*a lot*)/ *a bit* faster than the bus. It takes an hour by train and three
     by bus.

  1 I'm *much / slightly* taller than Becky – only a centimetre or two.

  2 Emily speaks Spanish *much / a bit* better than I do. I can hardly say anything,
     but she's fluent.

  3 It's *a lot / a little bit* hotter today than it was yesterday. It was twenty-five
     degrees yesterday and it's thirty-two today.

  4 My brother can cycle *far / slightly* more quickly than I can. He gets to college
     fifteen minutes earlier than I do and we leave home at the same time.

  5 This year I'm going to go running *far / a bit* more often: four times a week
     instead of three.

  6 People in the north are *much / a bit* friendlier than they are in the south. They
     very often talk to strangers and help them. In the south, people don't talk to
     strangers.

19b Complete the article. Use one word in each gap.

Parrots are popular pets mainly because they can do things that other birds
cannot. They are (0) .....*far*...... more intelligent and they are also (1) ....
lot more colourful than many other birds. They are (2) .... far the most
interesting birds to keep and they are easily (3) .... most rewarding as
they can be very playful, loyal and loving. They live a (4) .... longer than
other pets – often until they are fifty – so they will be a companion for a lifetime.

Some parrots are (5) .... bit better at copying speech than others, but in
general, most parrots can be trained to use words and imitate speech very

20 Adverbs of degree: *very, extremely,* etc.

- We use adverbs of degree to make adjectives and adverbs stronger or weaker.
- Gradable adjectives/adverbs refer to qualities that we can easily grade or compare and have a comparative and superlative form.
  - To make them stronger, we use *very, extremely* or *really*: *It's **very hot**.   I felt **extremely tired**.   He was driving **really fast**.*
  - To make them weaker, we use *a bit/quite/fairly* + positive adjective/adverb, or *rather* + negative adjective/adverb: *She works **quite/fairly quickly**.   Jack's **rather lazy**.*
- Ungradable adjectives/adverbs refer to extreme qualities that we don't usually grade or compare (e.g. *huge, tiny, awful, exhausted, brilliantly, wonderfully, terribly*) and do not have a comparative or superlative form.
  - To make them stronger, we use *absolutely* or *really*: *The food was **absolutely awful**!   He plays the piano **really brilliantly**!*
  - We can't make ungradable adjectives/adverbs weaker: ~~It was a bit awful.~~

P R A C T I C E

20a Complete the sentences. Use the words in the box.

> fairly quickly   quite good   quite well   really hungry
> very carefully   very fit   ~~very popular~~

0 That concert will be ....*very popular*.......... , so we need to get tickets for it soon.

1 I ate six sandwiches. I was ....

2 I can sing .... , but I'm not good enough to sing in a band.

3 That film was .... , but I think it was too long and the ending was disappointing.

4 They replied to my letter .... – after about ten days.

5 My brother's .... because he does a lot of running and swimming.

6 Please fill this form in .... You mustn't make a single mistake.

20b Circle the correct answer.

I had a (0) *very* / ⟨*really*⟩ great time paintballing. It was great fun,
but I was (1) *extremely* / *absolutely* exhausted at the end of it! I found it
(2) *very* / *absolutely* difficult at first. Luckily, by the end, I could play
(3) *fairly* / *extremely* well, but some people were much better than me.
Mark was (4) *really* / *a bit* brilliant!

At lunch, Justin said something about Hannah's clothes – which nobody
thought was funny – and she got so angry that she started shouting at
him. She was (5) *very* / *absolutely* furious! It was (6) *a bit* / *absolutely*
upsetting for the rest of us too, but it didn't spoil our afternoon.

Check 4 Adjectives and adverbs

1 Put the words in the correct order.

1 there / 've / eaten / never / we

....

2 food / serve / French / traditional / they / wonderful

....

3 she / hard / always / works

....

4 you / tonight / theatre / are / the / going / to?

....

5 's got / Tom / electric / new / guitar / a / fantastic

....

/ 5

2 Complete the conversation. Use the words in the box. You do not need all of them.

extremely happily happy hard
hardly loud loudly quite

A: Did you enjoy the film?

B: It was OK – not brilliant. And there were some annoying people behind us who kept talking (6) .... At times we could (7) .... hear the film.

A: What was it about?

B: It was about a man who sees a murder. The killers try (8) .... to catch him, but he keeps running away.

A: Did it have a (9) .... ending?

B: Yes, it did, although it was (10) .... disappointing. It wasn't terrible, but I thought it could have been better.

/ 5

3 Circle the correct answer.

╭───╮
│ ● ● ●   New Message   ⊖ │
├───┤
│ I had a(n) (11) ..... nice birthday, thanks. We went to │
│ a restaurant and had a (12) ..... enormous meal! Lisa │
│ gave me a (13) ..... bag which is very similar to yours. │
│ Yes, I've been on a few trips this summer. The │
│ (14) ..... one was a short trip to London and the │
│ (15) ..... best one was going to see my cousins in │
│ Cornwall. I get on well with my cousins Emily and │
│ Sarah. Emily's (16) ..... older than me – just three │
│ months, but Sarah's (17) ..... younger – six years. │
│ They live in a village near the coast. It's (18) ..... │
│ beautiful place I've ever seen! There are so many │
│ lovely beaches there. We went swimming once, but I │
│ couldn't swim far. My cousins are definitely (19) ..... │
│ fitter than me! I must say I enjoyed the hot chocolate │
│ we had afterwards more than the swim! It was │
│ (20) ..... the best hot chocolate I've ever had. │
╰───╯

11	A very	B absolutely	C rather	D bit
12	A very	B bit	C really	D far
13	A nice little black		B nice black little	
	C black little nice		D little nice black	
14	A most good	B better	C best	D most best
15	A first	B second	C less	D least
16	A a lot	B much more	C by far	D a bit
17	A slightly	B much more	C much	D easily
18	A more	B most	C the more	D the most
19	A very	B much	C more	D most
20	A very	B far	C slightly	D easily

/ 10

Total: / 20

Self-check

Wrong answers	Look again at	Try CD-ROM
2, 5, 13	**Unit 15**	Exercise 15
6, 7, 8, 9	**Unit 16**	Exercise 16
1, 3, 4	**Unit 17**	Exercise 17
14, 15, 18	**Unit 18**	Exercise 18
16, 17, 19, 20	**Unit 19**	Exercise 19
10, 11, 12	**Unit 20**	Exercise 20

Now do **Check 4**

Comparative structures

21 Making comparisons with nouns

- We can use *more, the most, less, the least, fewer* and *the fewest* with nouns to compare quantities.
- We use *more* and *the most* + uncountable/plural countable noun: *He's got **more money** than me.   Who won **the most medals**?*
- We use *less* and *the least* + uncountable noun: *My brother watches **less television** than I do.   Which fuel causes **the least pollution**?*
- We use *fewer* and *the fewest* + plural countable noun: *You've got **fewer points** than me.   The team with **the fewest points** comes last.*
- With *more, less* and *fewer*, we use *than* + noun/pronoun/clause: *She's got **more problems than me/than I have**.*

PRACTICE

21a Complete the sentences. Use *more, the most, less* or *the least*.

0   Philip's very creative. He has ......*more*...... ideas than me.

1   Steven scored .... goals. He scored three, Adam scored two and Ben scored one.

2   This car is much smaller, so it uses .... petrol than that one.

3   Laura always has .... energy than me. She's always ready to do something!

4   Mrs Bower is the best tutor even though she has .... experience of all the tutors here.

5   Paul gets .... telephone calls in the family. He's got lots of friends.

6   She buys .... clothes than I do. She loves them.

7   I've got .... money than I thought. I thought I had £500, but I've only got £350.

8   He isn't very hard-working, is he? Of all the people in our group, he does .... work.

21b Circle the correct answer.

There are (0) (*more*) / *most* young people here than in other parts of the region, but there are (1) *less / fewer* facilities for them. We need facilities like youth clubs and skate parks, which young people should be able to use for free. Young people here have (2) *less / the least* money than others in the region. We also need (3) *more / fewer* sports facilities if we want to encourage young people to get fitter by doing (4) *more / less* sport. Young people here do (5) *less / the least* sport than those in other parts of the country.

22 *as ... as, the same as, similar to, different from*

- We use (*just*) *as* + adjective/adverb + *as* to say that two people or things are the same or equal: *I'm **as tall as** you.   This cheap printer works **just as well as** the expensive ones.*

- We use *not as* + adjective/adverb + *as* to mean 'less ... than': *He's **not as intelligent as** his brother.* (= He's less intelligent than his brother.)   *I can't work **as quickly as** you can.* (= I work less quickly than you.)

- We use (*just*) *as much/many* + noun + *as* and *not (nearly) as much/many* + noun + *as* to compare quantities: *She earns **just as much money as** me/as I do.   This car **doesn't** use **as much petrol as** the old one.   I **don't** buy **nearly as many clothes as** you/**as** you do.*

- We can also use these expressions to compare things:
  - (*exactly*) *the same* (*as*): *Your car's **the same as** mine.   You've got **the same car as** me.   David's **exactly the same age as** me.   David and I are **exactly the same age**.*
  - (*quite/very*) *similar to, more or less the same*: *Your jacket's **quite similar to** mine. The two jobs are **more or less the same**.*
  - (*slightly/completely*) *different* (*from*): *They're **completely different from** each other.*

P R A C T I C E

22a **Complete the second sentence so that it means the same as the first.**

o His early pictures are less interesting than his more recent ones.
His early pictures ..... *aren't as interesting* ..... as his more recent ones.

1 Diet and exercise are equally important.
Diet is .... exercise.

2 Kirsty and Jo are equally sensitive.
Kirsty is .... Jo.

3 You can walk further than me.
I can't walk ....
you can.

4 Lucy and Kim work equally hard.
Lucy works .... Kim.

5 Michael's brother plays the violin better than he does.
Michael doesn't play the violin .... his brother.

6 Last year's holiday was more enjoyable than this year's holiday.
This year's holiday .... as last year's holiday.

7 The book was good and the film was equally good.
The film was .... the book.

8 Sarah drives faster than Jessica.
Jessica .... as Sarah.

22b Complete the sentences. Use *as much/many ... as* and the words in the box.

coffee ~~fun~~ money people photos success sweets

0 I like cycling, but it isn't ....*as much fun as*.... mountain biking. That's really exciting!

1 I don't eat .... she does. I don't like them very much.

2 I didn't take .... I took last summer. I took hundreds then!

3 We haven't had .... we had last year. We've lost a lot of games.

4 I don't know .... you. You know almost everybody here!

5 He doesn't spend .... me. He's very careful.

6 I drink .... you do – three or four cups a day.

22c Complete the conversation. Use one word in each gap.

A: Look! We've got exactly the (0) ....*same*........... trainers!

B: Really? No! Mine are white here and yours are black.

A: Oh, OK. Well, they're (1) .... or less the same. And your bag's very similar (2) .... mine. It's (3) .... same colour and size.

B: Yes, but mine hasn't got as (4) .... pockets as yours. Yours is nicer.

A: Yours is nice too. And your glasses are nice. Are they new?

B: Yes. They're slightly different (5) .... my old ones. They're the same (6) .... Lisa's.

23 *too, enough, very*

Too means 'more than you need'. *Enough* means 'as much as you need'. We use them in these patterns:

- *too* + adjective/adverb: *This car's **too old**. It goes **too slowly**.*
- adjective/adverb + *enough*: *Are you **warm enough**? Did she leave **early enough**?*
- *not* + adjective/adverb + *enough*: *This box **isn't big enough**. Ten minutes **isn't long enough**.*
- *too* + adjective/adverb + *for somebody* OR (*not* +) adjective/adverb + *enough* + *for somebody*: *The sea's **too cold for me**. This flat isn't **big enough for us**.*
- *too* + adjective/adverb + *to*-infinitive OR (*not* +) adjective/adverb + *enough* + *to*-infinitive: *He was **too ill to travel**. This tent's **light enough to carry**.*
- *too* + adjective/adverb + *for somebody* + *to*-infinitive OR (*not* +) adjective/adverb + *enough* + *for somebody* + *to*-infinitive: *This bag's **too heavy for me to carry**.* (= This bag is too heavy, so I can't carry it.) *The instructions were **simple enough for me to understand**.* (= The instructions were simple, so I could understand them.)

⚠ We use *very* to emphasise something that can be good or bad. We use *too* when something is a problem. Compare: *It's **very hot** today.* (This can be good or bad.) *It's **too hot** today.* (I don't like it.)

▶▶ **For enough + noun and too much/too many + noun, see Unit 3.**

PRACTICE

23a Circle the correct answer.

0 I don't want to go by bus. It takes (too)/ *very* long.

1 That film was *too / very* moving. I thought it was wonderful.

2 You can only get fit if you exercise *too regularly / regularly enough*.

3 You can't come to this club with us. You're *too / very* young.

4 I couldn't understand her. She spoke *too quickly / quickly enough*.

5 I'm sure you'll be fine at the interview. You've prepared for it *too / very* thoroughly.

6 Can we have the party in this room? Is it *very big / big enough* for fifty people?

23b Complete the second sentence so that it means the same as the first, using the word in bold. Use between two and five words.

0 They're too young to get married. **old**
   They .... *aren't old enough to* .... get married.

1 I'm not tall enough to see over everyone's heads in a crowd. **short**
   I'm .... over everyone's heads in a crowd.

2 She was very tired and she couldn't play tennis. **too**
   She .... tennis.

3 You walk too fast for me! **slowly**
   You don't .... me!

4 The box was very heavy and he couldn't lift it. **him**
   The box was .... lift.

5 He writes too badly to be a journalist. **well**
   He doesn't write .... a journalist.

6 They were speaking very quietly and I couldn't hear what they were saying. **for**
   They were speaking .... hear what they were saying.

23c Complete the letter. Use one word in each gap.

We moved into our new flat last week and everything went well. We hired a removal company because some of the furniture was too heavy for us (0) ....*to*........ lift. We were worried that the sofa was going to be (1) .... big for the sitting room, but it fits perfectly.

The flat's quite small – it's only just big enough (2) .... us. The balcony's nice – it's wide (3) .... for a table and some chairs. My bedroom looks out onto the street and is quite noisy. I think it's going to be too noisy (4) .... me to work in – I'll have to go to the library. At least it's too small for me (5) .... share with Molly! I'm glad we have our own rooms at last!

24   *so ... that, such (a/an) ... that*

- We use *so/such* to emphasise adjectives, adverbs and quantities. We use:
  - *so* + adjective/adverb: *Beth's **so nice**!   He drives **so slowly**!*
  - *such* + adjective + uncountable/plural noun: *We had **such good** weather!*
    *She wears **such lovely** clothes!*
  - *such a/an* + adjective + singular noun: *We had **such a good** time!*
  - *so* + much/many: *I've got **so much** work to do!*

- We use *so ... that/such (a/an) ... that* to talk about the result of something: *I was **so** tired **that** I fell asleep.   It was **such** hard work **that** I was soon exhausted. There were **so many** people in the hall **that** we could hardly move.*

P R A C T I C E

24a Complete the conversation. Use *so, such* or *such a*.

A: Jason's (0) ......*such*........ a lovely person! He's (1) .... kind and generous! And he has (2) .... good sense of humour too.

B: Yes, he has. He tells (3) .... hilarious jokes sometimes!

A: I know! We had (4) .... good fun with him last summer on holiday. He made friends with everyone (5) .... easily! He's been (6) .... good friend to me.

24b Complete the second sentence so that it means the same as the first. Use *so ... that* or *such (a) ... that*.

0 We couldn't see the band because we were very far from the stage.
   We were ....*so far from the stage that*.......... we couldn't see the band.

1 I couldn't hear her because there was too much noise.
   There was .... I couldn't hear her.

2 We couldn't cycle because the wind was very strong.
   The wind was .... we couldn't cycle.

3 We went to the beach because it was a beautiful day.
   It was .... we went to the beach.

4 I could see everything clearly because the moon was shining very brightly.
   The moon was shining .... I could see everything clearly.

5 We always go there because they have very good food.
   They have .... we always go there.

6 We can't sit outside because there are too many insects.
   There are .... we can't sit outside.

7 We left before the end because the play was boring.
   The play was .... we left before the end.

8 I've read the book three times because it's very good.
   It's .... I've read it three times.

25 Other comparative structures

- To show that something is increasing or decreasing, we can use comparative + *and* + comparative: *The party got **noisier and noisier**.   Change seems **less and less likely**.*

- We can also use *more and more/less and less/fewer and fewer* + noun: ***More and more people** are travelling by air.   She spends **less and less time** at home.*

- To say that one situation depends on another, we can use *the* + comparative + *the* + comparative: ***The earlier** we set out, **the sooner** we'll get there.*

- We can use *the* + comparative + *the better* on its own: *'Do you like hot weather?' 'Yes, **the hotter the better**.'*

PRACTICE

25a Complete the sentences. Use comparative + *and* **+ comparative.**

0   We're going to need .... *more and more* .... energy. (much)

1   The world's getting .... (hot)

2   Pollution's getting .... (bad)

3   Some countries are getting .... rain each year. (little)

4   There are .... forests. (few)

5   The ice in the Arctic is melting .... (quickly)

25b Complete the sentences. Use *the* **+ comparative +** *the* **+ comparative.**

0   When I'm busy, I'm happy. In fact, the busier I am,
.... *the happier I am* ....

1   If you cook it for a long time, it tastes nice. In fact, the longer you cook it,
....

2   Good clothes are often expensive. Usually, the better they are,
....

3   We drive more slowly on narrow roads. In fact, the narrower the road,
....

4   You'll make more mistakes if you're tired. In fact, the more tired you are,
....

5   You feel energetic when you're fit. Generally, the fitter you are,
....

25c Complete the conversations. Use *the* **+ comparative +** *the better*.

0   **A:** Do you like staying in smart hotels?   **B:** Yes. ..... *The smarter the better!* .....

1   **A:** Shall we get her a big bunch of flowers?   **B:** Yes. ....

2   **A:** Do you like puzzles that are really hard?   **B:** Yes. ....

3   **A:** This coffee's very strong. Is that OK?   **B:** Yes. ....

4   **A:** Are you looking for a cheap phone?   **B:** Yes. ....

5   **A:** Shall we meet soon?   **B:** Sure! ....

Check 5 Comparative structures

1 Complete the sentences. Use the words in the box. You do not need all of them.

> fewer and fewer   the fewest   less and less
> the least   more   more and more   more or less

1 .... people want to do sport, so we need another sports centre.

2 I don't often see Joe. He's spending .... time with me and my friends these days.

3 These are a little bit more expensive than the others, but they're .... the same price.

4 The person who gives me .... encouragement with my music is my brother. He thinks it's a waste of time.

5 This area has .... shops in the whole town. There's only a food shop, a newsagent's and a hairdresser's.

/ 5

2 Circle the correct answer.

A: That was (6) *such / such* a nice meal! And that fruit tart was (7) *so / such* gorgeous!

B: Thank you. I put (8) *less / fewer* sugar in it than I usually do. Was it OK?

A: Yes, it was great. Was it hard to make?

B: No, it was really easy. Often, the simpler the recipe is, (9) *nicer / the nicer* the food is.

A: Yes. Some recipes are (10) *too complicated / complicated enough*, so you can't follow them properly – and then the food tastes awful!

/ 5

3 Complete the second sentence so that it means the same as the first, using the word in bold. Use between two and five words.

11 I'm not confident enough to ask questions in class. **shy**
I'm .... questions in class.

12 Their new CD and their last CD are both very good. **as**
Their new CD is just .... their last one.

13 We've decided not to go to the concert because the tickets are too expensive. **that**
The tickets are .... we've decided not to go to the concert.

14 He watches more television than I do. **much**
I don't watch .... he does.

15 They didn't sleep in Tom's tent because it was too small. **them**
Tom's tent wasn't .... sleep in.

/ 5

4 Complete the e-mail. Use one word in each gap.

● ● ●	New Message	▭

Sorry you couldn't come with us on Saturday. It was such (16) .... shame! I hope you're better now. Maybe you had the same thing (17) .... Mark. He was ill last week too.

We went on a good ride. It was quite similar (18) .... the one you and I did in April. Jack thought it was too long, but I loved it – the longer (19) .... better, I think! It was a bit difficult in places, though. There were a few hills that were too steep (20) .... us, so we had to get off our bikes and walk, but the rest of the ride was quite easy.

/ 5

Total: / 20

✓ Self-check

Wrong answers	Look again at	Try CD-ROM
4, 5, 8	**Unit 21**	Exercise 21
3, 12, 14, 17, 18	**Unit 22**	Exercise 22
10, 11, 15, 20	**Unit 23**	Exercise 23
6, 7, 13, 16	**Unit 24**	Exercise 24
1, 2, 9, 19	**Unit 25**	Exercise 25

Now do **Check 5**

Present tenses

26   Present simple or present continuous?

Compare the uses of the present simple and present continuous:

We use the present simple:	We use the present continuous:
for habitual and repeated events/actions: *It **rains** a lot here.*	for actions in progress at the moment of speaking: *Oh no! It's **raining**!*
with adverbs of frequency (e.g. *always, never*), to say how often something happens: *I **always get up** at 6 a.m.*	with *always*, to show that something happens often and is surprising or annoying: *I'm **always losing** my keys!*
for situations/states that are true at the present time or usually true (permanent): *I **live** in Berlin.* *My brother **goes** to college in York.*	for situations/states that are true for a limited period (temporary): *I'm **living** in Hamburg **at the moment**.* *He's **doing** a work placement **this month**.*
for facts that are always true: *The sun **rises** in the east.*	for situations/states that are changing: *Our summers **are getting** hotter.*

▸▸   ***See Appendix 4: Spelling rules for present simple verbs, page 169, Appendix 5: Spelling rules for verbs + -ing, page 170 and Appendix 7: Verb forms, page 170.***

PRACTICE

26a Complete the sentences. Use the present simple or present continuous of the verbs in brackets.

0   The bus ....*doesn't stop*........ outside the cinema. (not stop)

1   Fiona .... today. She's at home. (not work)

2   The boys are outside. They .... in the garden. (sit)

3   I .... Spanish very well, but I understood what he said. (not speak)

4   My sister .... a lot. She's got lots of books. (read)

5   Is Emma on the phone to Kate again? She .... to her! (always / talk)

6   I .... work at seven. (always / start)

7   Who .... that awful noise? I can't stand it! (make)

8   .... very cold here in the winter? (it / get)

26b Circle the correct answer.

A: What's the matter? (0) *Do you get /* (*Are you getting*) tired?

B: Yes, a bit. And I'm cold.

A: Have you got a hat? I read somewhere that our body (1) *loses / 's losing* a lot of heat from the head. And you probably need something to eat. We (2) *use / 're using* a lot of energy during exercise. Would you like some chocolate?

B: No, thanks. I (3) *never eat / 'm never eating* chocolate. But I'll put my hat on!

A: Hi, Ben!

B: Hi, Adam! I haven't seen you for ages! How are you?

A: I'm fine. I (4) *live / 'm living* in Cardiff for a few months. I (5) *help / 'm helping* my uncle with his new house.

B: Really? My cousin (6) *lives / 's living* near Cardiff. She (7) *works / 's working* in a hospital there.

A: There are a lot of new shops near you, aren't there?

B: Yes, we (8) *become / 're becoming* quite trendy! New people (9) *move / are moving* in and a lot of new shops (10) *open / are opening*. I like it, but I hate the traffic.

27 State verbs

- Verbs that describe states are not usually used in the continuous form. Common state verbs include:

Mental/Thinking verbs	agree, believe, know, remember, think, understand
Attitude verbs	hate, like, love, need, prefer, want, wish
Sense/Perception verbs	hear, see, smell, taste
Appearance, qualities	appear, look (= seem), seem, sound
Being, possession	be, belong, contain, have, own
Other verbs	cost, fit, mean, owe

*I'm sorry, I **don't understand**.   Your job **sounds** really interesting.*
***Does** this car **belong** to you?   I **owe** Jessica £150.*

- Some state verbs can be used in the continuous form when they describe actions. They include: *be, have, see, smell, taste* and *think*. Compare: *I **think** (= believe) you're right.   I'm **thinking** about (= considering) it.   I **see** (= understand) what you mean.   I'm **seeing** (= meeting) Tom tomorrow.*

- With *feel* and *look*, we can use either the simple or the continuous form with no change in meaning: *I **feel**/'m **feeling** ill. You **look**/'re **looking** tired.*

- We often use *can* with sense/perception verbs: *I **can't hear** you.*

- *See* and *hear* are state verbs, but *look* and *listen* describe actions. Compare: ***Do** you **see** that girl over there?   I'm **looking** at your photos. I **can hear** voices next door.   Please be quiet. I'm **listening** to some music.*

PRACTICE

27a **Complete the sentences. Use the present simple or present continuous of the verbs in the box.**

cost   cry   not agree   not enjoy   prefer   ~~understand~~   wait

0 ....*Do*.... you ....*understand*.... how this works?

1 I'm sorry, but I .... with you.

2 Excuse me, how much .... these DVD players .... ?

3 What's the matter, Becky? Why .... you .... ?

4 I .... soul music to rap.

5 Hurry up! Nikki and Anna .... for us!

6 Actually, I'm unhappy because I .... my course.

27b **Circle the correct answer.**

0 We *have /* *'re having* dinner at the moment.

1 I'm not eating all the yoghurt! I *taste / 'm tasting* it to see if it's still OK.

2 *Do you see / Are you seeing* that blue car over there? It's Ben's.

3 I'm all right. I *think / 'm thinking* about what I have to do tomorrow.

4 This soup *tastes / 's tasting* awful!

5 I love this shampoo. It *smells / 's smelling* of coconuts.

6 Sophie *thinks / 's thinking* I watch too much television.

7 My college *has / is having* some very good sports facilities.

8 I took this photo last week. This is me and this is Kim. She *smells / 's smelling* the flowers.

27c **Complete the conversations. Use the present simple or present continuous of the verbs in brackets.**

A: (0) ......*Do you want*...... (you / want) to come to the cinema with us tomorrow evening?

B: Thanks, but I can't. I (1) .... (see) Nicole and Kelly then.

A: Is your driving test today? (2) .... (you / feel) nervous?

B: Yes, a bit. I (3) .... (think) it's going to be quite difficult.

A: Is Mark here?

B: Yes. He (4) .... (listen) to some music in his room.

A: Oh yes, I can hear it. It (5) .... (sound) good.

A: Are you OK? You (6) .... (look) a bit worried.

B: I'm OK. I (7) .... (think) about how to help my brother. He's got a lot of problems at college.

A: Maybe he (8) .... (need) professional help. There are some good advisors there.

Past tenses

28 Past simple

We use the past simple to talk about past actions or states, often with time expressions like *yesterday, last week, a year ago, when I was young,* etc.: **I *saw* Matt *yesterday*.** We ***were*** in France **two weeks ago**.

▶▶ **See Appendix 6: Spelling rules for verbs + -ed, page 170, Appendix 7: Verb forms, page 170 and Appendix 8: Irregular verbs, page 171.**

P R A C T I C E

28a Complete the sentences. Use the past simple of the verbs in brackets.

0   I .... *did* .... a cycle ride for charity last year. (do)

1   We .... from the most northerly point of Ireland to the most southerly. (go)

2   It .... us seven days to cover about 670 kilometres. (take)

3   On most days, we .... about 150 kilometres. (cycle)

4   We .... some beautiful lakes and rivers. (see)

5   We .... in expensive hotels. (not stay)

6   One man .... the ride because he .... ill. (not finish, be)

7   We .... very proud when we .... the end. (feel, reach)

8   I .... I had so many muscles that could hurt! (not know)

28b Complete the articles. Use the past simple of the verbs in the box.

admit	~~be~~	crash	have	lose	not have	not perform	not play	start

There (0) .... *was* .... a huge traffic jam on the M6 yesterday after two lorries (1) .... into each other. People (2) .... to wait in their cars for hours. 'We (3) .... any food or water, so it was very difficult for the children,' one driver said. Traffic eventually (4) .... moving at 5.00 p.m., eight hours after the accident.

City (5) .... their match against United, 2– 0. City's best striker, Anderson, (6) .... because of a recent injury. After the match, their manager, Jimmy Simmons, (7) .... , 'We (8) .... well and we know that we have to improve.'

29 Past simple and past continuous

- We use the past continuous to talk about an action or situation in progress at a particular time in the past: *I **was working** at eight o'clock last night.*

- We also use the past continuous to describe the background scene in a story: *The sun **was shining** and I **was walking** along the High Street.*

- When a short action interrupts an action in progress, we use *when* before the action in the past simple and *while/when* before the action in the past continuous: ***When he arrived**, I **was working**.   My car **broke down while/when** I **was driving** home.*

- When one action happens after another, we use the past simple: *When Sam **arrived**, I **cooked** a meal.* (= Sam arrived and then I cooked a meal.)

⚠ We don't usually use state verbs in continuous tenses: *When I met her, she **seemed** upset.* (Not *she ~~was seeming~~ upset*)

▶▶ *See Appendix 7: Verb forms, page 170.*

PRACTICE

29a Complete the sentences. Use the past simple or past continuous of the verbs in brackets.

   0 Sarah wasn't here in June. She ......*was travelling*...... round Europe. (travel)

   1 This time last year we .... that big concert. (plan)

   2 The museum was quite crowded when I visited it. A teacher .... a group of schoolchildren round and they .... some of the objects. (take, draw)

   3 The police .... his story. (not believe)

   4 It was eight o'clock in the morning. I was still in bed and my brother .... ready for school. (get)

   5 I didn't eat anything for lunch because I .... the food in the cafeteria. (not like)

   6 We .... anything at ten. We were really tired. (not do)

   7 It was chaos last night at the airport. Thousands of people .... for flights. (wait)

   8 We .... to go, but we had to. (not want)

   9 Rachel called earlier this morning. She .... very upset. (sound)

   10 I .... to my new CD, so I didn't hear the phone. (listen)

29b Circle the correct answer.

   0 **A:** What *were you saying* / (*did you say*) when she asked you?
      B: 'Yes'.

   1 **A:** Where *was Laura going* / *did Laura go* when we met her?
      B: She was on her way to London.

2 **A:** *Were you and Mark practising / Did you and Mark practise* your songs when I called?
  B: No. Mark wasn't here.

3 **A:** How *were you feeling / did you feel* when you passed your driving test?
  B: Incredibly pleased!

4 **A:** *Were people dancing / Did people dance* when you got to the party?
  B: No. Everybody was in the kitchen.

5 **A:** What *did you do / were you doing* when you left school in June?
  B: Nothing! I just wanted to rest.

6 **A:** Why *did you hide / were you hiding* your shopping bag when she came in?
  B: Because there's a present for her in it.

29C Complete the e-mail. Use the past simple or past continuous of the verbs in brackets.

I (0) ...**was walking**.... (walk) down the street this morning when I (1) .... (see) a lot of people in front of me. They (2) .... (watch) something. When I (3) .... (get) nearer, I saw what (4) .... (happen). A man (5) .... (lie) on the pavement. He (6) .... (bleed). Two other men (7) .... (stand) near him. One of them (8) .... (hold) a gun. A woman (9) .... (cry). I froze! Then suddenly, someone (10) .... (shout) 'Cut!' The woman (11) .... (stop) crying and the wounded man (12) .... (stand) up. Then I (13) .... (notice) a camera and (14) .... (realise) that they (15) .... (make) a film!

30 *used to, would, be/get used to*

- We use *used to* or *would* + infinitive to talk about something that happened regularly in the past: *I **used to go** jogging every day until I hurt my knee. He **would stay up** all night when he was younger.*
- We use *used to* (not *would*) for a situation that was true in the past: *She **used to have** long hair.   I **didn't use to like** pop music.   Where **did** they **use to live**?*
- We use *be/get used to* + noun/pronoun/*-ing* to talk about something that seems or becomes normal because we've experienced it before: *We don't mind the cold weather. We're **used to it**. (= It's normal for us.)   You'll soon **get used to wearing** glasses. (= It will become normal for you.)*

PRACTICE

30a **Complete the sentences. Use *used to* or *would* and the verbs in brackets. Sometimes both are possible.**

0 We .... *would go* .... to two or three films every week. (go)

1 We .... home very early in the morning when we went on holiday. (leave)

2 A few years ago, I .... many friends, but I do now. (not have)

3 .... near the airport? (you / live)

4 We .... hours talking about our dreams. (spend)

5 She .... us funny stories about the animals on the farm. (tell)

6 There .... many cars on the road in those days. (not be)

7 I .... all kinds of ball games when I was a child. (love)

8 My dad .... football with us on Sundays when we were little. (play)

30b **Circle the correct answer.**

0 I come from London, so *I'm* / *I'm getting* used to big cities.

1 After London, it's hard to *be* / *get* used to living in the country. It's very different.

2 It took me a few weeks to *be* / *get* used to my new surroundings.

3 *I'm not* / *I'm not getting* used to the silence. I miss the noise.

4 At the moment my parents have to drive me everywhere. I don't like that because *I'm* / *I'm getting* used to being independent.

5 The pace of life here seems a bit slow, but I'm sure I'll *be* / *get* used to it.

6 Change is hard for everyone, but we *'re* / *get* used to new things quite quickly.

30c **Complete the article. Use one word in each gap.**

Before the accident, I (0) ...... *used* ...... to be very sporty. I used (1) .... play tennis, swim, go running and go dancing. Every day I (2) .... come home from school and then go out and run or go swimming.

Now, after the accident, I can walk, but only with difficulty. I had to learn to walk again, really. I found it extremely frustrating and I (3) .... to get very angry and upset. But then I started learning to ride and things began to change. As a child, I was scared of horses and I (4) .... refuse to go near them, but I (5) .... used to them now. I really love them. Riding has given me more confidence.

I'm getting (6) .... to my body and the way I look, and I feel happy. I didn't use (7) .... go out with my friends because I didn't want people to look at me, but I don't mind now. I've (8) .... used to people looking and I just ignore it now. There are more important things to think about.

Check 6 Present and past tenses

1 Circle the correct answer.

1 Jamie *has* / *'s having* a shower at the moment.

2 *Did you live* / *Were you living* there for a long time?

3 Everybody *parks* / *'s parking* in this street because it's close to the shops.

4 We met each other while we *did* / *were doing* a course in Cardiff.

5 Everything *gets* / *'s getting* much more expensive, especially housing.

/ 5

2 Complete the sentences. Use the present simple, past simple or past continuous of the verbs in the box.

last not answer see send wait

6 He .... when I asked him his name.

7 At eleven o'clock last night, we .... for our bus in the rain!

8 Winter .... a long time in northern countries like Russia and Canada.

9 .... you .... that red car over there? It's Paul's. He bought it last week.

10 Kate always .... me a postcard when she's on holiday.

/ 5

3 Complete the letter. Use the present simple, past simple or past continuous of the verbs in brackets.

I (11) .... (leave) university in 2002 and (12) .... (get) an administrative job in my local hospital. While I (13) .... (work) there, I (14) .... (become) very interested in health care, especially nursing. I would like to become a nurse because I (15) .... (want) to learn how to help people.

/ 5

4 Complete the second sentence so that it means the same as the first, using the word in bold. Use between two and five words.

16 I told Louise everything when we were close friends. **used**
I .... Louise everything when we were close friends.

17 My mother made fantastic birthday cakes for us when we were children. **would**
My mother .... fantastic birthday cakes for us when we were children.

18 My new bike felt strange at first, but it soon felt normal. **used**
My new bike felt strange at first, but I soon .... it.

19 It isn't normal for her to go everywhere by bus. **going**
She isn't .... everywhere by bus.

20 I didn't like olives at all when I was younger, but I love them now. **use**
I .... olives at all when I was younger, but I love them now.

/ 5

Total: / 20

✓ Self-check

Wrong answers	Look again at	Try CD-ROM
3, 5, 8, 10	**Unit 26**	Exercise 26
1, 9, 15	**Unit 27**	Exercise 27
6, 11, 12	**Unit 28**	Exercise 28
2, 4, 7, 13, 14	**Unit 29**	Exercise 29
16, 17, 18, 19, 20	**Unit 30**	Exercise 30

Now do **Check 6**

Perfect tenses

31 Present perfect for recent events

- We use the present perfect to talk about an action that happened at some time in the recent past. We don't say when it happened because this isn't important. We are thinking about the present result of the action: *I've met* Tom. (= I know him now.) *He's broken his leg.* (= His leg is broken now.)

- We use the past simple (not the present perfect) to talk about an action that happened at a specific time in the past. We usually say when it happened: *I met Tom last year.* *He broke his leg two years ago.* *She passed her driving test yesterday.*

- To emphasise that something happened in the very recent past, we can use *just, recently* (= a short time ago), *already* (= before now or before a particular time) or *yet* (= up to now). Note that we can't use *just* at the end of a sentence: *Sophie's just left.* *Have you seen Molly recently?* *Jack's already left.* *Have you already eaten?* *The film's started already.* *I haven't read that book yet.* *Have you finished yet?*

- We use the past simple (not the present perfect) to give more details about recent events: *'Have you heard? Mary's had a baby!'* *'When did she have it?'* *'Last night!'*

▶▶ **See Appendix 6: Spelling rules for verbs + -ed, page 170, Appendix 7: Verb forms, page 170 and Appendix 8: Irregular verbs, page 171.**

PRACTICE

31a Complete the sentences. Use the present perfect of the verbs in brackets.

0 I haven't got my rucksack because Matt ....*'s borrowed*............ it. (borrow)

1 Your hair .... a lot! (grow)

2 The kitchen's in a mess because no one .... the washing-up. (do)

3 Has she still got her car or .... it? (she / sell)

4 A lot of new people .... our drama group. (join)

5 We .... the map, so we'll have to try to remember the way. (not bring)

6 Are you coming with us or .... to stay at home? (you / decide)

7 I .... my new address to many people. (not give)

8 Are they still doing exams or .... ? (they / finish)

9 Lisa .... I don't know if she's coming with us. (not call)

10 I .... all my photos in this album. (put)

31b Circle the correct answer.

0 **A:** What's your new CD like? **B:** I haven't listened to it *yet* / *just*.

1 **A:** How's Josh? **B:** I haven't seen him *recently* / *just*.

2 **A:** Would you like some coffee? **B:** No, I've *recently* / *already* had four cups.

3 **A:** Are you OK? You sound tired. **B:** I'm fine. I've *recently* / *just* woken up.

4 **A:** Will she help us? **B:** Maybe. I haven't asked her *already* / *yet*.

5 **A:** Have you played *recently* / *just*? **B:** No, not for a few weeks.

6 **A:** Have they gone *recently* / *yet*? **B:** No, they're still here.

7 **A:** What's the matter? **B:** I've *already* / *just* banged my elbow!

8 **A:** I want to lose three more kilos. **B:** But you've *already* / *yet* lost five!

31c Complete the articles. Use the present perfect or past simple of the verbs in brackets.

Two students (0) ....*have raised*........ (raise) £500 for charity. They (00) ....*cooked*........ (cook) a three-course meal for seventy people.

Our local volleyball team (1) .... (win) a place in the regional final. The Gantley Ladies (2) .... (beat) the Colewood Ladies in an extremely exciting match.

Firefighters (3) .... (return) to work after a two-day strike. They (4) .... (agree) to go back after a meeting with fire service managers.

A millionaire (5) .... (give) Whitford Hospital £100,000. Mr Brian Jackson gave the money to the children's ward, where his son (6) .... (receive) treatment a year ago.

31d Circle the correct answer.

○ ○ ○   New Message   ⊖

I'm having a good time with Justine and her family. They (0) *moved* / *'ve moved* here last summer, so they're still getting used to their new place. It's quite big and modern and they (1) *decorated* / *'ve decorated* it beautifully. Justine (2) *didn't change* / *hasn't changed*. She's just the same – full of fun!

My French (3) *improved* / *has improved* a lot – I can understand more now than when I arrived – and I (4) *learnt* / *'ve learnt* to ride a scooter, so we go out on our scooters every day. Justine (5) *bought* / *'s bought* one last year, and I (6) *hired* / *'ve hired* one.

Yesterday we (7) *had* / *'ve had* a wonderful time at the swimming pool. We go there quite often and I (8) *got* / *'ve got* quite good at diving.

32 Present perfect for general experiences

- We use the present perfect to talk about things that have happened and experiences we've had in our lives up to now: *There **have been** a few problems.   She's **had** a lot of different jobs.*

- We can use *always, often, once, twice,* etc. to talk about frequency: *He's **always wanted** to be an actor.   I've **met** her **once**.*

- We use *ever* and *never* to ask or say if something has happened or not: ***Have** you **ever been** to Spain?   I've **never climbed** a mountain.*

- We also use the present perfect with *ever* and *never*:
  - to talk about something that is happening for the first time: *This is **the first time** she's **ever flown**.   She's **never flown before**.*
  - with the comparative and superlative: *This is **the best** film I've **ever seen**. I've **never seen** a **better** film.*

 Notice the difference between *have/has been* and *have/has gone*:

*Mike's **been** to Rome.* (He went to Rome in the past but he's back now.)   *Mike's **gone** to Rome.* (He's in Rome now.)

- We use the past simple to give more details about our experiences: *Tina's **travelled** all over the world. She **went** to New Zealand last year and last month she **spent** a week in Iceland.*

PRACTICE

32a Complete the conversations. Use the present perfect of the verbs in brackets.

- **0** **A:** *Have you ever been* .... to hospital? (you / ever / be)
  B: No, I haven't. I ......*'ve never been*......... seriously ill. (never / be)

- **1** **A:** .... to you about her course? (Sophie / ever / talk)
  B: No. She .... it. (never / mention)

- **2** **A:** .... golf? (you / ever / play)
  B: No. I .... it looked boring. (always / think)

- **3** **A:** .... their songs in public? (they / ever / perform)
  B: No. They .... the chance. (never / have)

- **4** **A:** .... bungee jumping? (you / ever / try)
  B: No. I .... afraid of heights. (always / be)

- **5** **A:** .... at you? (he / ever / shout)
  B: No. He .... very kind and polite. (always / be)

- **6** **A:** .... an e-mail to the wrong person?
  (you / ever / send)
  B: No, I .... that. That sounds awful! (never / do)

32b Complete the second sentence so that it means the same as the first, using the word in bold. Use between two and five words.

   0 I haven't been to Scotland before. **first**
     This is the ....*first time I've ever*.......... been to Scotland.

   1 They've never invited us to dinner before. **time**
     This is .... ever invited us to dinner.

   2 This is the first time we've ever been camping. **never**
     We .... camping before.

   3 She hasn't tried to ride a bike before. **ever**
     This is the first .... to ride a bike.

   4 This is the first time I've made this, but it tastes nice. **before**
     I .... , but it tastes nice.

   5 Have you never watched this before? **first**
     Is this .... ever watched this?

32c Complete the letter. Use *ever* and the present perfect of the verbs in brackets.

> This is definitely the biggest city (0) ....*I've ever lived*........ (I / live) in.
> There are lots of interesting places and fantastic restaurants. The food is
> brilliant. It's the best food (1) .... (I / have) anywhere!
>
> It's very hot at the moment. Luckily, the flat I'm in is quite cool. It's a
> lovely place and it has the most amazing kitchen (2) ....
> (I / see)! It's huge!
>
> The family I work for are lovely. In fact, they're the nicest family
> (3) .... (I / work) for. The children are sweet but quite
> shy. The little girl hardly says anything! But she's the sweetest little girl
> (4) .... (I / meet)!
>
> Coming here was the scariest thing (5) .... (I / do) –
> because it's so far from home – but it's exciting too.

32d Circle the correct answer.

   0 They *wrote* / *('ve written)* some great songs together. They *(recorded)* / *'ve recorded* some of them on their CD last year.

   1 Caroline's *been* / *gone* to the sports centre. She'll be back at eight.

   2 I *only was* / *'ve only been* skiing once. I *didn't enjoy* / *haven't enjoyed* it much!

   3 Rob's *been* / *gone* to the DVD shop, so we've got two DVDs for tonight.

   4 I *was* / *'ve been* to the Globe Theatre. I *saw* / *'ve seen* a play there last summer.

   5 She *didn't always live* / *hasn't always lived* here. She *moved* / *'s moved* here in 2001.

   6 I *met* / *'ve met* a lot of Sarah's family and I know them quite well. Her brother *was* / *'s been* in the same class as my sister.

33 Present perfect with stated time reference

- We use the present perfect with *for* and *since* to talk about something that started in the past and has continued up to the present. We use *for* + a period of time and *since* + a time or date: ***for** a month/three years/ages*   ***since** 2004/yesterday/I was four*

- The past simple focuses on a finished action in the past. The present perfect focuses on a continuing situation. Compare these pairs of sentences: *I **met** Sam **two years ago**. = I've **known** Sam **for two years**.   I **moved** to London **in 2002**. = I've **lived** in London **since 2002**.*

- To refer to a period of time that is still continuing, we use the present perfect with expressions like *today, this week, this year,* etc. Compare: *I've **seen** Beth **this morning**.* (It's still morning.)   *I **saw** Beth **this morning**.* (It's now the afternoon or evening.)

P R A C T I C E

33a **Write sentences. Use *for* or *since* and the present perfect.**

0 I / be / very busy / January   *I've been very busy since January.*

1 I / not watch / TV / ages ....

2 I / not tidy / my room / weeks ....

3 I / not speak / to Emma / Friday ....

4 I / not check / my e-mails / ten days ....

5 I / not see / Nikki / last month ....

6 I / not hear / from her / she left ....

33b **Complete the second sentence so that it means the same as the first, using the word in bold. Use between two and five words.**

0 I bought these jeans on Saturday. **had**
I .... *'ve had these jeans since* .... Saturday.

1 Jodie moved here six months ago. **lived**
Jodie .... six months.

2 I started wearing glasses when I was ten. **worn**
I .... I was ten.

3 Mark went upstairs twenty minutes ago. **been**
Mark .... twenty minutes.

4 We met them in June. **known**
We .... June.

5 I got a job here a month ago. **worked**
I .... a month.

6 They got married in 2005. **been**
They .... 2005.

33c **Complete the sentences. Use the present perfect or past simple of the verbs in brackets. The time in brackets is the time now.**

   0 (8.00 p.m.) What ....*did you do*............ this afternoon? (you / do)

   1 (10.00 a.m.) I .... two letters this morning. (write)

   2 (4.00 p.m.) Tim .... round to see you this morning. (come)

   3 (11.30 p.m) .... a good time this afternoon? (you / have)

   4 (2.00 p.m.) I .... four cups of coffee today. (have)

   5 (9.30 p.m.) They .... two DVDs tonight. (watch)

33d **Circle the correct answer.**

I live in a small village in the north of England. We've been here (0) *for /* (*since*) 1998. I've got a lot of friends here. We (1) *knew / 've known* each other (2) *for / since* a long time.

I'm studying Biology. Last year the course (3) *was / has been* a bit boring, but we (4) *did / 've done* some very interesting things this year and I'm enjoying it more.

I work in a supermarket on Saturdays. I've worked there (5) *for / since* the beginning of September. It's quite good fun. I (6) *had / 've had* quite a good time there today, but it's nice to be home now.

34 Present perfect continuous

Compare the present perfect continuous with the present perfect simple:

Present perfect continuous	Present perfect simple
You've been cooking! I can smell it! (focus on a recent action)	*You've cooked the dinner! Thanks!* (focus on the present result of a recent action)
I've been painting the kitchen. I've got one wall to do. (The action is not complete.)	*I've painted the kitchen. It looks lovely, doesn't it?* (The action is complete.)
It's been raining for two hours! (focus on how long)	*It's rained twice this week.* (focus on how often/how many)
I've been living here this summer, but I'm leaving next week. (temporary situation)	*I've lived here all my life.* (permanent situation)

- With *work, teach, study* and *live*, we can use the present perfect simple or continuous + *for/since* with no change in meaning: *I've worked/'ve been working here for years.*
- We use the present perfect simple with state verbs: *I've known him since 2003.*

▶▶ *See Appendix 7: Verb forms, page 170.*

PRACTICE

34a The picture shows people doing different things and the times they started doing them. Look at it and complete the sentences. Use the present perfect continuous of the verbs in the box.

| jog read ~~shop~~ sit stand talk work |

The time now is 11.30 a.m.

0 She ....*'s been shopping*.......... since ten past ten.

1 They .... at the bus stop since quarter past eleven.

2 He .... for twenty minutes.

3 She .... there since eleven o'clock.

4 He .... on his computer since half past ten.

5 He .... his newspaper for fifteen minutes.

6 They .... to each other for forty-five minutes.

34b Complete the conversation. Use the present perfect continuous of the verbs in brackets.

A: Hello! Sorry, but we're going to be a bit late. We're stuck in traffic. We (0) ....*'ve been sitting*.......... (sit) here for about fifteen minutes. Are you still at home?

B: Yes. Has your journey been awful?

A: No, not too bad, but I'm tired. I (1) .... (drive) all day.

B: How are Emily and Beth?

A: They're fine. They (2) .... (sleep) since six!

B: (3) .... (Emily / sing) to you? She sang to us when we went to France.

A: No! I hope she doesn't! Anyway, what (4) .... (you / do) today?

B: Oh, not much. I (5) .... (read) the book you lent me.

A: Is your brother there?

B: Yes. He's in his room. He's revising for a test. He (6) .... (not do) very well at school lately.

A: Well, we're moving again, so we'll see you in about half an hour.

34c **Complete the sentences. Use the present perfect simple or present perfect continuous of the verbs in brackets. Sometimes both are possible.**

o I ....*'ve written*........... three really long essays this term. (write)

1 He .... here since 1998. (work)

2 Philip .... this car for about two years. (have)

3 Can I sit down? I .... round town in the heat and I feel tired. (walk)

4 He .... Spanish for six months now. (learn)

5 They .... in London for eight years. (live)

6 Be careful! I .... some water by the door. (spill)

7 How long .... ? (it / rain)

8 I .... some tea. Would you like some? (make)

9 Jenny .... a poster for the play. Look. Isn't it brilliant? (design)

10 Hi! How long .... there? (you / stand)

35 Present perfect, past simple or present simple?

- We use the present perfect (not the past simple):
  - for past actions that have a clear result in the present: *Oh, dear! I've spilled my coffee!* (Not *I spilled my coffee!*)
  - for past actions, if we aren't interested in when they happened: *I've been to China.* (Not *I went to China.*)
- We use the past simple (not the present perfect):
  - for actions or situations that finished in the past: *Pelé played football for Brazil.* (Not *Pelé's played football for Brazil.*)
  - when we say the time when something happened in the past: *I bought that CD last weekend.* (Not *I've bought that CD last weekend.*)
- We use the present perfect (not the present simple) for actions or situations that started in the past and continue to the present: *I've worked here since 2003.* (Not *I work here since 2003.*)

P R A C T I C E

35a **Circle the correct answer.**

A: Emma (o) *painted* / (*'s painted*) a picture of a forest on her wall. It looks amazing!

B: (1) *Did anybody help* / *Has anybody helped* her?

A: No, I don't think so. She (2) *did* / *'s done* it all herself.

_____

A: I'm thinking of getting a motorbike. (3) *Did you ever ride* / *Have you ever ridden* one?

B: Yes, but only as a passenger. Steven (4) *took* / *'s taken* me on his once, about a year ago.

_____

A: Do you know that Internet café near the cinema – the One World? They
(5) *added / 've added* another room, so it's much bigger now.
B: Oh. I (6) *didn't go / haven't been* there. Is it nice?

A: My dad (7) *grew up / 's grown up* in Dublin.
B: Really? I (8) *went / 've been* there lots of times. It's a beautiful city.
A: Yes, it is.

35b **Complete the sentences. Use the present simple or present perfect of the verbs in brackets.**

0 I ....*haven't been*........ well for a couple of months. (not be)

1 I .... from ten at night to ten in the morning. (sleep)

2 After lunch I .... quite tired. (feel)

3 I .... these headaches for weeks. (have)

4 I .... any work since the beginning of February. (not do)

5 I .... my friends for a long time. (not see)

6 Most of them .... me every day. (phone)

35c **Complete the article. Use the present simple, past simple or present perfect of the verbs in brackets.**

People who love their jobs

Ahmed Malik (0) ....*sells*............ (sell) newspapers and sweets from his shop in north London. He (1) .... (have) the shop for thirty years. His wife (2) .... (work) in the shop with him and they (3) .... (employ) two assistants. In 2005, they (4) .... (buy) another shop in another part of London and their son now (5) .... (manage) that for them.

Emily Saunders is the head of English in a large secondary school. 'I (6) .... (come) to this school ten years ago as a teacher,' she told us. 'Since last September, I (7) ....

(be) head of the English department. I (8) .... (not teach) as many classes as I used to, but I have other responsibilities. It's a very good school and I'm very happy here.'

David O'Brien is a driver for the Post Office. 'I (9) .... (collect) mail from post offices in my van. I (10) .... (work) for the Post Office for twenty-three years. I was a postman until 1990 and then I (11) .... (get) my own van. I (12) .... (enjoy) the job more since I became a driver. It's more responsible and you don't get wet!'

Check 7 Present perfect (simple and continuous)

1 Circle the correct answer.

1 I *burnt* / *'ve burnt* these burgers a bit. Do you think they're OK?

2 We haven't bought our tickets for the festival *already* / *yet*.

3 Kelly *works* / *'s worked* here since March.

4 He *'s had* / *'s been having* this computer for three years.

5 They *live* / *'ve lived* in the same house since 1967.

/ 5

2 Complete the conversations. Use the present perfect or past simple of the verbs in brackets.

A: Shall we go and see this band?
(6) .... (you / hear) of them?

B: Yes. Becky (7) .... (tell) me about them a few weeks ago. I think they're good.

A: I (8) .... (forget) to ask David for his address last night. Do you think you can remember where his house is?

B: I'll try. I (9) .... (be) there twice. I (10) .... (go) there with Rob in the summer.

/ 5

3 Complete the second sentence so that it means the same as the first, using the word in bold. Use between two and five words.

11 It started raining four hours ago and it hasn't stopped yet. **been**
It .... four hours.

12 This is the first time I've ever driven a van. **never**
I .... a van before.

13 They moved to Stockport in 2003. **lived**
They .... 2003.

14 Ben and Mark started working at six and they haven't finished yet. **been**
Ben and Mark .... six.

15 I met Rob ten years ago. **known**
I .... ten years.

/ 5

4 Circle the correct answer.

```
● ● ●                New Message                ⊖

Hi, Laura!

How are you? I (16) got / 've got your
message on Tuesday, but I (17) haven't had
/ haven't been having time to reply. Sorry!
I (18) was / 've been very busy this week,
mainly with work for college.

Also, Claudia, a friend of mine from Italy,
(19) has stayed / has been staying with
me. She's leaving on Friday, so I could
meet you on Saturday if you're free. We
could go shopping if you like. Claudia
(20) bought / 's bought some really nice
sandals at the market last week and I
think I'd like a pair.

Anyway, give me a ring and we can
arrange something.

Isabel
```

/ 5

Total: / 20

Self-check

Wrong answers	Look again at	Try CD-ROM
2, 7, 8, 16, 20	Unit 31	Exercise 31
6, 9, 10, 12	Unit 32	Exercise 32
13, 15, 18	Unit 33	Exercise 33
4, 11, 14, 17, 19	Unit 34	Exercise 34
1, 3, 5	Unit 35	Exercise 35

Now do **Check 7**

36 Past perfect

● We use the past perfect to show that one action happened before another action in the past: *I phoned Carla's home, but she'd gone out.* (= First Carla went out. Then I phoned Carla's home.)

● We use many of the same time expressions we use with the present perfect, e.g.:
  – *already* and *just*: *We got to the cinema late and the film **had already started**. I **had just had** lunch, so I wasn't hungry.*
  – *for* and *since*: *I was sad to leave because I'd lived there for ten years.   Tim was my best friend. We'd known each other since we were five.*
  – *ever* and *never*: *He was very excited because he'd never been to America before. It was the funniest thing she'd ever seen.*

 We use the past simple (not the past perfect) to talk about single actions in the past: *I **left** London a year ago.* (Not *I'd left London a year ago.*)

▶▶ **See Appendix 6: Spelling rules for verbs + -ed, page 170, Appendix 7: Verb forms, page 170 and Appendix 8: Irregular verbs, page 171.**

PRACTICE

36a Complete the sentences. Use the past perfect of the verbs in brackets.

0 The car stopped because we ....*'d run*............... out of petrol. (run)

1 I was cold because I .... any warm clothes. (not take)

2 We wanted to visit our cousins last weekend, but they .... to go to London. (arrange)

3 The computer crashed. Luckily, I .... all my work on it. (save)

4 He felt very tired because he .... well. (not sleep)

5 Did they send you the wrong books or .... the wrong ones? (you / order)

6 The soup didn't taste nice because I .... to put salt in it. (forget)

36b Complete the sentences. Use *already, ever* or *never* and the past perfect of the verbs in brackets.

0 It was the first time she ....*'d ever competed*............... in the Olympics. (compete)

1 She wanted an Olympic medal because she .... one before. (win)

2 She had done very badly in her last race. It was the worst race she .... (run)

3 Her trainer .... her to rest, and he told her again that she was not fit enough. (advise)

4 A month later, she .... , so she began training for the next competition. (recover)

5 She began writing a book about her career. She was quite nervous because she .... a book before. (write)

37 Past perfect and past simple

- We can use the past perfect and the past simple in one sentence with linking words and expressions such as:
  - *by the time*: **By the time** we **got** to the airport, our flight **had left**.
  - *after, as soon as, before*: **After** we**'d done** the washing-up, we **went** for a walk. **As soon as** he**'d left**, I **phoned** Anna.   She**'d finished** her project **before** she **went out**.

- It's often possible to use either the past perfect or the past simple with *after, as soon as* and *before*: **As soon as** he **left**, I **phoned** Anna.

- Compare these sentences with *when*: *When I* **arrived**, *Tim* **left**. (= I arrived. Then Tim left.)   *When I* **arrived**, *Tim* **had left**. (= Tim left. Then I arrived.)

⚠️ We don't use the past perfect for both actions in a sentence if one happened after the other: *They***'d eaten** *all the food by the time we* **got** *there*. (Not ~~They'd eaten all the food by the time we'd got there.~~)

P R A C T I C E

37a Complete the sentences. Use the past perfect or past simple of the verbs in brackets. Sometimes both are possible.

   0 By the time he ....*started*........ his exams, I ....*'d finished*......... mine. (start, finish)

   1 As soon as they .... the car, they .... it. (repair, sell)

   2 Beth .... round after she .... Rob to the station. (come, take)

   3 I .... my room before I .... to bed. (tidy, go)

   4 As soon as we .... our bags in our rooms, we .... lunch. (put, have)

   5 They .... by the time I .... (leave, arrive)

   6 After I .... to him, I .... better. (talk, feel)

37b Complete the sentences. Use the past perfect or past simple.

   0 I asked him to help me. He agreed.
      When I ....*asked*................ him to help me, he ....*agreed*........... .

   1 Joe left college. Then I met him.
      By the time I .... Joe, he .... college.

   2 They had lunch. Then I saw them.
      When I .... them, they .... lunch.

   3 I spent all my money. Then I left the fair.
      By the time I .... the fair, I .... all my money.

   4 She failed her Maths exam. She was very disappointed.
      When she .... her Maths exam, she .... very disappointed.

5 The fire destroyed most of the shop. Then the firefighters arrived.

When the firefighters .... , the fire .... most of the shop.

6 We ate two tubs of popcorn. Then the film started.

By the time the film .... , we .... two tubs of popcorn.

7 We looked on the Internet. We found a lot of information.

When we .... on the Internet, we .... a lot of information.

37C **Complete the stories. Use the past perfect or past simple of the verbs in brackets. Sometimes both are possible.**

When she went into the kitchen, she (0) .... *saw* .... (see) the letter on the table. After she (1) .... (read) it, she (2) .... (tear) it into small pieces. Then she went for a long walk. By the time she (3) .... (come) home, she (4) .... (form) a plan. She began to pack a small suitcase. She (5) .... (leave) the house by the time he (6) .... (phone) her the next morning.

As soon as I (7) .... (sign) the form, he (8) .... (take) me down a corridor and into a small room. He told me to wait and then he left. Half an hour later, a woman walked into the room. When I (9) .... (ask) her if I could leave, she (10) .... (smile). 'Not yet, Mr Evans,' she said. 'Not yet.' I began to feel anxious.

38 Past tenses in narratives

Read this short narrative:

*Jack **got up** early and **opened** his curtains. The sun **was shining**. He **went** downstairs. A letter **was lying** on the floor by the front door. The postman **had delivered** it earlier. Jack **opened** the letter and **was** delighted to learn that he **had won** a car in a competition.*

● We use the past simple for the main events, to say what happened next: *Jack **got up**. He **went** downstairs.   He **opened** the letter.*

● We use the past continuous for background actions that continued while the main events happened: *The sun **was shining**.   A letter **was lying** on the floor.*

● We use the past perfect when we refer back to something that happened earlier: *The postman **had delivered** it earlier.   He **had won** a car in a competition.*

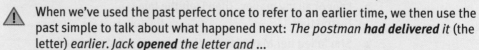 When we've used the past perfect once to refer to an earlier time, we then use the past simple to talk about what happened next: *The postman **had delivered** it (the letter) earlier. Jack **opened** the letter and ...*

PRACTICE

38a **Circle the correct answer.**

> Amy and I went to Lucy's house on Friday night. We (0) (arrived)/ 'd arrived late, but she (1) *didn't prepare / hadn't prepared* any food. In fact, she (2) *had / was having* a bath!

> I (3) *found / 'd found* somebody's diary on the train last week. It (4) *was / had been* on the floor near a seat. Obviously, somebody (5) *dropped / had dropped* it. The owner's name and address (6) *were / had been* inside, so I (7) *sent / was sending* it back to him.

> I (8) *got / was getting* lost on my way to college on the first day. I (9) *forgot / 'd forgotten* to bring a map, so I walked a long way in the wrong direction. The streets were very busy and everybody (10) *walked / was walking* very fast.

38b **Complete the article. Use the past simple, past continuous or past perfect of the verbs in brackets.**

Avalanche survivors in good health

A survivor of Monday's avalanche (0) ......*described*..... (describe) his experience to reporters yesterday.

Duncan Wood and his friend Steven Taylor (1) .... (return) from a climb when the avalanche (2) .... (hit) them. 'We (3) .... (check) the weather reports before leaving, of course, and we (4) .... (chose) an area that was safe – we thought,' Mr Wood said. 'The weather was OK – it (5) .... (not snow). We (6) .... (walk) down the mountain when suddenly, the snow under me (7) .... (start) moving and (8) .... (carry) me down the mountain. I was terrified! Snow and rocks (9) .... (fall) everywhere around me!

'When it (10) .... (stop), I was covered in snow, but I could still see the sky above me. I (11) .... (manage) to dig a hole and get out. Then I (12) .... (see) an arm in the snow near me. Steven (13) .... (land) right next to me! I (14) .... (dig) a hole for him and he (15) .... (get) out. We weren't badly injured and we feel fine now. We were very lucky.'

Check 8 Narrative tenses

1 **Complete the sentences. Use the past perfect or past simple of the verbs in brackets. Sometimes both are possible.**

1 By the time it .... dark, we .... a good place to camp. (get, find)

2 When we .... , Ben .... (arrive, already / leave)

3 She .... after she .... lunch. (go out, have)

4 As soon as I .... my work, I .... very relieved. (finish, feel)

5 She .... a lot about him before she .... to his exhibition. (read, go)

6 The plane .... by the time we .... to the airport. (take off, get)

/ 6

2 **Complete the conversations. Use the past perfect or past simple of the verbs in brackets.**

A: Did your performance go well?
B: No, it didn't. We played really badly because we (7) .... (not practise) enough.

A: Didn't you go to the cinema with Ben and Philip on Friday?
B: No. I (8) .... (already / see) the film they were going to see.

A: How did you get home last night?
B: Sarah (9) .... (give) us a lift.

A: Kevin and Mark were really excited because they (10) .... (never / be) to London before.
B: Yes, I know. Mark told me.

A: I like this photo of you! Is it recent?
B: Yes. Nina (11) .... (take) it about a month ago.

A: Does Luke live here?
B: No. He (12) .... (move) to Cambridge in 2005.

/ 6

3 **Circle the correct answer.**

When I opened the front door, I (13) ..... Lucy in the kitchen. She (14) ..... quite loudly. I (15) ..... for a few moments and then I went into the kitchen. Lucy and my mother (16) ..... at the table. My mother (17) ..... a cake and they were eating it. I (18) ..... a glass of water and went to my room. It was a mess. I (19) ..... it at all before I left. I (20) ..... my computer and checked my e-mails.

13 A heard   B was hearing
   C were hearing   D had heard

14 A talked   B was talking
   C had talked   D had talking

15 A listened   B have listened
   C was listening   D had listened

16 A have sat   B was sitting
   C were sitting   D had sat

17 A made   B has made
   C was making   D had made

18 A got   B was getting
   C were getting   D had got

19 A didn't tidy   B wasn't tidying
   C weren't tidying D hadn't tidied

20 A turned on   B was turning on
   C were turning on D had turned on

/ 8

Total: / 20

✓ **Self-check**

Wrong answers	Look again at	Try CD-ROM
7, 8, 9, 10, 11, 12	**Unit 36**	Exercise 36
1, 2, 3, 4, 5, 6	**Unit 37**	Exercise 37
13, 14, 15, 16, 17, 18, 19, 20	**Unit 38**	Exercise 38

Now do **Check 8**

Future forms

39   *will* and *be going to*

We use *will*:	We use *be going to*:
for general predictions about the future: *It **will be** hot tomorrow. In ten years' time, people's lives **won't be** very different.*	for general predictions about the future. *Be going to* is more informal than *will*: *It's **going to be** hot tomorrow.*
We often use *I think, I'm sure, probably, definitely,* etc. to show how certain we feel: ***I think** he'**ll do** well in his exams.* ***I'm sure** we'**ll win**.*	for things we expect to happen because of what we know or can see now: *Be careful with that knife! Someone's **going to get** hurt!*
for decisions we make at the time we are speaking: *I'm tired. I think I'**ll stay** in this evening.*	for intentions, when we have already decided to do something: *I'm **going to stay** in today. I've got to write an essay.*
for offers and promises: *I'**ll make** some coffee. Don't worry, I'**ll pay** you back soon.*	

▶▶   **See Appendix 7: Verb forms, page 170.**

P R A C T I C E

39a **Complete the sentences. Use *will* or *be going to* and the verbs in brackets.**

0   The traffic's very bad this morning.
     We ....*'re going to be*........ late for our lecture. (be)

1   We could have the party here. I'm sure
     the neighbours .... the noise.
     (not mind)

2   Matt probably .... with us. He
     doesn't like football. (not come)

3   She's working too hard. She ....
     ill. (get)

4   In twenty years' time, the tree in our garden
     .... really tall. (be)

5   I .... some horrible dreams
     tonight after that film! It was really scary! (have)

6   Don't worry about the ink on your shirt. I'm sure
     nobody .... it. (notice)

7   It .... a lovely day. Look at that clear blue sky! (be)

8   I think we .... enough time to eat before the film, so let's find
     a café. (have)

39b Circle the correct answer.

o **A:** What are your plans for the weekend?
B: I *'ll* / (*'m going to*) go shopping on Saturday and then stay at home on Sunday.

1 **A:** I don't think we've got enough chairs for everyone.
B: I *'ll* / *'m going to* get some more from next door.

2 **A:** Look! Our bus is coming! Hurry up!
B: I don't want to run. I think I *'ll* / *'m going to* wait for the next one.

3 **A:** Are you free this afternoon?
B: No, I've got to go to the library. I *'ll* / *'m going to* look at their collection of old newspapers for my History project.

4 **A:** Please don't tell Kate or Lucy.
B: OK. I *won't* / *'m not going to* tell anybody. Don't worry.

5 **A:** Have you sold your car yet?
B: Yes. I *'ll* / *'m going to* get a new one next month.

39c Complete the conversation. Use *will* or *be going to* and the verbs in the box.

be	call	give	live	move	rent	~~study~~

A: Do you plan to go to university?
B: Yes. I (o) ....*'m going to study*.... medicine in London.
A: Brilliant! I'm sure you (1) .... a great doctor!
B: Thanks!
A: Where (2) .... ?
B: I don't know. I haven't arranged anything yet. I think I (3) ....
a room in a house with some other students. The problem is that everywhere is very expensive.
A: My brother (4) .... to London next month. He's just bought a flat there. I (5) .... you his phone number. He might be able to help.
B: Thanks very much! I (6) .... him tomorrow.

40 Present simple and continuous for future

- We use the present simple for events in the future that are part of a timetable:
*Our train **leaves** at ten o'clock.* *The library **closes** at six this evening.*

- We use the present continuous (not the present simple) to talk about future events that we have planned and arranged: *We're **having** a party next week.* ***Are** you **doing** anything this evening?* *I'm **meeting** Jess at eight tonight.*

 We use *will* (not the present simple) for decisions we make at the time of speaking, or for offers and promises: *Wait. **I'll come** with you.* (Not *I come with you.*) ***I'll meet** you at the cinema.* (Not *I meet you at the cinema.*)

P R A C T I C E

40a **Complete the sentences. Use the present simple or present continuous of the verbs in brackets.**

   0 The kite festival .... *starts* .... on Friday evening. (start)

   1 We .... by bus. (go)

   2 Our bus .... here at seven thirty. (leave)

   3 We .... buses in Birmingham. (change)

   4 The bus .... to Hereford at four thirty. (get)

   5 We .... , so I hope the weather's nice. (camp)

   6 We .... – we just like kites. (not compete)

   7 My sister .... with us. (not come)

   8 The festival .... on Sunday afternoon at about four. (end)

40b **Complete the e-mail. Use the present simple or present continuous of the verbs in brackets.**

● ○ ○	New Message	⊖

What (0) .... *are you doing* .... (you / do) on Saturday? Amy and I
(1) .... (go) to the sale at Zara's. We
(2) .... (meet) outside the shop at nine. We won't have
much time there because our dance lesson (3) ....
(start) at ten thirty. It (4) .... (finish) at twelve, so I
could meet you after that.

Do you want to come to our house for lunch? I don't think anybody will
be there, but I can make you something. My parents
(5) .... (take) my sister to a swimming competition
which (6) .... (begin) at one, I think.

40c **Circle the correct answer.**

  A: I (0) *get* / ⟨*'m getting*⟩ the bus to town tonight. There's one that (1) *leaves* /
     is leaving here at seven and (2) *gets* / *is getting* there at half past.

  B: That sounds good. I (3) *see* / *'ll see* you outside McDonald's at about half past.

       —————————

  A: Do you want to come round tomorrow afternoon?

  B: Thanks, but I can't. I (4) *look* / *'m looking* after my little brother. He's not
     very well. You haven't got any good board games, have you? He likes playing
     games.

  A: Yes, we've got a few. I (5) *bring* / *'ll bring* them round this evening.

       —————————

  A: Could you give me a lift into town tomorrow morning, please? My hair
     appointment (6) *is* / *is being* at ten.

  B: I can't, I'm afraid. I (7) *help* / *'m helping* in the café tomorrow.

  C: Don't worry. I (8) *give* / *'ll give* you a lift.

41 Future continuous

- We use the future continuous to talk about an action that will be in progress at a particular time in the future: *'Can we meet tomorrow morning at ten?' 'No, I'll be working* then.'* (= I'll start working earlier than ten and continue later than ten.)

- Compare the future with *will* and the future continuous: *Come at seven thirty. We'll eat at eight.* (= We'll start eating at eight.)   *Don't phone at eight. We'll be eating.* (= We'll be in the middle of eating.)

▶▶ **See Appendix 7: Verb forms, page 170.**

PRACTICE

41a Complete the conversation. Use the future continuous of the verbs in brackets.

A: Can you meet me in town tomorrow at one?

B: Um … no. I'll be out at one. I (0) .... *'ll be having* .... (have) lunch with Peter. What about later? Two thirty or three? Or (1) .... (you / watch) the match then?

A: Yes, I will. Are you playing tennis with Jamie in the afternoon?

B: Yes, at half past four.

A: Well, I could meet you at the tennis court at about six. Is that OK?

B: Yes, that's fine. We (2) .... (practise) for our match on Sunday.

A: Yes, I can imagine it. He (3) .... (try) to do all kinds of clever shots and you (4) .... (not pay) attention! And you (5) .... (shout) at each other!

B: No, no! You haven't seen us for ages! We (6) .... (work) together perfectly. Like a machine!

A: A broken machine, you mean!

41b Circle the correct answer.

0 Our exams finish on Friday. This time next week I *'ll relax /* ('*ll be relaxing*) at home.

1 Bring your books round tonight. My brother *will help / will be helping* you with your Maths.

2 I'll still be awake at midnight. I *'ll have / 'll be having* my fifth cup of coffee!

3 I *won't go / won't be going* without you, but please don't be late.

4 Good luck with your exam on Wednesday. I *'ll think / 'll be thinking* of you.

5 Meet me in the library on Thursday morning. We *'ll revise / 'll be revising* together.

6 Come round on Saturday morning for a chat. I *won't do / won't be doing* anything.

42 Future perfect

- We use the future perfect to talk about an action or situation that will be finished before a particular time in the future: *I can meet you at six tomorrow. My football match **will have finished** by then.* (= It will finish some time before then.)
- We often use the future perfect with *by* or *by the time* + present simple: ***We'll have finished** dinner by eight.   **By the time** I **get** back, he'll have left.*
- Compare the future with *will* and the future perfect: ***We'll leave** at six o'clock.* (= Six o'clock is the time we'll leave.)   ***We'll have left** by six o'clock.* (= We'll leave before six o'clock.)

▶▶   **See Appendix 7: Verb forms, page 170.**

P R A C T I C E

42a **Complete the sentences. Use the present simple or future perfect of the verbs in brackets.**

0   I ....*'ll have finished*........... my project by the end of this month. (finish)

1   We .... any food by the time they .... (not make, arrive)

2   We .... to Scotland by the beginning of May. (move)

3   .... your course by the time I .... you again? (you / start, see)

4   Don't call late tonight. I .... to bed by ten. (go)

5   He .... by eight. He gets up at seven thirty. (not leave)

6   By the time we .... the play on Saturday, we .... it thirty times. (perform, rehearse)

42b **Complete the sentences. Use *will* or the future perfect of the verbs in the box.**

| disappear   experience   improve   land   move   need   ~~rise~~ |

0   Global temperatures ....*will have risen*........... by at least 1 °C by the end of this century.

1   Many of us .... more extreme weather events, such as storms, heat waves and floods.

2   The world .... much more energy in the future.

3   They say that the treatment of cancer .... enormously by 2025.

4   Experts predict that half of today's languages .... by 2100.

5   More and more people .... from the countryside to cities in this century.

6   They say that people .... on Mars by 2040.

43 Future in the past

- We use *was/were going to* + infinitive to talk about a planned action in the past that didn't happen: *I'm sorry. I **was going to phone** you, but I didn't have time.* (= It was my intention to phone you, but I didn't.)

- We also use *was/were going to* for a prediction in the past, often after *think* or *know*: *At last we were safe. Everything **was going to be** OK.   I knew my exams **were going to be** difficult.*

▶▶ ***See Appendix 7: Verb forms, page 170.***

P R A C T I C E

43a **Complete the sentences. Use *was/were going to* and the verbs in the box.**

> be   earn   go   ~~not get~~   not share   not stay   set up

0 I ....*wasn't going to get*.......... married, but now I'm married with two children!

1 I .... to Canada, but I didn't. I'm still here!

2 Rob and I .... a flat, but then he needed someone, so I moved in.

3 I .... a lot of money very quickly, but that hasn't happened yet!

4 Sarah and I .... dancers, but we both have office jobs.

5 I .... in London, but actually, I really enjoy living here.

6 Matt and Duncan .... their own company, but then Matt moved to Paris.

43b **Complete the texts. Use *was/were going to* and the verbs in brackets.**

> I (0) ....*was going to go*............ (go) shopping with a friend yesterday, but then she got ill, so I went by myself. I wanted some trainers, but the ones I liked were too expensive. I knew they (1) .... (cost) a lot, but I didn't realise how much! I bought a T-shirt instead. I (2) .... (not / get) any clothes, but I couldn't resist it!

> Lucy (3) .... (meet) me at six, but she didn't turn up. Kate and Ben picked me up at six thirty. I thought Ben (4) .... (not come) with us, so I was surprised to see him. I (5) .... (not say) anything about the previous weekend, but he asked me. I had to tell him the truth. I thought he (6) .... (be) angry, but he laughed when I told him what had happened.

Check 9 Future forms

1 Complete the conversation. Use *will* or *be going to* and the verbs in brackets.

A: I'm sorry you don't feel well.

B: Thanks. I'm sure I
(1) .... (feel) better
soon. I've decided to stay in bed
today. I (2) ....
(not do) any work on my essay.

A: (3) .... (you /
come) into college tomorrow?

B: I don't know. I haven't decided
yet.

A: I could give you a lift if you like.

B: Really? That would be great! I
don't think my brother
(4) .... (let) me
borrow his car.

A: I (5) .... (pick) you
up at about eight. OK?

B: Yes, lovely! Thank you very much.

/ 5

2 Complete the sentences. Use *was/ were going to*, the future continuous or the future perfect of the verbs in brackets.

6 Come and join us in the park
later. We ....
(play) volleyball near the little
lake.

7 Let's go to the beach at six. Most
people .... (go)
home by then.

8 That was horrible! I thought that
car .... (hit) us!

9 Could I talk to you tonight at nine
or .... (you /
get) ready for your trip?

10 Don't worry!
We ....
(not eat) everything by the time
you get here!

/ 5

3 Circle the correct answer.

Dear Choir Members,

As you know, the choir we met in France last year
(11) *are coming / will have come / were going to
come* here in May.

On 25th, 26th and 28th May, they (12) *'ll perform /
're performing / were going to perform* here in
Cheltenham. (They (13) *'ll give / 're going to give /
were going to give* another concert on the 27th, but
we couldn't find a suitable venue, unfortunately.)
I'm glad to say that the tickets are going fast and I
think we (14) *sell / 're selling / 'll have sold* them
all by the end of this week, so if you want some,
hurry!

On the 29th, they (15) *go / 'll go / 're going*
sightseeing in Stratford. I (16) *'ll book / 'm going
to book / 'll have booked* the coaches for this trip
next week, so please phone me this week if you
want a place. The cost is £15 per person and the
coaches (17) *leave / are leaving / are going to leave*
the bus station at 8.30 a.m. I (18) *won't be / won't
have been / 'm not being* here on Thursday between
eight and ten – I (19) *'m going to rehearse / 'll
rehearse / 'll be rehearsing* in London – but you can
leave a message on the answerphone.

I don't know yet about the party on the 30th. I
(20) *'ll start / was going to start / 'll have started*
organising it last week, but I didn't have time. I'll
give you the details as soon as I can.

/ 10

Total: / 20

✓ Self-check

Wrong answers	Look again at	Try CD-ROM
1, 2, 3, 4, 5, 16, 18	Unit 39	Exercise 39
11, 12, 15, 17	Unit 40	Exercise 40
6, 9, 19	Unit 41	Exercise 41
7, 10, 14	Unit 42	Exercise 42
8, 13, 20	Unit 43	Exercise 43

Now do **Check 9**

Modal verbs

44 Ability and possibility

- We use *can, could* and *be able to* to express ability and possibility.

Present	can, am/is/are able to
Past	could, was/were able to
Future	can + time expression, *will be able to*

- We usually use *can* to express present ability or possibility: *I **can speak** English. You **can buy** cold drinks in that shop.*
  Be able to is more formal and not as common: *We **are not able/unable to attend** the opening ceremony.*
- We use *could* or *was/were able to* for general ability in the past: *Tom **could/was able to swim** when he was four.*
- We use *was/were able to* (not *could*) for a single completed action: *They **were able to swim** to safety.*
- We use *couldn't* or *wasn't/weren't able to* for both general ability and single actions: *Jane **couldn't/wasn't able to read** when she was five.   They **couldn't/weren't able to solve** the problem.*
- We use *manage to* to suggest difficulty, usually for single actions: ***Did** you **manage to get** home all right?*
- We use *can* or *will be able to* + a time expression to talk about a future possibility: *I **can see** you tomorrow.   She**'ll be able to meet** us this evening.*
- For a future ability, we use *will be able to* (not *can*): *After this course, I**'ll be able to speak** English much better.* (Not *~~I can speak English much better~~*)

P R A C T I C E

44a **Complete the sentences. Use *can, could* or *will be able to*.**

0 Joe ....*could*.......... beat me at chess when he was only eight.

1 She's only four, but she .... play the piano.

2 In the future, people like us .... travel to other planets!

3 Don't worry. You .... hire a racket at the sports centre.

4 I .... do karate when I was younger, but I've forgotten it now.

5 After my exams, I .... visit them more often.

6 Luke .... speak Italian really well when he lived in Milan.

44b **Cross out one of the options if it is incorrect.**

Becky worked in a group on her Business Studies
course last term. Here she describes what they did.

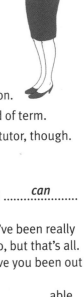

0 Joe ~~could~~ / *managed to* think of three different
products for our group project in about fifteen minutes!

1 Lisa *could* / *was able to* write very well when we were at school,
but the report she wrote for our project wasn't very good.

2 She *could* / *was able to* express herself really well then,
but she can't write very well now.

3 I *couldn't* / *didn't manage to* find any useful information
on the Internet.

4 But I *could* / *managed to* draw some pictures for our presentation.

5 We *could* / *were able to* prepare a good presentation for the end of term.

6 We *couldn't* / *weren't able to* discuss the presentation with our tutor, though.

44c **Complete the conversation. Use one word in each gap.**

A: Do you want to go to the cinema at the weekend? Mark and I (0) ....*can*..........
go on Saturday or Sunday.

B: No, sorry. I'm going to be too busy. I'd love to go soon, though. I've been really
busy this term. I (1) .... to go to a gig a few weeks ago, but that's all.
I (2) .... be able to go out more next term, I hope. Have you been out
a lot?

A: Not really. But I went to a play last week in London. We (3) .... able
to get cheap tickets for some seats near the front. We (4) .... see
everything!

B: That sounds great!

A: Yes, it was. You (5) .... get some really good seats sometimes.

B: I'd love to come with you if you go again.

A: Sure. I'll send you the new programme next week.

B: Thanks. Will we (6) .... able to get cheap tickets, do you think?

A: Yes, I think so. I think there are always some cheap ones.

B: Great!

45 Degrees of certainty (present and future)

- We use *must, may, might, could* and *can't* to show how certain we are that something is true, or that something will happen.
- We use *must* when we are sure that something is true now: *You **must be** tired.*
- We use *may, might* or *could* when we think that something is possible now or in the future: *That **might be** Paul's car.* (= Maybe it's his.) *I **may go** out tonight.* (= Maybe I'll go out.) *You **could be** right.* (= Maybe you're right.) *It **could rain** tomorrow.* (= It's possible that it will rain tomorrow.)
- We use *may not* or *might not* (but not *could not*) to refer to the present or future: *He **may not be** at home today. We **might not see** you next week.*
- We use *can't* when we think that something is impossible now. Notice the difference between *may/might not* and *can't*: *He **might not be** in London.* (= It's possible that he isn't in London.) *He **can't be** in London.* (= It's impossible that he's in London.)

PRACTICE

45a **Complete the sentences. Use *must* or *might*.**

o The girl standing next to Joe looks a lot like him, doesn't she? She ....*must*........ be his sister.

1 The woman in the green dress .... be his aunt. I'm not sure.

2 Joe .... be really excited about his new job in Paris. He's wanted to live in France for ages.

3 He .... stay there for a year or two. It depends if he likes the job.

4 His brother .... move there too next year. He hasn't decided yet.

5 Joe's been studying French for ages. He .... speak it really well.

6 I .... visit him in the spring. I'm not sure.

45b **Circle the correct answer.**

o We *can't / couldn't /* (*may not*) drive to the beach. We haven't decided yet.

1 I don't believe it! They *can't / may not / mustn't* be the winners! They were awful!

2 She *could / may / must* have a lot of money. She buys very expensive clothes.

3 He *can't / couldn't / may not* come to the party. I don't know if he's free on Saturday.

4 £11.00 and £3.99 is £25.98? That *can't / may not / mustn't* be right!

5 I *could / can't / mustn't* get a job in the holidays, but I'm not sure that I will.

6 What's the time? It *can't / might / must* be very early. It's still dark.

7 We *might / can't / mustn't* stay at home. It depends how tired we are.

8 There *can't / couldn't / might not* be many buses early in the morning. I don't know.

45c **Complete the second sentence so that it means the same as the first, using the word in bold. Use between two and five words.**

0 I'm sure that's Rob's bag. **must**
That .... *must be* .... Rob's bag.

1 Maybe he's in the cafeteria. **could**
He .... in the cafeteria.

2 Perhaps he'll come back for it. **might**
He .... back for it.

3 Maybe I won't see him this evening. **may**
I .... him this evening.

4 Perhaps Jamie knows his address. **might**
Jamie .... his address.

5 I'm sure somebody has it. **must**
Somebody .... it.

45d **Complete the letter. Use *must, may (not), might (not), could* or *can't*. There may be more than one possible answer.**

Congratulations on your exam results! You (0) .... *must* .... be really pleased!

I'm looking forward to seeing you next month. I'm thinking of things we can do. We (1) .... get bored here, so let's try to go to London. There (2) .... be a good show on. I'll check. We can also visit Jane in Scotland. I've never been to her house, but I know it's in a small village outside Edinburgh, so it (3) .... be beautiful! It (4) .... be big enough for all of us, though – I don't know. If we can't stay there, we can easily stay in a hostel. It (5) .... be difficult to find one.

46 Speculating about the past

- We use *must/may/might/could/can't* + *have* + past participle to speculate about the past, to show how certain we are that something happened.

- We use *must* + *have* + past participle when we are certain that something happened: *I sent the letter two weeks ago. He **must have received** it.*

- We use *may/might/could* + *have* + past participle when we think it's possible that something happened: *She **might have left**.*

- We use *may/might not* + *have* + past participle (but not *couldn't*) when we think it's possible that something didn't happen: *They **may not have seen** us.*

- We use *can't* + *have* + past participle when we think it's impossible that something happened. Notice the difference between *may/might not have* and *can't have*: *She **might not have passed** her exam.* (= It's possible that she didn't pass.) *She **can't have passed** her exam!* (= It's impossible that she passed.)

PRACTICE

46a **Complete the sentences. Use *must have* or *might (not) have* and the verbs in brackets.**

0 I ......*might have bought*...... the wrong book. Is this the one you wanted? (buy)

1 We .... the door. I can't remember. (not lock)

2 That party was amazing! They .... a lot of money on it. (spend)

3 Michael's finished his essay and he only started it last night! He .... all night. (work)

4 He .... your message. Why don't you leave another one? (not get)

5 I .... her phone number in my file. I'm not sure. (write)

6 That sounds awful! You .... terrified! (be)

46b **Circle the correct answer.**

0 I *can't* / *might not* have thrown away that letter. I never throw away letters.

1 They *can't* / *might not* have gone to the zoo. I'm not sure if it was open.

2 I *can't* / *may not* have brought my camera. I'll go and look for it in the car.

3 There *can't* / *might not* have been many people in town this afternoon. Everyone was watching the football match at home.

4 Sophie *can't* / *might not* have taken these photos. I'm not sure she was at that party.

5 They *can't* / *might not* have painted the whole flat in one day! It's too big.

6 The cat *can't* / *might not* have got out. All the doors and windows were shut.

46c **Complete the conversations. Use *must have, could have, might have* or *can't have* and the verbs in brackets.**

A: Are you ready?

B: Um ... hang on a minute. I'm just looking for my MP3 player. I don't know where it is. Maybe it's in my bag. No, it isn't. Oh dear! I hope I haven't lost it.

A: Lisa (0) ......*could have borrowed*...... (borrow) it. She uses it sometimes, doesn't she?

B: Yes, but she hasn't been at home today, so she (1) .... (take) it.

A: Let me look in your bag. You (2) .... (not see) it. Ah, here it is!

A: Why didn't Lucy come to Kate's last night?

B: I don't know. She (3) .... (forget) all about it. Do you think Kate was upset?

A: She didn't say anything, but she (4) .... (be) very disappointed. She really wanted Lucy to come.

B: Lucy's often ill. She (5) .... (not be) well yesterday.

A: She (6) .... (be) ill. Ben saw her in the afternoon. She was fine.

47 Permission

- To express permission or lack of permission, we use *can/can't* (present), *could/ couldn't* (past) and (*not*) *be allowed to* (all tenses): *You **can give** me the money tomorrow.   You **can't bring** food into class.   **Can** we/**Are** we **allowed to talk** in the library?   When I was a child, I **couldn't**/**wasn't allowed to stay** out after nine. Next year, students **will be allowed to use** dictionaries in exams.*

- *May* (*not*) is sometimes used in notices: *Students **may borrow** CDs from the library. Visitors **may not take** photographs of the paintings.*

- Compare the use of *could* and *was/were allowed to*: *In my last job, I **could**/**was allowed to start** at ten.* (general permission: *could* or *was/were allowed to*) *I **was allowed to leave** early yesterday.* (on a particular occasion: *was/were allowed to*, not *could*)

- To ask for permission, we use *can, could* (more polite) or *may* (formal). We don't use *be allowed to*: **Can I go** now?   **Could I use** your phone?   **May I sit** here? To answer *yes*, we can say: *Yes, sure/all right/of course/certainly.* To answer *no*, we can say: (*No,*) *I'm sorry, but* (+ a reason).

PRACTICE

47a Circle the correct answer.

0 You *can't* / *'re allowed to* / *couldn't* smoke here. It's a no-smoking area.

1 You *can't* / *couldn't* / *weren't allowed to* use your mobile phone in the exam. Switch it off.

2 Members *may* / *can't* / *could* use the members' restaurant on the top floor. Please show your membership card to the waiter.

3 I'm sorry, sir. You *can't* / *weren't allowed to* / *couldn't* come in here. Please wait outside.

4 We *may* / *'re allowed to* / *could* use the computer centre at lunchtime, so I often go there.

5 Next year, we *'re allowed to* / *'ll be allowed to* / *could* design a real building as part of our course.

6 He *can't* / *isn't allowed to* / *couldn't* ride a motorbike last year because he wasn't old enough.

7 We *can't* / *aren't allowed to* / *couldn't* park near the stadium because all the streets near it were closed.

8 We *may not* / *can't* / *weren't allowed to* wear jeans at school when I was a student.

9 You *can* / *can't* / *couldn't* take the car if you want. I don't need it.

10 We took some photographs, but we *can't* / *may not* / *weren't allowed to* record the interview.

MEMBERS ONLY

DO NOT ENTER

47b Cross out one of the options if it is incorrect.

o Last weekend, I ~~could~~ / *was allowed to* drive the family car for the first time.

1 My brother *could* / *was allowed to* get a motorbike a few weeks ago.

2 When I was a child, I *could* / *was allowed to* ride my bike whenever I wanted.

3 I *could* / *was allowed to* watch television every evening.

4 I *could* / *was allowed to* choose most of my own clothes.

5 My brother and I *could* / *were allowed to* decorate our bedroom with pictures that we liked.

6 On my thirteenth birthday, I *could* / *was allowed to* stay at a friend's house for the first time.

7 Two years ago, I *could* / *was allowed to* visit my cousin in Scotland by myself.

8 Last week, our little sister *could* / *was allowed to* go shopping with her friends for the first time.

47c Complete the conversations. Use one word in each gap.

A: Excuse me, (0) ......*may*...... I take a photo of the painting?

B: No, I'm (1) .... Visitors are not (2) .... to take photographs of the paintings. But you (3) .... photograph the sculptures outside.

A: Hi, Becky. How are you? Are you feeling better?

B: Yes, but I have to stay in bed. I'm not allowed (4) .... get up yet.

A: (5) .... I come and see you?

B: Yes, of (6) .... ! Come as soon as you like.

48 Obligation and necessity

- We use *must, have to* and *have got to* to talk about something that is important or necessary. The meanings are similar, but there are some differences.

- *Must* shows that the speaker feels the action is necessary and important: *I **must remember** to phone Sam.   You **must be** back by ten.*

- *Have to* and *have got to* show that the action is necessary because someone else says so, or because of a rule or law: *I **have to take** these tablets every day. You **have to show** your passport to get into the country.*

- *Have to* is more common than *must* in speech. *Must* is often used for written instructions and rules: *All drivers **must be** at least twenty-one years old to hire a car.*

- *Have got to* is spoken and informal: *I've **got to see** you right away!*

- We use *have to* (not *must* or *have got to*) to talk about the past or the future: *Our flight was at six, so we **had to leave** the house at three.   It's going to be cold, so we'll **have to take** warm clothes with us.*

- We usually use *have to* (not *must* or *have got to*) in questions: *Is this a direct train or **do** we **have to change**?*

⚠ Compare *don't have to* and *mustn't*: *You **don't have to tell** him.* (= It's not necessary.)   *You **mustn't tell** him.* (= It's important that you don't.)

PRACTICE

48a Complete the sentences. Use *must* or *have/has to*.

o I've been feeling ill for a week. I ....*must*............ go to the doctor today.

1 You can't buy a ticket on the train. You .... get one before you get on.

2 They .... work in a hospital for six months as part of their course.

3 In some countries, everyone .... vote. It's the law.

4 I .... wash my jeans before the party. They're really dirty.

5 I .... wear a uniform for my job at the supermarket.

6 We .... practise our songs again. Some of them don't sound very good.

48b Complete the conversation. Use the correct form of *have to* or *have got to*. Do not use *have to* if *have got to* is possible.

A: Have you ever been in a play? I've joined a drama group and it's great!

B: Yes, I was in a play at school. It was quite hard work because we
   (0) ....*had to*............ rehearse every week.

A: (1) .... you .... do a lot of acting exercises?

B: Yes, some. They were good fun. (2) .... you .... do them?

A: Yes, every week. Last week we (3) .... pretend to be film stars.

B: That sounds fun. Are you doing a play too?

A: Yes, a short one. I hate learning all my lines! It's quite boring, isn't it?

B: Yes, you (4) .... sit down and learn them. It is a bit boring.
   I wish I could join your group, but I've got exams next term and I
   (5) .... concentrate on them. But I'd love to come to your play.
   When is it?

A: I don't know yet. I (6) .... check with the teacher and tell you later.

48c Circle the correct answer.

o You (*don't have to*)/ *mustn't* buy any equipment to go walking.

1 *Do you have to* / *Must you* wear special shoes for aerobics?

2 You *don't have to* / *mustn't* eat a lot before exercising. It isn't good for you.

3 Joe was ill, so he *had to* / *must* miss football practice.

4 I *don't have to* / *mustn't* cycle to college, but I do it because I love cycling.

5 At my running club we *have to* / *must* jog slowly before we start running.

6 That was great! We *have to* / *must* play more often.

7 These jogging bottoms don't fit me properly. I *have to* / *must* get some new ones.

8 Everyone can enjoy sport. You *don't have to* / *mustn't* be good at it.

49 *need (to)*

- *Need* is a main verb with present, past, future and participle forms (*need, needs, needing, needed*), followed by *to*-infinitive: *She **needs to talk** to you.*   ***Do** you **need to wash** your hands?*   *We **needed to be** home by five.*   *They **didn't need to pay** for the damage.*   *You**'ll need to be** careful.*

- It can also be a modal verb, followed by infinitive without *to*. This form is mainly used in negatives: *You **needn't look** so frightened!* (= It isn't necessary.)

- Compare these uses of *need* when talking about the past: *We **didn't need to hurry** because we had plenty of time.* (= We didn't hurry because it wasn't necessary.) *We **needn't have hurried** because the train was delayed.* (= We hurried, but it wasn't necessary.)

PRACTICE

49a Complete the sentences. Use *need/needs to* or *needn't*.

  0 You ....*needn't*........ change your clothes. Those are fine.

  1 We .... stop during the journey. We can't drive all the way without a break.

  2 We .... take our bikes. We can walk there.

  3 He .... make some new friends. His old friends have moved away.

  4 They .... work harder. They aren't doing enough at the moment.

  5 You .... walk home with me. I'll be all right on my own.

  6 She .... meet us at the station. We can get the bus to her house.

49b Circle the correct answer.

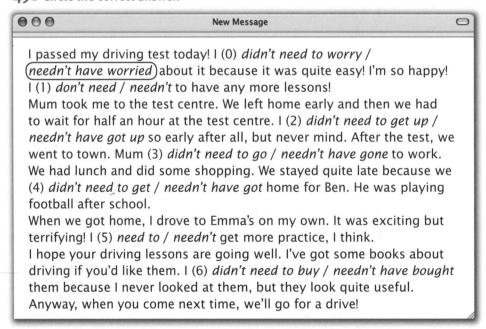

New Message

I passed my driving test today! I (0) *didn't need to worry /* (needn't have worried) about it because it was quite easy! I'm so happy! I (1) *don't need / needn't* to have any more lessons!

Mum took me to the test centre. We left home early and then we had to wait for half an hour at the test centre. I (2) *didn't need to get up / needn't have got up* so early after all, but never mind. After the test, we went to town. Mum (3) *didn't need to go / needn't have gone* to work. We had lunch and did some shopping. We stayed quite late because we (4) *didn't need to get / needn't have got* home for Ben. He was playing football after school.

When we got home, I drove to Emma's on my own. It was exciting but terrifying! I (5) *need to / needn't* get more practice, I think.

I hope your driving lessons are going well. I've got some books about driving if you'd like them. I (6) *didn't need to buy / needn't have bought* them because I never looked at them, but they look quite useful.

Anyway, when you come next time, we'll go for a drive!

50 Advice and recommendations

- We use *should/shouldn't* or *ought* (*not*) *to* to say that something is or isn't a good idea: *You **should try** this recipe.   She **shouldn't watch** so much TV.   We all **ought to do** something for the environment.   I **ought not to tell** you this.*

- We can also use *must, have to* and *mustn't*. *Must, have to* and *mustn't* are stronger than *should* and *ought to*: *You **have to see** the new exhibition.   You **mustn't miss** Tom's talk – it'll be very interesting.*

- We use *had better* (*not*) + infinitive to give strong advice or a warning: *You'd better tell* the police!   *You'd better not be* late!*

- We use *should/shouldn't* + *have* + past participle to express criticism of someone's behaviour in the past: *I **should have known** that he'd be late!   She **shouldn't have lied** to me.*

PRACTICE

50a Complete the conversation. Use *should/shouldn't* or *ought/ought not*.

A: We (0) ......*shouldn't*...... stop for a coffee. We're going to be late.

B: I'm always late for everything! I (1) .... to organise my time better.

A: Actually, you (2) .... to agree to do too much. You (3) .... learn to say no. And you (4) .... help your sister with her homework every night. It's not good for her or you.

B: Yes, she (5) .... to depend on me so much.

A: Exactly. She (6) .... try to work on her own.

50b Complete the second sentence so that it means the same as the first, using the word in bold. Use between two and five words.

0 I think it's necessary for you to decide what you want to do. **must**
   You ....*must decide*................ what you want to do.

1 I really think we ought to start cooking now. **better**
   We .... cooking now.

2 You really should try that new Chinese restaurant. **have**
   You .... that new Chinese restaurant.

3 I think it's very important that you don't tell him about this. **must**
   You .... him about this.

4 I think you must call her tomorrow. **had**
   You .... her tomorrow.

5 It's essential that you don't go without me. **not**
   You'd .... without me.

6 I think it's important that you ask your doctor. **must**
   You .... your doctor.

7 I really think you should apologise to her. **better**
   You .... to her.

8 You really should see that film. **have**
   You .... that film.

50C Complete the messages from a message board on the Internet. Use *should/ shouldn't* or *should have/shouldn't have* and the verbs in brackets.

Message 1: posted by citygirl

Can anyone help me? I want to be a singer, but my parents want me to study medicine. I've applied to university, but I really don't want to go. I haven't told my parents how I feel. I think my dad wants me to be a doctor because he feels he (0) ....*should have been*........... (be) one.

Message 2: posted by LisaR

You (1) .... (tell) your parents how you feel. They need to know.

Message 3: posted by africanprincess

I was in your situation a few years ago and didn't do anything. I (2) .... (talk) to my parents. I definitely (3) .... (go) to university as I was really unhappy there. You (4) .... (do) something you don't want to do. Good luck!

Message 4: posted by citygirl

Thanks, everyone. I know I (5) .... (apply) to university. I didn't think about it enough. I think I (6) .... (explain) how I feel to my parents. I hope they'll understand.

51   Requests, offers and suggestions

- To ask someone to do something for us, we use:
  - *Can you ... ?* (informal): **Can you help** me, please?
  - *Could you ... ?* (polite): **Could you close** the door, please?
  - *Will you ... ?* (neutral): **Will you wait** here and look after my bags?
  - *Would you ... ?* (a polite order): **Would you be** quiet, please?
  - *Would you mind ... (+ -ing)?* (very polite): **Would you mind shutting** the window?
- To offer to do something for someone, we use:
  - *Shall I/we ... ?* (polite): **Shall I drive**?
  - *I/We can/could* (polite): **I could give** you a lift to the station.
  - *I'll/We'll* (informal): **I'll show** you how this works.
  - *Let me/us* (informal): **Let me pay** for the coffee.
- To make suggestions, we use:
  - *Shall we ... ?* (neutral): **Shall we have** some lunch?
  - *We can/could* (more polite): **We can go** to a restaurant.
  - *Why don't we ... ?* (informal): **Why don't we sit** here?
  - *Let's* (informal): **Let's watch** a movie.

PRACTICE

51a **Complete the requests. Use the verbs in the box and the verbs in brackets**

do   pick   ~~play~~   post   put   take

0 ....*Can you play*........................ that again? (can)

1 .... the washing-up? (will)

2 .... this letter for me? (mind)

3 .... your feet off the seat, please? (would)

4 .... some water in this vase? (could)

5 .... me up at six thirty? (can)

51b **Complete the conversations. Use one word in each gap.**

Anna: We (0) ....*could*........ play tomorrow afternoon if you like.

Jenny: Yes, that would be great.

Anna: OK. (1) .... we try to get a court at four?

Jenny: Sure.

Anna: I (2) .... phone them now if you like, and find out if there's one free. (3) .... I say we want it for an hour?

Jenny: Yes. That sounds fine.

Matt: (4) .... don't we go to the Beautiful Days festival next year?

Rob: Yes, good idea. (5) ....'s camp there, like we did at Latitude last year.

Matt: OK. I (6) .... get the tickets for us both. We (7) .... get them on the Internet. When is it on? Do you know?

Rob: Actually, I saw an advert for it in a magazine. (8) .... me go and get it. It's in my bag.

Check 10 Modal verbs

1 Circle the correct answer.

1 He's lived here for fifteen years. He *can't* / *must* / *might* know the area very well.

2 I had been ill, so I *was allowed to* / *could* / *should* hand in my essay late.

3 When I got to the hotel, I found that there was a hair-dryer in my room, so I *couldn't have taken* / *didn't need to take* / *needn't have taken* my own.

4 Although the train was crowded, we *might* / *were able to* / *could* get seats.

5 You *can't* / *must* / *might* have slept through all that noise! It was really loud!

/ 5

2 Complete the conversation. Use *might, must, mustn't, needn't* or *ought*.

A: I want to go for a walk this afternoon. Do you want to come?

B: Yes! I (6) .... have something to eat first, though. I'm really hungry.

A: Jamie (7) .... come too. He hasn't decided yet.

B: OK. Are you going for a long walk?

A: I don't know. We (8) .... go very far if you don't want to.

B: OK. I (9) .... get back too late as I've got some work to do.

A: That's fine. I (10) .... to do some work too. But let's go for a walk first!

/ 5

3 Complete the second sentence so that it means the same as the first, using the word in bold. Use between two and five words.

11 It is not necessary for me to get up early. **have**
I .... up early.

12 They couldn't get tickets for the concert. **able**
They .... tickets for the concert.

13 We can't park here. **allowed**
We .... here.

14 Could you take your shoes off? **mind**
Would .... your shoes off?

15 I really think you should go to the doctor. **better**
You .... to the doctor.

/ 5

4 Complete the note. Use one word in each gap.

I'm going to get the food for our picnic tomorrow. (16) .... I get some chicken? Do you like it? I'm going to have a lot to carry and I don't think I'll manage (17) .... carry it on my bike, so I'm going to get the bus. (18) .... don't you come with me?

Oh, and please remind Kim about the picnic. She said she was going to call me this morning, but she didn't. She (19) .... have forgotten. I should (20) .... reminded her yesterday, but I forgot. Thanks!

/ 5

Total: / 20

✓ Self-check

Wrong answers	Look again at	Try CD-ROM
4, 12, 17	Unit 44	Exercise 44
1, 7	Unit 45	Exercise 45
5, 19	Unit 46	Exercise 46
2, 13	Unit 47	Exercise 47
6, 9, 11	Unit 48	Exercise 48
3, 8	Unit 49	Exercise 49
10, 15, 20	Unit 50	Exercise 50
14, 16, 18	Unit 51	Exercise 51

Now do **Check 10**

Statements and questions

52 Basic sentence types and word order

- In English, there are four basic sentence structures: statements, questions, imperatives and exclamations.
- We use these basic patterns to make simple statements. A statement must have a subject and a verb:
  - subject + intransitive verb (e.g. *come, wait*). Intransitive verbs don't need an object: *The bus is coming.*
  - subject + intransitive verb + adverbial. An adverbial can be a prepositional phrase or an adverb: *They're waiting outside.*
  - subject + transitive verb + object: *I like apples.*
  - subject + transitive verb + direct object + *to/for* + indirect object: *I gave the keys to Tim.* (For this pattern, see Unit 53.)
  - subject + transitive verb + object + adverbial/object complement. An object complement gives us information about the object: *I put the bag on the table. He called me a liar. We painted the door blue.*
  - subject + linking verb (e.g. *be, become, seem, feel, smell*) + complement. A complement can be an adjective, a noun phrase or an adverbial: *Jo seems very nice. He has become an important man. My car is over there.*
- We can add adverbs to all the basic patterns.
- We use imperatives to give orders or make requests. We use the base form of the verb with no subject: *Come here, please. Don't forget the money.*
- We use exclamations to express strong feelings. We form exclamations with:
  - *what* + noun phrase (+ subject + verb): **What** a lovely day (*it is*)!
  - *how* + adjective (+ subject + verb): **How** kind (*you are*)!

▶▶ *For direct and indirect objects, see Unit 53. For adverbs, see Units 17 and 20.*

PRACTICE

52a Put the words in the correct order.

0 saw / at the Dome / Dan and I / a band   *Dan and I saw a band at the Dome.*

1 a big venue / it / is   ....

2 we / at the front / stood   ....

3 brilliant / the band / were   ....

4 me / the music / made / happy   ....

5 had / a great voice / the singer   ....

6 Dan / a natural performer / her / called   ....

7 with my phone / I / some pictures / took   ....

8 look / they / great   ....

52b Write the sentences from 52a in the table.

	Subject	Verb	Object	(Object) Complement	Adverbial
0	*Dan and I*	*saw*	*a band*		*at the Dome.*
1					
2					
3					
4					
5					
6					
7					
8					

52c Circle the correct answer.

0 What (*awful weather*) / *awful weather is*!

1 *Not leave* / *Don't leave* the door open.

2 *How* / *What* a beautiful picture this is!

3 Please *not* / *do not* write on this page.

4 How heavy *your bag is* / *is your bag*!

5 What a clever idea *is this* / *this is*!

6 How *lovely* / *lovely was*!

7 How wonderful *sounds* / *it sounds*!

8 *Tell* / *Don't tell* me about your holiday.
I want to hear everything.

53 Direct and indirect objects

- Some verbs can be followed by two objects: a direct object and an indirect object.
  Two patterns are possible:
  – verb + direct object + *to/for* + indirect object: *Natalie **gave the book to Jenna**.*
  *He **bought a present for me**.*
  – verb + indirect object (without *to/for*) + direct object: *Natalie **gave Jenna the book**.*
  *He **bought me a present**.*

- We use *to* with these verbs: *give, hand, lend, offer, pass, post, sell, send, show*:
  *He **lent** the book **to** a friend.   I **sent** a card **to** my aunt.*

- We use *for* with these verbs: *book, buy, choose, cook, find, get, make, order, save*:
  *They **booked** a table **for** us.   I **bought** a present **for** my brother.*

- When the direct object is a pronoun, we usually choose the pattern that puts the
  pronoun first: *We wrote some postcards and sent **them** to our friends.* (Not ~~We wrote
  some postcards and sent our friends them.~~)   *He bought a book and lent **it** to Rob.*
  (Not ~~He bought a book and lent Rob it.~~)

PRACTICE

53a Circle the correct answer.

He handed a brown envelope (0) (to)/ *for* the short man in the dark suit. 'Give it (1) *to* / *for* him,' he said, 'and then find his brother (2) *to* / *for* me. I need to speak to him.' The short man nodded and left. Then Vince turned to me. 'You must leave now,' he said. 'I've ordered a car (3) *to* / *for* you. It will be here in a minute. Get some flowers (4) *to* / *for* your wife and go home. Say that you had to work late at the office. I've sent a message (5) *to* / *for* Lenny and he'll pick you up at seven tomorrow.' I nodded, but I decided not to get the flowers. I'd bought a lot of flowers (6) *to* / *for* Jenny in the past month and she was starting to think I had a secret.

53b Complete the sentences. Use *to* or *for* and the words in brackets.

o Zoe's written the invitations, so she's going to post ....*them to everyone*........ .
    (them / everyone)

1 Is she sending .... ? (one / Lucy)

2 She loves chocolate cakes, so her mother's ordered ....
    (one / her)

3 Zoe liked the sweets I made last year, so I'm going to make
    .... (some / her)

4 Adam's seen some nice earrings, so he's going to buy ....
    (them / her)

5 I'm not going to wear my blue dress, so I'm going to lend ....
    (it / Zoe)

6 I've bought some new shoes for the party, but I haven't shown
    .... yet. (them / anyone)

7 I'd like a bracelet to go with my dress and my mother's promised to get
    .... (one / me)

8 Zoe and I both had some nice bracelets, but then I gave ....
    (mine / a friend)

53c Re-write the sentences.

o I showed the brochure to my friends.   *I showed my friends the brochure.*

oo I've booked us a table.   *I've booked a table for us.*

1 I'm cooking some sausages for Ben.   ....

2 Have you sold your bike to Jamie?   ....

3 Could you pass Matt this note?   ....

4 She's saving Kim those chocolates.   ....

5 Tom offered his seat to an old lady.   ....

6 I've found you some information.   ....

54 Making questions

● *Yes/No* questions ask if something is true or not. The word order is:

Auxiliary/ Modal verb	Subject	Verb	Completion	Short answers
Are	you	leaving?		Yes, we are.
Can	you	remember	her address?	No, I can't.
Did	Martin	phone	last night?	No, he didn't.

● Alternative questions ask which of two alternatives is true. The word order is the same as for *yes/no* questions: *Is she Spanish or French?*

● *Wh-* questions start with a question word (e.g. *what, who,* etc.) and ask for missing information. The question word comes before the auxiliary/modal verb. If the main verb has a preposition after it, we put the preposition at the end.

Question word	Auxiliary/ Modal verb	Subject	Verb	Completion
Why	are	you	crying?	
How	will	they	get	home?
Who	were	you	talking	to?

● Notice these phrases with *what* and *how*:
  – *what* + noun: ***What time** is it?*   ***What kind** of food do you like?*
  – *how* + adjective/adverb: ***How tall** are you?*   ***How far** is it?*
  – *how much/many* + noun: ***How much food** do we have?*

● There is a difference in meaning between *what* and *which*: ***What** music do you like?* (out of all the different kinds)   ***Which** film did you prefer – the first or the second one?* (choosing from a limited number)

▶▶   **For question words as the subject of a question, see Unit 55.**

PRACTICE

54a Complete the questions. Use the words in brackets.

o I know her brother quite well. .... *Do you know* .... him? (you)

1 We'll bring some drinks. .... the food? (they)

2 I live in a flat. .... in a flat or a house? (you)

3 I should tell Emma. .... Lisa too? (I)

4 We've been working in the library. .... at home? (you)

5 We came by train. .... by train or by bus? (Jack)

6 They have to get up at six. .... to get up early too? (we)

7 She sent me a text message. .... you one? (she)

8 He often plays tennis with us. .... with you too? (he)

54b **Complete the questions. Use the words in brackets.**

    0 Question: ....*Why did you decide*........... to do your last film?
               (why / you / decide)

         Answer: I wanted to do a comedy.

    1 Q: .... it? (where / you / make)
       A: In Chicago and Hollywood.

    2 Q: .... in Hollywood? (how long / you / spend)
       A: A month. It was very exciting!

    3 Q: .... about your performance in it?
       (how / you / feel)
       A: I'm quite pleased with it.

    4 Q: .... next year? (what / you / do)
       A: A thriller. I'm going to be a police officer!

    5 Q: .... on it? (who / you / work / with)
       A: I'm not sure. Maybe someone really famous!

    6 Q: .... ? (whose / performances / you / admire)
       A: I really love all Johnny Depp's work.

54c **Circle the correct answer.**

    0 A: (What) / Which time does our train get here?   B: Ten fifteen.

    1 A: What / Which colour is Ben's car?   B: Black, I think.

    2 A: What / Which platform does the train go from?   B: Three.

    3 A: What / Which dress do you like best?   B: The long one.

    4 A: What / Which food have you brought?   B: Just a sandwich.

    5 A: What / Which time's the meeting?   B: Four o'clock.

    6 A: What / Which bag is yours?   B: The green one.

54d **Complete the conversation. Use one word in each gap.**

A: (0) ....*Do*........ you want to come to a dance
course on Saturday at the Arts Centre?

B: Maybe. (1) .... kind of dance is it?

A: Ballet and jazz.

B: (2) .... difficult will it be?

A: Not too difficult. You'll be fine!

B: OK. (3) .... will you get there?

A: I think I'll get the bus.

B: (4) .... bus goes that way? Is it the
23 or the 27?

A: I usually get the 23. It stops near the Arts
Centre.

B: How (5) .... do you go there?

A: Once a term.

B: (6) .... the courses usually good?

A: Yes. I usually learn a lot.

55 Question words as subject or object

● *Who* and *what* can be the subject or object of a question. Compare:

Subject	Object
Who phoned you? (**Someone** phoned you.)	**Who** did you phone? (You phoned **someone**.)
What happened? (**Something** happened.)	**What** did you say? (You said **something**.)

● When *who* or *what* is the subject of a question, the word order is the same as for a statement: *Who **phoned Pat**?   Tom **phoned Pat**.*

● When *who* or *what* is the object of a question, we use an auxiliary/modal verb before the subject: *What **does he want**?   What **are they doing**?   Who **can we ask**?*

● *Which*, *whose* and *how many/much* can also be the subject or object of a question:
– Subject: *Which one **looks** better?*   Object: *Which one **do** you like?*
– Subject: *How much money **is** left?*   Object: *How much money **can** we spend?*

P R A C T I C E

55a Write questions. Use *who* or *what*.

  o A: I did something stupid.   B: Really? *What did you do?* ....

  1 A: Somebody took the money.   B: What? ....

  2 A: Something large fell off.   B: Oh no! ....

  3 A: I can see something.   B: ....

  4 A: Somebody's meeting us.   B: ....

  5 A: Something's happening.   B: Really? ....

  6 A: We should tell somebody.   B: I know. ....

  7 A: He bought something.   B: ....

  8 A: Someone helped him.   B: Really? ....

55b Complete the questions.

  o A: We watched a DVD.   B: Which DVD .... *did you watch* .... ?

  1 A: Lots of people came.   B: Really? How many .... ?

  2 A: Some money is missing.   B: What? How much .... ?

  3 A: He'd borrowed a camera.   B: Really? Whose .... ?

  4 A: The bag costs £100.   B: What? Which .... ?

  5 A: We've got some milk.   B: How much .... ?

  6 A: Her friend might join us.   B: Whose .... ?

  7 A: I'd like to buy that shirt.   B: Which .... ?

  8 A: We can get a few tickets.   B: How many .... ?

56 Negative questions

- We can make *yes/no* and *wh-* questions negative by adding *not* to the auxiliary/ modal verb: ***Don't** you like your present?*   ***Can't** you keep still?*
- We use negative *yes/no* questions:
  - to ask for confirmation: ***Isn't** that your brother?*
  - to express surprise: *It's a great film.* ***Haven't** you seen it?*
  - to express annoyance: ***Haven't** they arrived yet?*
- Notice how we use *yes* and *no* in answers: *'**Haven't** you **finished**?' 'Yes.'* (= I have finished.) / *'No.'* (= I haven't finished.)
- We use negative *wh-* questions:
  - to ask for information: ***Who doesn't want** ice cream?*
  - to criticise: ***Why didn't** you **tell** me?* (= You should have told me.)

P R A C T I C E

56a Write negative questions. Then complete the answers. Use *yes* or *no*.

A: She lives in your street. (0) .....Don't you know her?.....
(you / know / her)
B: (oo) .....No..... . Who is she?

A: You've been writing that for ages. (1) ....
(you / finish / yet)
B: (2) .... I'll finish it in a minute.

A: (3) .... (your sister / go to / Highfield School)
B: (4) .... She didn't like it.

A: (5) .... (you / call / Tom / last night)
B: (6) .... I was too busy.

56b Read the diary entry and complete the negative questions. Use *why*.

> I had an interview for a job on a magazine, but I won't get the job.
> I hadn't dressed well for the interview. I couldn't answer some of the
> questions. And I wasn't able to think of any questions for them. I won't
> apply for another job on a magazine. I don't want to be a journalist!

0 .....Why won't you get..... the job?
1 .... well for the interview?
2 .... some of the questions?
3 .... of any questions for them?
4 .... for another job on a magazine?
5 .... to be a journalist?

57 Question tags

- We form question tags with an auxiliary/modal verb + pronoun. We use negative question tags after positive statements and positive question tags after negative statements: *He's French,* **isn't he**? *She likes animals,* **doesn't she**? *You didn't enjoy the meal,* **did you**? *He can't swim,* **can he**?

- If there are two auxiliary verbs in a statement, or a modal and an auxiliary verb, we use the first one in the question tag: *You've been painting,* **haven't** *you?* *He* **should** *have phoned,* **shouldn't** *he?*

- We often use question tags when we think that something is true and expect the listener to agree with us.
  In this case, our voice goes down: *It's a good film,* **isn't it**? ➔

- We also use question tags as 'real questions', when we are not sure if something is true and want to check.
  In this case, our voice goes up: *His mother's a teacher,* **isn't she**? ➔

- The question tag for *I am* is *aren't I*: *I'm in the team,* **aren't I**?
- The question tag for *let's* is *shall we*: *Let's go for a swim,* **shall we**?

PRACTICE

57a Complete the questions. Use question tags.

- **0** We can't cycle along this path,
  ....*can we*.......... ?

- **1** We'd better cross the road at the crossing,
  .... ?

- **2** The new cycle bridge will be open next month,
  .... ?

- **3** It's going to be very convenient for you,
  .... ?

- **4** There didn't use to be traffic lights here, ... ?

- **5** Let's leave our bikes here, ... ?

- **6** We shouldn't leave them unlocked, ... ?

- **7** You haven't forgotten your lock, ... ?

- **8** You bought this bike last year, ... ?

57b Circle the correct answer.

- **0** We could have walked here, (*couldn't*) / *haven't* we?

- **1** You haven't been waiting long, *were* / *have* you?

- **2** She'll have finished her course by then, *hasn't* / *won't* she?

- **3** They can't have already gone, *have* / *can* they?

- **4** It won't be raining all the time, *will* / *is* it?

- **5** I needn't have worried, *need* / *have* I?

- **6** He should have talked to his father about this, *hasn't* / *shouldn't* he?

57c **Write a sentence for each situation. Use question tags. Then add** ↗ **or** ↗
above the question tags, to show if the speaker's voice goes up or down.

0 You're talking to a friend. You're almost sure that he doesn't like jazz.

You ...*don't like jazz, do you* .... ?

1 You're talking to someone on a train. It's very hot.

It's .... ?

2 You're talking to a friend. You're almost sure that you're older than her cousin.

I'm .... ?

3 You're talking to your brother. Someone's told you that the film starts at eight,
but you don't think this is right. You want to check.

The film .... ?

4 You're talking to a friend. You think her mother is a doctor, but you aren't sure.

Your mother .... ?

5 You're talking to a friend. Someone's told you that his sister works in a bank,
but you don't think this is right. You want to check.

Your sister .... ?

58 Reply questions

- We use reply questions to show that we are interested in or surprised by what
someone is saying: '*He left six weeks ago.*' '***Did he?*** *I didn't realise that.*'
- We form reply questions with an auxiliary/modal verb + pronoun. We use a positive
question after a positive statement and a negative question after a negative
statement: '*I **can** speak German.*' '***Can** you?*' '*Sarah**'s not** feeling very well.*'
'***Isn't** she?*'
- If there are two auxiliary verbs in a statement, or a modal and an auxiliary verb, we
use the first one in the reply question: '*He**'s** been working very hard.*' '***Has** he?*'

P R A C T I C E

58a **Circle the correct answer.**

0 A: Nikki's already gone.   B: (Has)/ Hasn't she?
1 A: She didn't stay long.   B: *Did* / *Didn't* she?
2 A: She was in a hurry.   B: *Was* / *Wasn't* she?
3 A: She left at about one.   B: *Did* / *Didn't* she?
4 A: She'll be back at four.   B: *Will* / *Won't* she?
5 A: She hasn't bought the cinema tickets.   B: *Has* / *Hasn't* she?
6 A: She isn't having dinner with us.   B: *Is* / *Isn't* she?

58b **Write reply questions.**

    o **A:** It was snowing this morning.   **B:** *Was it?* ....

    1 **A:** I didn't go to college.   **B:** ....

    2 **A:** I've got an awful cold.   **B:** ....

    3 **A:** Adam and I can't come tomorrow.   **B:** ....

    4 **A:** He's starting a new job.   **B:** ....

    5 **A:** They're going to be annoyed with us.   **B:** ....

    6 **A:** They don't often invite us.   **B:** ....

58c **Circle the correct answer.**

    o **A:** My cousins will be staying with us.   **B:** .... they?
    A Are   **(B)** Will   **C** Aren't   **D** Won't

    1 **A:** I've been thinking about this since the weekend.   **B:** .... you?
    A Are   **B** Have   **C** Aren't   **D** Haven't

    2 **A:** They shouldn't have come round last night.   **B:** .... they?
    A Should   **B** Have   **C** Shouldn't   **D** Haven't

    3 **A:** He hasn't been learning the guitar for long.   **B:** .... he?
    A Is   **B** Has   **C** Isn't   **D** Hasn't

    4 **A:** I will have left home by then.   **B:** .... you?
    A Will   **B** Have   **C** Won't   **D** Haven't

    5 **A:** Your idea could have made a lot of money.   **B:** .... it?
    A Could   **B** Has   **C** Couldn't   **D** Hasn't

    6 **A:** She won't be playing in the final tomorrow.   **B:** .... she?
    A Will   **B** Is   **C** Won't   **D** Isn't

59   Avoiding repetition: *so, too, neither*, etc.

- To avoid repeating the same words when we add more information to a statement, we can use these structures:
  - *so* + auxiliary verb + subject: *I enjoyed this book and **so did Kate**.*   *'I've been to America.' **'So has Laura.'***
  - subject + auxiliary verb + *too*: *Tim's done well in his exams and **Mike has too**.* *'Jenny liked the film.' **'Peter did too.'***
  - *neither/nor* + auxiliary verb + subject: *I wasn't there and **neither/nor was Lucy**.* *'Sam isn't coming.' **'Neither/Nor is Ben.'***
  - subject + negative auxiliary verb + *either*: *Matt won't buy a ticket and **I won't either**.*   *'I've never been skiing.' **'Kim hasn't either.'***

- We can also use *so, too, either, neither* and *nor* to agree with someone: *'I love spicy food.' **'So do I.'**/**'I do too.'***   *'I don't want to go.' **'I don't either.'***   *'I didn't like that programme.' **'Neither/Nor did I.'***

- To answer a question, we can use *I (don't) think so, I hope so* and *I hope not*: *'Did Rob enjoy the party?' **'I think so.'***   *'Is Paul here?' 'No, **I don't think so.'*** *'Is he still ill?' **'I hope not.'***

PRACTICE

59a **Complete the sentences. Use the words in brackets.**

  o I don't like cheese. Jessica doesn't like cheese. (either)
I don't like cheese and ...*Jessica doesn't either*........................ .

  1 We got to the cinema early. They got to the cinema early. (so)
We got to the cinema early and ....

  2 Lisa's lent me some magazines. Kirsty's lent me some magazines. (too)
Lisa's lent me some magazines and ....

  3 Adam wasn't listening. I wasn't listening. (neither)
Adam wasn't listening and ....

  4 The shops will be shut tomorrow. The museum will be shut tomorrow. (so)
The shops will be shut tomorrow and ....

  5 I hadn't noticed her message. My brother hadn't noticed her message. (either)
I hadn't noticed her message and ....

  6 Tom didn't call me last night. Nick didn't call me last night. (nor)
Tom didn't call me last night and ....

  7 They live in a small flat. We live in a small flat. (too)
They live in a small flat and ....

  8 Becky won't understand. Rachel won't understand. (neither)
Becky won't understand and ....

59b **Complete the conversation. Use one or two words in each gap.**

  A: I'm really enjoying the course.
  B: So (o) ....*am I*.......... . It's really interesting. I like the practical parts the best.
  A: Yes, (1) .... too. Sometimes I don't understand the lectures.
  B: No, (2) .... either. I have to read about the topic later. I didn't realise it was going to be so difficult!
  A: No, neither (3) .... I was very tired at first.
  B: So (4) .... ! But I've got used to the timetable now.
  A: (5) .... too, but I don't get enough sleep.
  B: No, nor (6) .... There's too much to do!

59c **Complete the conversations. Use one or two words in each gap.**

  o **A:** Is Jack ill?   **B:** Yes, I ......*think*...... so.

  1 **A:** Has he got flu?   **B:** No, I don't .... so.

  2 **A:** Will he be able to play on Saturday?   **B:** I hope ....

  3 **A:** Do you think it's going to rain?   **B:** I hope ....

  4 **A:** Can we beat them?   **B:** I think ....

  5 **A:** Are they good?   **B:** No, I .... think so.

  6 **A:** Have we got a practice session tomorrow?   **B:** I .... not!

Check 11 Statements and questions

1 Put the words in the correct order.

1 's become / it / very popular / café / a

....

2 some / ice cream / who / wants?

....

3 cooked / us / she / great / a / meal

....

4 should / we / what / tomorrow / bring?

....

5 don't / on the table / your dirty plate / leave

....

/ 5

2 Circle the correct answer.

6 A: I'll have finished work by then.
   B: *Will / Have* you?

7 A: They're really famous! *You haven't /*
   Haven't you heard of them?
   B: No.

8 A: Will you be able to come tomorrow?
   B: I hope *so / not*. I'd like to.

9 A: Which one *belongs / does belong* to Lisa?
   B: I don't know.

10 A: Why *did / didn't* you tell him?
   B: I didn't want to.

11 A: *What / Which* time do you have to be
   there?
   B: Ten fifteen. Jenny's picking me up at nine.

12 A: Amy wants to move there.
   B: *Is / Does* she? I think she'd miss all the
   shops here.

/ 7

3 Complete the e-mail. Use one word in each gap.

New Message

How are you? When (13) .... you
get back? Thanks for your postcard. It's
beautiful. (14) .... an amazing beach
that is! And the weather was really good!
You weren't expecting that, (15) ....
you?

Do you want to play tennis some time?
I can play again – I've got a new racket.
My parents bought it (16) .... me
for my birthday. I can play on Monday or
Wednesday evening and (17) ....
can Jamie and Craig. Are you free then?
By the way, what's the leisure centre like
in Hendon? How big is it? It hasn't got a
football pitch, (18) .... it? Jamie's
team are looking for somewhere to play
and I couldn't think of anywhere and
(19) .... could Craig.

I'll bring the DVD for you when we meet.
I've actually lent it (20) .... Kate, but
I'm sure I can get it back at the weekend.

/ 8

Total: / 20

Self-check

Wrong answers	Look again at	Try CD-ROM
1, 5, 14	Unit 52	Exercise 52
3, 16, 20	Unit 53	Exercise 53
4, 11, 13	Unit 54	Exercise 54
2, 9	Unit 55	Exercise 55
7, 10	Unit 56	Exercise 56
15, 18	Unit 57	Exercise 57
6, 12	Unit 58	Exercise 58
8, 17, 19	Unit 59	Exercise 59

Now do **Check 11**

-ing forms and infinitives

60 Verbs followed by *-ing* form or *to*-infinitive (1)

- Some verbs are followed by an *-ing* form: *I **enjoy watching** films.   I **miss seeing** my friends every day.*

▶▶ **See Appendix 9: Verbs followed by -ing form, page 172.**

- Some verbs are followed by a *to*-infinitive: *They **promised to meet** us.   I **want to go** home.*

▶▶ **See Appendix 10: Verbs followed by to-infinitive, page 172.**

- Some verbs are followed by either a *to*-infinitive or an *-ing* form with no change in meaning: *It began **to rain/raining**.   She continued **to talk/talking**.   He started **to laugh/laughing**.*

▶▶ **See Appendix 11: Verbs followed by -ing form or to-infinitive, page 173.**

- Sometimes there is a difference between *like + -ing* and *like + to*-infinitive. Compare: *I **like swimming**. (= I enjoy it.)   I **like to keep** my room tidy. (= I don't enjoy tidying it, but I prefer to do it.)*

- *Would like, would prefer* and *would love* are followed by a *to*-infinitive, not an *-ing* form: *I'd **like to talk** to you. (Not I'd like talking to you.)*

- To make an *-ing* form or infinitive negative, we put *not* in front of it: *We decided **not to go** with them.   I hate **not having** enough time to visit my cousins.*

PRACTICE

60a Complete the sentences. Use the correct form of the verbs in brackets. There may be more than one possible answer.

0 I miss ....*living*.......... in the country. (live)

1 I can't help .... about our old house. (think)

2 I hate .... able to see my old friends. (not be)

3 My parents decided .... here a month ago. (move)

4 They intend .... here for a few years. (work)

5 I've given up .... my bike because there's too much traffic. (ride)

6 I've started .... friends, so I feel happier. (make)

7 My new friends have promised .... me to get used to the city. (help)

8 I managed .... lost on my last trip to the centre. (not get)

9 One of my friends has offered .... me to a fabulous café. (take)

10 I can't imagine .... here all my life, but it's all right. (stay)

6ob Circle the correct answer.

0 I'd like *being* / *(to be)* a chef.

1 I'd love *having* / *to have* my own restaurant.

2 I really like *cooking* / *to cook*. It's my favourite activity.

3 But I don't feel like cooking tonight. I'd prefer *eating* / *to eat* out.

4 I don't enjoy cleaning the kitchen, but I hate mess, so I like *leaving* / *to leave* it clean and tidy.

5 My mother likes *planning* / *to plan* a meal in advance, but I prefer to plan it on the same day.

6oc Complete the texts. Use the correct form of the verbs in brackets. There may be more than one possible answer.

I'd like (0) ......**to get**...... (get) a job in computing. There are all kinds of computer courses that you can do. Some are very expensive and I can't afford (1) .... (do) those, but I've managed (2) .... (save) enough money for a cheaper one.

I can't stand (3) .... (sit) at a desk and I enjoy (4) .... (be) outside, so I need a job that's quite physical. Maybe a builder.

I hope (5) .... (become) a singer. I'd love (6) .... (sing) in front of a big audience. I sometimes write songs too. I started (7) .... (write) them when I was fourteen. I also play the guitar, but I've never considered (8) .... (play) it professionally.

61 Verbs followed by *-ing* form or *to*-infinitive (2)

Some verbs can be followed by an *-ing* form or a *to*-infinitive with a change in meaning. We usually use an *-ing* form to talk about an action that is completed or in progress, and a *to*-infinitive to express an intention to do something. Compare:

He **stopped talking** to his friend.
(= He was talking and then he stopped.)

He **stopped to talk** to a friend.
(= He stopped in order to talk.)

Try taking more exercise.
(= Take more exercise and see if it helps.)

Try to take more exercise.
(= Make an attempt to take more exercise.)

I **remember telling** Georgia.
(= I told him and I can remember it.)

I must **remember to tell** Georgia.
(= I must remember and then tell him.)

I won't **forget seeing** that film.
(= I saw it and I won't forget it.)

I **forgot to phone** my aunt.
(= I forgot, so I didn't phone her.)

▶▶ *See Appendix 11: Verbs followed by -ing form or to-infinitive, page 173.*

P R A C T I C E

61a Circle the correct answer.

  o   We drove for two hours and then stopped *having* / (*to have*) some lunch.

  1   I try *arriving* / *to arrive* on time, but I'm often late for things.

  2   He doesn't play rugby now. He stopped *playing* / *to play* a year ago.

  3   If you make something that's too salty, try *adding* / *to add* some sugar to it.

  4   We went for a walk when it stopped *raining* / *to rain*.

  5   Could you turn down your radio? I'm trying *working* / *to work*.

  6   She saw a beautiful sunset, so she stopped *taking* / *to take* a picture of it.

61b Complete the conversation. Use the correct form of the verbs in brackets.

  A: I'm sorry, I forgot (o) ....*to ask*........ (ask) you about your birthday. Did you have a good time?

  B: Yes, thanks. I had a lesson at the snowboard centre with some friends.

  A: I went there last year. I remember (1) .... (fall) over a lot!

  B: Me too! I forgot (2) .... (move) my weight on the board properly.

  A: And you have to remember (3) .... (look) up, not down at the board, don't you?

  B: Yes. There was a lot to learn! But I really enjoyed it.

  A: So did I! I'll never forget (4) .... (ride) down the slope at top speed!

  B: Yes. I remember (5) .... (feel) really excited! I'd love to do it again. I've got some good photos of us. I must remember (6) .... (show) them to you next time.

  A: Great! I'd love to see them.

61c Complete the second sentence so that it means the same as the first, using the word in bold. Use between two and five words.

  o   I thought that talking to her would help, but it didn't. **tried**
      I ....*tried talking*............... to her, but it didn't help.

  1   It's important for us to book our train tickets tomorrow. **remember**
      We must .... our train tickets tomorrow.

  2   He didn't tell Jack about the party because he didn't remember. **forgot**
      He .... Jack about the party.

  3   Do you still have piano lessons? **stopped**
      Have you .... piano lessons?

  4   I'll always have the memory of scoring the winning goal in the final. **forget**
      I'll never .... the winning goal in the final.

  5   Why don't you click on that icon and see if that works? **try**
      Why don't you .... on that icon?

  6   I cried on my first day at school and I'll never forget it. **remember**
      I'll always .... on my first day at school.

62 Verbs followed by object + (*to-*)infinitive

- Some verbs can be followed by an object + *to*-infinitive: *She **wanted us to go** with her.   They didn't **allow us to enter** the room.*
- Some verbs must have an object before the *to*-infinitive: *He taught **me** to swim.* (Not *He taught to swim.*)
- Other verbs can have an object, depending on the meaning of the sentence. Compare: *I'd **like to pay** for the tickets.* (= I'll pay.)   *I'd **like you to pay** for the tickets.* (= You'll pay.)
- We use object + infinitive without *to* after *make* and *let*: *She **made me pay** for the damage.   Please **let me speak**.*
- We can use object + *to*-infinitive or object + infinitive without *to* after *help*: *I **helped him** (**to**) **mend** the fence.*

▶▶ **See Appendix 12: Verbs followed by object + to-infinitive, page 173.**

P R A C T I C E

62a Complete the sentences. Use an object and the correct form of the verbs in the box.

| buy   come   give   ~~miss~~   phone   play   visit |

0 Her illness caused ....*her to miss*............ a lot of last term. She didn't come to college for four or five weeks.

1 She's brilliant! Who taught .... the guitar like that?

2 They forced .... them the briefcase. I had no choice.

3 His parents didn't allow .... a motorbike because they thought it was dangerous.

4 Tom's expecting my call. Remind .... him before I go out.

5 Kirsty's invited .... her while she's in Italy. Shall we go?

6 Try to persuade .... with us. She's been working too hard lately.

62b Complete the conversation. Use an object if necessary. If a sentence does not need an object, write – on the line.

A: We've got our end-of-year exhibition next week. Would you like (0) ......–...... to come?

B: Yes! Thanks! I really want (1) .... to see your pictures.

A: Thanks. I want (2) .... to see them. I'd like (3) .... to know what you think. And I'd like (4) .... to meet my parents. They'll be there on the last night. I need (5) .... to take the pictures home for me afterwards.

B: Are you nervous about it? Are you worried about people's reactions?

A: Not really. You can't please everyone. So, I expect (6) .... to hear a few criticisms!

62c **Complete the second sentence so that it means the same as the first, using the word in bold. Use between two and five words.**

0   We couldn't take our bags into the museum. **let**
They .... *didn't let us take* .... our bags into the museum.

1   They forced him to sign the document. **made**
They .... the document.

2   I thought that she'd be angry with me, but she wasn't. **expected**
I .... angry with me, but she wasn't.

3   Why do you allow her to borrow all your clothes? **let**
Why do you .... all your clothes?

4   If you need advice from someone, ask one of your tutors. **advise**
If you need .... you, ask one of your tutors.

5   The heat caused everyone to feel tired. **made**
The heat .... tired.

6   Lisa never allows anyone to use her laptop. **lets**
Lisa never .... her laptop.

7   The manager sent them an invitation to meet him for a discussion. **invited**
The manager .... him for a discussion.

8   He said that I should take the DVD back. **reminded**
He .... the DVD back.

62d **Circle the correct answer.**

Each year about 12,000 American teenagers are sent to treatment centres by their parents. These are places that take teenagers who are behaving badly and help (0) *to change* / *them to change*. Many of these teenagers refuse to go to these centres – they do not want (1) *to change* / *them to change*. Their parents often have to force (2) *to go* / *them to go* because they want (3) *to behave* / *them to behave* better. They feel their children need (4) *to get away* / *them to get away* from their normal lives and get special help.

Programmes at the centres vary, but most last several weeks. They aim to teach (5) *to respect teenagers* / *teenagers to respect* other people. Counsellors invite (6) *to talk* / *them to talk* about any problems they have in the family. Often the teenagers start to think about how their problems are making them (7) *behave* / *to behave* badly. Without their usual distractions – centres do not let them (8) *watch* / *to watch* TV or listen to music – they can think more clearly about their lives and their goals for the future.

63 Infinitive of purpose, *in order to, for + -ing* form

- We use (*in order*) *to* + infinitive to say why we do something: *I went into town (**in order**) **to meet** some friends.   She came round (**in order**) **to watch** a DVD.*

- We use *for + -ing* form to talk about the purpose of something, or how we use it: *This knife is **for cutting** bread.   You can use this soap **for washing** your hands.*

- We can use *what ... for* to ask about the purpose of something, or to ask why someone does something: *'**What's** this bag **for**?' 'It's **for keeping** food cold.'* *'**What** are you phoning him **for**?' '**To tell** him about the film tonight.'*

- We can also *for + noun* to talk about the purpose of or reason for something: *This drawer is **for** your clothes.   I sat down **for** a rest.*

PRACTICE

63a **Complete the sentences. Use *to* or *for* and the correct form of the verbs in brackets.**

0   I came here ....*to see*.......... you. (see)

1   This is really good .... stains from your clothes. (remove)

2   We had to run fast .... the train. (catch)

3   This tool is .... small holes in wood. (make)

4   You need to rest for a few days .... properly. (recover)

5   I want to buy today's paper .... about the match. (read)

6   The blue cloth is .... the floor. (clean)

7   He pretended to be rich .... his friends. (impress)

8   Have you got any glue .... china? (mend)

63b **Complete the conversation. Use one word in each gap.**

Lucy's tidying her room and throwing some things away. Emma's helping her.

Lucy: I definitely want to keep the blue boxes.

Emma: (0) ......*What*...... do you use them for?

Lucy: (1) .... storing my things in. I put them under the bed.

Emma: What about those plastic boxes over there? (2) .... are they for?

Lucy: Oh – they're (3) .... CDs. I've been keeping them (4) .... give them to my cousin. I don't use them any more and I need the space (5) .... my new computer.

Emma: (6) .... do you need a computer for?

Lucy: (7) .... lots of things! Mainly my college work. I use the Internet at college in (8) .... to find information, and it would be very convenient to do that at home.

Emma: So you aren't going to use it (9) .... chatting to your friends?

Lucy: No, my phone's (10) .... that!

64 Expressions with *-ing* forms

- We can use *go* + *-ing* form to say that we spend time doing an activity, usually a sport: *We **went swimming** yesterday.*   *I **go jogging** every morning.*
  We also say: *We're **going shopping**.*   *I want to **go sightseeing**.*

- These expressions are followed by an *-ing* form:
  - *I can't talk now. I'**m busy cleaning** the kitchen.*
  - *I **spent/wasted** a lot of **time/hours looking** for information on the Internet.*
  - ***There's no point in complaining**.* (= Complaining won't achieve anything.)
  - ***It's a waste of time cleaning** your car.* (= You spend time cleaning your car, but it'll just get dirty again.)
  - ***It's no good/use asking** me.* (= You won't get anything by asking me.)
  - ***It's not worth getting** a taxi. Let's walk.* (= It's not necessary to get a taxi.)

PRACTICE

64a **Complete the sentences. Use *go* and the correct form of the verbs in the box.**

| ~~camp~~   cycle   hike   sail   shop   sightsee   swim |

0   I decided to .... *go camping* .... , so I bought a tent.

1   The shops were great, so we .... a few times.

2   We .... in Rome and saw lots of famous places.

3   The beach was very close, so we .... every day.

4   My friend and I .... with our new bikes last Saturday.

5   I .... a couple of times on the lake near our hotel.

6   I was going to .... in the mountains, but the weather was awful.

64b **Complete the second sentence so that it means the same as the first, using the word in bold. Use between two and five words.**

0   Talking about it won't achieve anything.   **point**
    There's .... *no point in talking* .... about it.

1   She watched TV for four hours last night.   **spent**
    She .... TV last night.

2   I'm not going to try to get tickets because there won't be any.   **good**
    It's .... to get tickets.

3   You won't improve things by feeling sorry for yourself.   **use**
    It's .... sorry for yourself.

4   It's not a good idea to buy those goggles if you don't go swimming.   **worth**
    It's .... those goggles if you don't go swimming.

5   It's useless calling her because she never answers the phone.   **waste**
    It's .... her because she never answers the phone.

65 Adjectives followed by *to*-infinitive

- We can use a *to*-infinitive after adjectives that describe feelings (e.g. *amazed, disappointed, sorry*): *I was **glad to see** Kate.   We were very **surprised to win**.*
- We can use adjective + *to*-infinitive to give our opinion about someone's actions. We use adjectives such as *careless, crazy, nice* and *wrong*: *He was **stupid to leave** the key in the lock.   You were **wrong not to inform** the police.*
- We can also use *it* + *be* + adjective (+ *of someone*) + *to*-infinitive: *It was **wrong (of Josh) to shout** at them.*
- We can use adjective + *to*-infinitive or *it* + *be* + adjective (+ *for someone*) + *to*-infinitive to describe an action, with adjectives such as *difficult, exciting, fun* and *impossible*: *Some pets are **expensive to keep**.   **It's expensive to keep** some pets. These books are **easy for children to read**.   **It's easy for children to read** these books.*

P R A C T I C E

65a Join the sentences.

o I got on the course. I was pleased.   *I was pleased to get on the course.*

1 Sam was silly. He didn't apply for it.   ....

2 I was right. I listened to Jack.   ....

3 I got his advice. I was grateful.   ....

4 I had some very good tutors. I was lucky.   ....

5 I didn't get an A in the exam. I was sorry.   ....

6 I didn't work hard enough. I was stupid.   ....

65b Complete the second sentence so that it means the same as the first.

o This race can be hard for beginners to complete.
It can be .... *hard for beginners to complete* .... this race.

1 I was stupid not to bring my file.
It was .... my file.

2 That train will be difficult for us to get.
It will be .... that train.

3 He was wrong not to help the people who were injured.
It was .... the people who were injured.

4 Most scientific reports are impossible for ordinary people to understand.
It's .... most scientific reports.

5 They were kind to invite us.
It was .... us.

6 Is the equipment safe for children to use?
Is it .... the equipment?

Check 12 -ing forms and infinitives

1 **Complete the conversation. Use the correct form of the verbs in brackets.**

A: I was sorry (1) .... (not see) you on Saturday.

B: Yes – sorry I missed you. I'd gone into town (2) .... (look) at cameras. I need one for my project.

A: Can't you borrow your brother's?

B: No. He won't let me (3) .... (borrow) anything! Anyway, I got a cheap one, and I got some paper for (4) .... (print) photos.

A: Your camera looks nice. Is it easy (5) .... (use)?

B: Yes.

/ 5

2 **Complete the sentences. Use one word in each gap if it is necessary. If it is not necessary, write – on the line.**

6 Our coach wants .... to come to more training sessions because we're not fit enough.

7 There's .... point in going now – we're already too late.

8 Do you need special trainers .... running or will ordinary ones be all right?

9 These trousers make me .... look fat!

10 It was very nice .... them to pay for us.

/ 5

3 **Complete the second sentence so that it means the same as the first, using the word in bold. Use between two and five words.**

11 We haven't got enough money to hire a car. **afford**
We can't .... a car.

12 She left her job at the bakery a couple of months ago. **stopped**
She .... at the bakery a couple of months ago.

13 Do you want to watch a DVD? **fancy**
Do you .... a DVD?

14 You won't get anything by asking Tom about this. **use**
It's .... Tom about this.

15 He walks around town for hours every weekend. **spends**
He .... around town every weekend.

/ 5

4 **Circle the correct answer.**

SECRETS OF SUCCESS

Martha Wilkins decided (16) *becoming / to become* a florist when she read an article about someone who supplied flowers to film stars. 'I remember (17) *thinking / to think*, "What an amazing job!" And when I started work at a florist's, I found that I liked (18) *working / work* with my hands. I really enjoyed it,' she explains. 'The owner of the shop was very experienced and she taught (19) *to arrange / me to arrange* flowers.' Several years later, Wilkins set up her own shop, which is now very successful. 'The key is to listen to the customers,' she says. 'I talk to every customer about what they want and then I try (20) *giving / to give* it to them.'

/ 5

Total: / 20

✓ Self-check

Wrong answers	Look again at	Try CD-ROM
11, 13, 16, 18	Unit 60	Exercise 60
12, 17, 20	Unit 61	Exercise 61
3, 6, 9, 19	Unit 62	Exercise 62
2, 4, 8	Unit 63	Exercise 63
7, 14, 15	Unit 64	Exercise 64
1, 5, 10	Unit 65	Exercise 65

Now do **Check 12**

The passive

66 The passive

- In an active sentence, the subject of the sentence is the 'doer' who performs the action of the verb. In a passive sentence, the object of the active verb becomes the subject. We use the passive only with verbs that take an object. Compare:

	Subject	Action	Object
Active	He	has painted	the house.
Passive	The house	has been painted.	

- We use the passive when:
  - we want to focus on the action, not the doer of the action: *The house **has been painted**. It looks great!*
  - the doer is not known or not important: *Oh no! My bag's **been stolen**!* (= I don't know who stole it.)   *This house **was built** in 1970.* (= Somebody built it. It's not important who.)
  - the doer is obvious or 'people in general': *He **was arrested**.* (Obviously, the police arrested him.)   *The show **is watched** all over the world.*

- If we want to mention the doer of the action, we use *by* + agent (= the person/thing that does the action): *I was hit **by a car**.*

- The passive is more common in writing than speech.

- We form the passive with an appropriate form of *be* + past participle.

PRACTICE

66a Circle the correct answer.

0   Very little *knows* / *is known* about this disease because it is very rare.

1   The government *has spent* / *has been spent* a huge amount of money on education.

2   Traffic on the M11 is very slow this week as repairs *are carrying out* / *are being carried out* on two lanes.

3   The shopkeeper chased the thieves for a few minutes, but then they *disappeared* / *were disappeared* into the crowd.

4   'I've done a lot of work for them, but they *haven't paid* / *haven't been paid* me,' an electrician complained.

5   The shopping centre *is going to knock down* / *is going to be knocked down*.

6   'We should *inform* / *be informed* about the dangers to our health,' a factory worker said.

7   Representatives from sixty-five countries *will attend* / *will be attended* the conference.

8   The missing boy *has not found* / *has not been found* yet.

66b **Complete the second sentence so that it means the same as the first, using the word in bold. Use between two and five words.**

0 They have planted a lot of trees along the river. **been**
A lot of trees ....*have been planted*.......... along the river.

1 Andrew Black wrote this article. **by**
This article .... Andrew Black.

2 They sell these computer games all over the world. **are**
These computer games .... all over the world.

3 They're planning a music festival for next summer. **planned**
A music festival .... for next summer.

4 I'm sure somebody will sort everything out soon. **sorted**
I'm sure everything .... soon.

5 We can arrange a meeting for next week. **arranged**
A meeting .... for next week.

6 Caitlin didn't take this photo. **by**
This photo .... Caitlin.

7 He was unhappy because the coach had not chosen him for the team. **been**
He was unhappy because he .... for the team.

8 Are we doing enough about climate change? **done**
Is .... about climate change?

66c **Circle the correct answer.**

Stolen Goya painting recovered

A painting by Francisco Goya that (0) ..... stolen while it was (1) ..... to an exhibition in New York earlier this month has (2) ..... . *Children with a Cart* (1778) (3) ..... at about $1.1m.

Apparently, the FBI were called on Saturday (4) ..... a lawyer who offered to reveal where the painting was.

It is unlikely that the painting will now (5) ..... in the show in New York. It will instead (6) ..... back to its home in Ohio.

0	A is	B was	C had	D been
1	A transport	B transporting	C being transported	D been transported
2	A recovered	B be recovered	C was recovered	D been recovered
3	A is valued	B has valued	C been valued	D valued
4	A from	B for	C by	D of
5	A include	B be included	C have included	D been included
6	A take	B taking	C taken	D be taken

(0 B circled)

67 The causative: *have/get something done*

- We use the causative form (subject + *have* + object + past participle) when we don't do something ourselves, but arrange for someone else to do it for us. Compare: *Emma **cleaned** her car.* (= She did it herself.)　*Sarah had her car **cleaned**.* (= She arranged for someone else to do it for her.)

- All tenses are possible: *We're **having our house decorated** at the moment.* ***Have** you **had your car repaired**?*　*I want **to have new curtains made**.*

- We can use *get something done* in a similar way, especially in informal English: *I **must get my hair cut**.*

- But we don't usually use *get* in the present perfect tense: *She's **had** her ears pierced.*　(Not *She's got her ears pierced.*)

- We can also use *have something done* (but not *get something done*) when something unpleasant happens to us: *I **had my bag stolen** at the airport.*

PRACTICE

67a **Complete the sentences. Use the causative form with *have*.**

Ben's opening a café. It used to be a clothes shop.

0 I ....*'ve had the floor replaced*........ . It's completely new. (the floor / replace)

1 There used to be some steps up to the shop, but I decided to
.... (them / remove)

2 I .... It's fine. (the air-conditioning / check)

3 I .... yesterday. (some tables / deliver)

4 Sorry about the noise. I .... in the kitchen.
(some new equipment / install)

5 I .... a warm orange colour last week. Do you
like it? (the walls / paint)

6 I may .... at the back next year.
(another room / add)

67b **Complete the sentences. Use the causative form with *get* where possible. If *get* is not possible, use the causative form with *have*.**

0 I need to ....*get the car serviced*........ . (the car / service)

1 The windows in this shop are usually dirty. The owners
.... regularly. (them / not clean)

2 I .... , so I had to apply to another college.
(my application / turn down)

3 We should .... (that tap / fix)

4 I .... while I was on the underground.
(my money / steal)

5 Where .... ? Was it expensive?
(you / your bike / repair)

6 They .... last week. (their electricity / cut off)

Check 13 The passive

1 Complete the sentences. Use the correct form of the verbs in brackets.

1 The winning goal in last night's match .... by Scott in the 87th minute. (score)

2 The number of road accidents .... by six per cent last year. (rise)

3 Police have found the plane's voice and flight recorders, so they can now .... by experts to establish the cause of the crash. (examine)

4 Michael Norris, who wrote many popular television series, ... yesterday, aged seventy-three. (die)

5 More than 2,000 people .... at next week's conference. (expect)

/ 5

2 Complete the conversations. Use the causative form.

A: Your hair looks nice! (6) .... you .... (it / cut)?

B: Yes. I (7) .... (it / do) yesterday.

A: Our kitchen's a mess at the moment. We (8) .... (just / the windows / replace) and now we (9) .... (some new cupboards / fit). It's taking them ages.

B: When are they going to finish it?

A: Friday, I think. Then next week, we (10) .... (the sitting room / decorate), so there'll be a few more weeks of mess!

/ 5

3 Circle the correct answer.

We (11) 've given / 've been given the afternoon off, so I'm going into town. I want to get some posters (12) print / printed for the play. I'm going to try the place that Jamie (13) used / was used last year, as he says it's good. I'll have to go by bus as I haven't had (14) my bike fixed / fixed my bike yet. I hope I'll see you later although I might (15) ask / be asked to paint some of the scenery for the play tonight.

/ 5

4 Complete the second sentence so that it means the same as the first, using the word in bold. Use between two and five words.

16 Two companies have proposed plans for apartment blocks. by
Plans for apartment blocks .... two companies.

17 Someone stole their cameras from their hotel room. stolen
They .... from their hotel room.

18 I'm going to arrange for someone to repair the computer next week. get
I'm going to .... next week.

19 Carol Hicks directed this film. was
This film .... Carol Hicks.

20 Your eyes should be tested every year. have
You .... every year.

/ 5

Total: / 20

✓ Self-check

Wrong answers	Look again at	Try CD-ROM
1, 2, 3, 4, 5, 11, 13, 15, 16, 19	Unit 66	Exercise 66
6, 7, 8, 9, 10, 12, 14, 17, 18, 20	Unit 67	Exercise 67

Now do Check 13

Reported speech

68 Reported statements: tense changes

- We use reported speech to report what someone said earlier. After a past tense reporting verb (e.g. *said, told*), the original verb forms usually move one tense into the past, and the pronouns and possessive adjectives change: **'I like** pizza,' Tim said. (direct speech) → Tim said (that) **he liked** pizza. (reported speech)
  'You look great,' I told Anna. → I told Anna (that) **she looked** great.

Direct speech (actual words)		Reported speech
present simple	→	past simple
present continuous	→	past continuous
present perfect/past simple	→	past perfect
past continuous/ present perfect continuous	→	past perfect continuous
past perfect	→	past perfect
will	→	*would*
am/is/are going to	→	*was/were going to*
can	→	*could*
may	→	*might*
must	→	*must/had to*

- *Could,* *would* and *might* don't change in reported speech: **'I might** come with you,' she said. → She said (that) she **might** come with us.

- *Say* and *tell* are the most common reporting verbs for statements. Notice how they are used:
  - He **said** (**to me**) (**that**) he was tired. (Not He ~~said me that~~ he was tired.)
  - He **told me** (**that**) he was tired. (Not He ~~told that~~ he was tired.)

PRACTICE

68a Report the statements.

0 'I've got an awful headache.'   Kim said *(that) she had an awful headache* .

1 'I haven't been feeling well all day.'   She ....

2 'I've found some great trainers.'   Tom ....

3 'I wasn't looking for them.'   He ....

4 'I'm going to wear them to college.'   He ....

5 'I didn't see David.'   Lisa ....

6 'I called him.'   She ....

7 'I'm staying at home.'   Ben ....

8 'I don't feel like going out.' He ....

9 'I'm late.' Amy ....

10 'I have to be there at eight.' She ....

68b Report the conversation.

0 'I'm going to the park with my brother,' Paul said.
Paul said (that) he was going to the park with his brother.
....

1 'We're going to have a game of football,' he said.
....

2 'I might come too,' Stephen said.
....

3 'We'll be in our usual place,' Paul said.
....

4 'I can't stay long because my friends are coming at six,' Stephen said.
....

5 'They're taking me to the skate park in Burnley,' he said.
....

6 'I've never been there before,' he said.
....

7 'I'd like to go to the skate park in Manchester,' Paul said.
....

8 'We could go together,' Stephen said.
....

68c Read the conversation. Then complete the diary entry. Use one word in each gap.

Emma: I'm really stressed! Someone at college is being horrible to me.

Becky: Someone did the same thing to me once. I spoke to her and she stopped criticising me.

Emma: Speaking to her will make things worse!

Becky: You must do something. You can't ignore it.

Emma (0) ......*told*...... me that she (1) .... really stressed. She (2) .... that someone at college was being horrible to (3) ....
I said that someone (4) .... done the same thing to me once. I (5) .... her that I'd spoken to the girl and that she (6) .... stopped criticising me. Emma said that speaking to her (7) .... make things worse. I told (8) .... that she (9) .... to do something and that she (10) ....n't ignore it.

69 Reported statements: other changes

- Place and time references often change when we report what someone said in a different place or at an earlier time. Compare:

Actual words	Words reported later
Spoken outside the cinema: *'I'll meet you **here**,'* Kate said.	Spoken somewhere else: *Kate said she'd meet us **there**/**at the cinema***.
Spoken on Sunday: *'I'm going to a party **tonight**,'* Matt said.	Spoken the following Tuesday: *Matt said he was going to a party **on Sunday night***.

- These words/phrases often change in reported speech:

Direct speech		Reported speech
this/that (+noun)	→	*the*
this morning	→	*that morning, on Friday morning*, etc.
now	→	*then*
today, tonight	→	*that day/night, on Friday/Friday night*, etc.
yesterday	→	*the day before, the previous day, on Friday*, etc.
tomorrow	→	*the next/following day, on Friday*, etc.
last week, last Friday	→	*the week/Friday before, the previous week/Friday*
next week, next Friday	→	*the week/Friday after, the following week/Friday*
an hour ago	→	*an hour before*

PRACTICE

69a **Complete the reported statements. Use one word in each gap.**

0 'I can't understand this film,' she said.
She said she couldn't understand ......*the*...... film.

1 'I'm playing football this evening,' I told Tom.
I told Tom I was playing football .... evening.

2 She said, 'There was an accident here last year.'
She said there had been an accident .... the year ....

3 'I ordered two books three weeks ago,' I told the shop assistant.
I told the shop assistant I'd ordered two books three weeks ....

4 On Sunday, Adam told me, 'I've got an exam tomorrow.'
Adam told me he had an exam on ....

5 'I'll be in your group next term,' she said.
She said she'd be in my group the .... term.

6 'I'm leaving now,' she told us.
She told us she was leaving ....

7 'It's really cold today,' Lucy told me.
Lucy told me it was really cold .... day.

8 'I finished my exams last week,' he said.
He said he had finished his exams the .... week.

69b Complete the reported statements.

Nikki and Jessica met in a café two weeks ago. Now Nikki is reporting their conversation to a friend.

0 'I love the food at this café,' Jessica said.
Jessica said that she loved the food ....*at the café*........... .

1 'I saw Helen this afternoon,' she told me.
She told me that she'd seen Helen ....

2 'I saw her yesterday,' I said.
I said that I'd seen her ....

3 'My brother called two hours ago. He's going to meet me here,' I told her.
I told her that my brother had called two hours .... and that he was going to meet me ....

4 'We're going bowling tonight,' I said.
I said that we were going bowling ....

5 'I don't have enough money for my coffee now. I'll pay you back next week,' she said.
She said that she didn't have enough money for her coffee .... and that she'd pay me back ....
She still hasn't paid me!

70 Reported statements with no tense change

- If the reporting verb is in the present tense (e.g. *says*), the tense does not change in reported speech: *'I'll meet you there.'* → He *says he'll meet* us there.

- If the statement we are reporting is still true in the present, we don't have to change the tense after a past tense reporting verb: *'It's a good restaurant.'* → Helen said *it's a good restaurant.* (This is still true now.) *'I've got a brother.'* → He told me *he's got a brother.* (This is still true now.)

- But if the reporting verb is in the past tense, we can change the tense: *Helen said it was a good restaurant.* *He told me he had a brother.*

PRACTICE

70a Report the statements.

0 'We've got football practice.'
They say ....*(that) they've got football practice*................ .

1 'I'm exhausted.'
He says ....

2 'I'll be back at six.'
Paul says ....

3 'The film is wonderful!'
Everybody says ....

4 'I didn't borrow Kate's earrings.'
Caroline says ....

5 'We've never been to the theatre.'

A lot of my friends say ....

6 'We're going to be away next month.'

Our neighbours say ....

70b Complete the e-mail. Use the correct form of the verbs in brackets. There may be more than one possible answer.

New Message

I've been asking my friends about webcams for you. Marco says that you (0) ....*can get*............ (can / get) them for about £20. He says he (1) .... (buy) his last year on the Internet. Another friend tells me that the more expensive ones (2) .... (have) a better picture and audio quality, and that you (3) .... (need) to get a special program too. He says they (4) .... (be) very easy to install. I think they're great!

I tried to persuade my sister in America to get one, but she said she (5) .... (not want) one. She said she (6) .... (not like) cameras. It's a shame because I'd like to see her and talk to her more often.

---

71   Reporting verbs

- We don't always use *say* or *tell* to report someone's words. We often use other reporting verbs to summarise what someone said: *'I'm sorry I'm late,'* Lisa said. → Lisa **apologised** for being late.   *'I didn't steal the money,'* Joe said. → Joe **denied** stealing the money.

- We use the following structures. The verbs marked * can be followed by more than one structure:

verb + *to*-infinitive agree*, offer, promise*, refuse	She **offered to give** us a lift. Mike **refused to help** me.
verb + object + *to*-infinitive advise, invite, persuade*, remind*, warn*	I **advised him not to leave**. He **reminded me to** phone Tim.
verb (+ object) + -*ing* form admit*, accuse somebody of, apologise for, congratulate somebody on, deny*, suggest*	She **admitted lying** to me. He **accused me of stealing**. We **suggested getting** a taxi.
verb + *that* clause admit*, agree*, complain, deny*, explain, promise*, suggest*	I **agreed that I'd made** a mistake. She **denied that she'd cheated**. I **promised that I'd be** there.
verb + object + *that* clause inform, persuade*, remind*, warn*	The waiter **informed us that** our table was ready.

PRACTICE

71a **Report the statements. Use the verbs in the box.**

| accused advised ~~agreed~~ apologised denied |
| invited offered refused warned |

0 'Yes, OK. I'll book the tennis court for Monday,' Jack said.
Jack .... *agreed to book* .... the tennis court for Monday.

1 'No, I'm not going to pay for your ticket,' he told me.
He .... for my ticket.

2 'I didn't start the fight!' Scott said.
Scott .... the fight.

3 'Don't go near that dog,' he told us.
He .... near the dog.

4 'You took my money!' he told Emma.
He .... his money.

5 'I'm sorry I shouted at you,' she said.
She .... at me.

6 'Would you like to play volleyball with us?' Kim's sister asked me.
Kim's sister .... volleyball with them.

7 'Shall I wrap the chocolates for you?' the shop assistant asked me.
The shop assistant .... the chocolates for me.

8 'I think you should do engineering,' his tutor said.
His tutor .... engineering.

71b **Complete the second sentence so that it means the same as the first, using the word in bold. Use between two and five words.**

0 'You'll get your exam results on 7th May,' the principal told us. **informed**
The principal .... *informed us that we'd* .... get our exam results on 7th May.

1 'My computer's very slow,' Becky said. **complained**
Becky .... very slow.

2 'The bus is much cheaper than the train,' Jamie said. **explained**
Jamie .... much cheaper than the train.

3 'We're meeting Adam tonight,' I told Mark. **reminded**
I .... meeting Adam that night.

4 'I don't do enough exercise,' he said. **admitted**
He .... do enough exercise.

5 'I'll call you tomorrow,' he said. **promised**
He .... me the next day.

6 'I didn't give him the password,' she said. **denied**
She .... him the password.

72 Reported questions

- Reported questions have the same tense and word changes as reported statements.

▶▶ **For reported statements, see Units 68–70.**

- Common reporting verbs/phrases in questions are *ask* and *want to know*.
  They **asked** me what I was doing.   She **wanted to know** where Jack was.

- When we report a *yes/no* question, we use *if/whether* after the reporting verb:
  'Do you speak French?' → She asked me **if I spoke** French.
  Are you coming? → He asked her **whether she was coming**.

- When we report a *wh-* question, we use the question word: **'Where's the station?'** →
  She wanted to know **where the station was**.

- The word order in reported questions is the same as in statements. We don't use the
  auxiliary *do/does/did*: **'Where are you going?'** → He asked me where **I was going**.
  (Not ~~He asked me where was I going.~~)   **'Do you like** swimming?' → She asked me
  if I liked swimming. (Not ~~She asked me did I like swimming.~~)   **'What do you want**
  to do?' → They asked me what **I wanted** to do. (Not ~~They asked me what did I want
  to do.~~)

- We don't use a question mark (?) in reported questions.

PRACTICE

72a **Report the questions.**

Yesterday Rob asked his friend Philip for advice about flats in London. Now he's
telling another friend about their conversation.

0 'Is your room very expensive?'
I asked him ..*if his room was very expensive*.. .

1 'Are you looking for somewhere cheap?'
He asked me ....

2 'Is your flat near the city centre?'
I asked him ....

3 'Can you get there easily?'
I wanted to know ....

4 'Does your flat have a washing machine?'
I asked him ....

5 'Was it very hard to find your room?'
I asked him ....

6 'Did you look at a lot of flats?'
I wanted to know ....

7 'Have you looked on the Internet?'
He asked me ....

8 'Would you like to stay with me for a few days?'
He asked me ....

72b **Report the questions.**

0 'Where can I get some tissues?' she asked.
She asked ....*where she could get some tissues*.. .

1 'When are you going to visit us?' he asked us.
He asked ....

2 'Why is everybody looking at me?' I asked.
I wanted ....

3 'What sports do you do at college?' Joe asked me.
Joe asked ....

4 'What has your brother decided to do?' I asked her.
I wanted ....

5 'How did you get to the beach?' I asked them.
I asked ....

6 'How long have you been here?' they asked us.
They asked ....

7 'Who won't be here next week?' the tennis coach asked.
The tennis coach wanted ....

8 'How much did you pay for your ticket?' she asked him.
She asked ....

9 'How often do your cousins stay with you?' I asked her.
I asked ....

10 'Where's Kate?' I asked.
I wanted ....

72c **Read the questions from a survey. Then complete the e-mail.**

0 How old are you?	**5** How many films do you see a month?
1 Do you live with your parents?	**6** What kind of films do you like?
2 How do you spend your free time?	**7** Do you do any sport?
3 How often do you go out?	**8** Do you have any hobbies?
4 Do you go to the cinema?	

⬤⬤⬤ New Message ⊖

Last week I had a call from somebody who was doing a survey. It was
quite interesting. She asked me (0) ....*how old I was*............. and
(1) .... with my parents. She asked me
(2) .... free time and (3) ....
out. She also wanted to know (4) .... to the
cinema and (5) .... a month. She was surprised
when I said ten! Then she asked me (6) .... I said
I liked everything! She also asked me (7) .... any
sport and (8) .... any hobbies. I had to say no to
both of those!

73 Reported commands and requests

- We form reported commands and requests with verb + person + *to*-infinitive.
- We use *ask* to report requests: *'Can you help me, please?'* → *I **asked him to help** me.*
- We use *tell* or *order* to report commands: *'Sit down.'* → *She **told me to sit** down.* *'Open your suitcase!'* → *He **ordered me to open** my suitcase.*
- For negative requests and commands, we use *not* before the *to*-infinitive: *'Please don't make a noise.'* → *He **asked us not to make** a noise.* *'Don't touch the paintings!'* → *She **ordered me not to touch** the paintings.*
- We don't use *that* to report a command or request: ~~He asked me that I tell him the time.~~
- We don't use *say* to report a command or request: ~~I said you to clean your shoes.~~
- Compare reported statements and commands: *Ann **told me that** she was leaving.* (reported statement) *Ann **told me to** leave.* (reported command)
- Compare reported questions and requests: *My boss asked me if I'd stay late.* (reported question) *My boss **asked me to stay** late.* (reported request)

PRACTICE

73a Report the commands and requests.

0 'Could you get the tickets, please?'
He asked me ....*to get the tickets*... .

1 'Can you save a seat for me, please?'
Rachel asked me ....

2 'Bring your essays on Monday.'
The tutor told us ....

3 'Stay at home for the rest of the week.'
The doctor told me ....

4 'Please don't tell Sarah.'
She asked me ....

5 'Stop fighting!'
The police officer ordered the men ....

6 'Don't be late.'
I told them ....

7 'Could you lend me some money, please?'
Ryan asked his brother ....

8 'Don't be afraid of the other team.'
The captain told us ....

9 'You must pay a fine of £2,000.'
The judge ordered Mr Taylor ....

10 'Can you turn the computer off, please?'
I asked Mark ....

73b **Circle the correct answer.**

Jessica works at a theatre. Last week there was a small fire there. Now she's telling a friend about it.

0 'Open the fire exits!' the manager said.
The manager *asked* / (*ordered*) some people *open* / (*to open*) the fire exits.

1 'Stay calm and don't run,' he said to the audience.
He told the audience *stay* / *to stay* calm and *to not* / *not to* run.

2 'Help the audience leave,' he said.
He *told* / *said* some of us *to* / *that we* help the audience leave.

3 'Could you get my coat from the cloakroom, please?' a woman in the audience said.
A woman in the audience *asked* / *ordered* me *get* / *to get* her coat from the cloakroom!

4 'I'll get it for you later,' I said.
I *told* / *said* her *to* / *that I'd* get it for her later.

5 'Move away from the building,' the fire officers said to us.
The fire officers *asked* / *said* us *move* / *to move* away from the building.

6 'Are you OK?' the manager asked me.
After the fire, the manager *told* / *asked* me *if* / *that* I was OK.

74   *I think that ... , Do you know if ... , I wonder why ...*

- After verbs which express thoughts and feelings (e.g. *believe, forget, hope, imagine, know, realise, remember, think, understand, wonder*), we can use a *that* clause, a question word or *if/whether*.

- We can use *that* to introduce a statement: *I can't believe **that David's thirty**!*
  *We hope **that you'll come**.*

- A question word introduces an indirect question: *I wonder **who that is**.*   *Do you remember **where he lives**?*   *I can't imagine **why he did** it!*

- If there is no question word, we use *if/whether*: *Do you know **if** they've left?*

- Other expressions we often use in indirect questions include: *I'm not sure ... , I've no idea ...* : *I'm **not sure when** they're arriving.*   *I've **no idea who** that is.*

- We often use indirect questions instead of direct questions to sound more polite, using expressions like *can/could you tell me ... , do you know ... , have you any idea ... ,* etc.: *Where's the ticket office?* → ***Could you tell me** where the ticket office is, please?*   *What time is it?* → ***Do you know** what time it is?*   *Where's Sophie?* → ***Have you any idea** where Sophie is?*

- In indirect questions, the word order is the same as in statements: *Where's the museum?* → *Could you tell me where **the museum is**, please?*

⚠ - We only use a question mark if the first part of the sentence is a question.
  Compare: ***Do you know** where he is?*   ***I wonder** where he is.*

- After a past tense verb, the next verb usually moves one tense back into the past: *I **couldn't** believe (that) he **was** thirty!*   *I **wondered** who the man **was**.*

PRACTICE

74a **Re-write the sentences. Use the verbs in brackets and a *that* clause.**

  0 He's gone. (can't believe)   *I can't believe that he's gone.*

  1 He likes it there. (hope)   ....

  2 He's still looking for a flat. (know)   ....

  3 He's sold his car. (think)   ....

  4 He's made new friends. (imagine)   ....

  5 His career's important to him. (realise) ....

  6 He's been very busy. (understand)   ....

74b **Re-write the direct questions as indirect questions.**

  0 Is this their latest CD?
      Could you tell me *if this is their latest CD* ?

  1 How much does it cost?
      Do you know .... ?

  2 Are they going to do a tour soon?
      Have you any idea .... ?

  3 Where are they going to play?
      Can you tell me .... ?

  4 Will they be at any of the festivals next summer?
      Do you know .... ?

  5 Why did their drummer leave?
      I wonder .... ?

  6 Have they found a new drummer yet?
      Do you know .... ?

  7 Are they as good as they used to be?
      Do you think .... ?

  8 When is their next CD coming out?
      Have you any idea .... ?

74c **Circle the correct answer.**

I went to the British Museum today and had a great time. I had no idea
that I (0) will / (would) enjoy it so much! I really liked the chessmen
from Lewis in Scotland. I thought that they (1) are / were amazing.
I can't remember how old (2) they are / are they, but I think that they
(3) were / had been made in Norway. Nobody knows who (4) brought
/ had brought them to Lewis, but they say it was probably a merchant
on his way to Ireland. I wondered (5) what / that had happened to him.
Maybe he died on the island or maybe he went back to Norway and left the

75 Question words + *to*-infinitive

We can use a *wh-* question word + *to*-infinitive after verbs which express thoughts and feelings, or after verbs of reporting and communicating:

Verbs of thinking/feeling	
decide, find out, forget, know, learn, remember, see, think, understand, wonder	I don't know **what to do.** I've forgotten **how to ride** a bike.
Verbs of reporting/communicating	
ask, describe, discuss, explain, show, suggest, tell	He explained **how to fill in** the form. She showed us **where to wait.**

- *Ask, show* and *tell* need an object before the question word: *The shop assistant **told me** where to find the belts.*
- We can use *whether* + *to*-infinitive after *decide, know* and *wonder*: *I can't decide **whether to buy** it (or not).* (= whether I should buy it)

PRACTICE

75a Re-write the questions. Use the *to*-infinitive.

   o 'What do I do?' I didn't understand .... *what to do* ....

   1 'How do I use a drill?' I didn't know ....

   2 'I'll show you. Hold it like this.' He showed me ....

   3 'How do I cut it?' I asked ....

   4 'Where do I put the glue?' I didn't know ....

   5 'What colour should I paint it? I couldn't decide ....

   6 'How much paint should I buy?' I asked ....

75b Complete the sentences. Use the words in the box on the left and the correct form of the verbs in the box on the right.

how (x2) ~~how long~~ what what time where whether (x2) which places	bring camp get get up join make ~~practise~~ sign visit

   o My piano teacher never told me ...... *how long to practise* ...... each day.

   1 We don't know .... or stay in hostels.

   2 I can't see .... my name on this form.

   3 Have you decided .... a drama group or not?

   4 They asked us .... to the barbecue – food or drink.

   5 I can't remember .... lemonade, but I think it's quite easy.

   6 We've been discussing .... tomorrow for our early train.

   7 We couldn't decide .... to the airport. I suggested getting a taxi.

   8 Let's get a guidebook. I want to find out .... in Paris.

Check 14 Reported speech

1 Report the sentences.

1 'We want to go to Oakham next Sunday.'
Sarah explained that ....
....

2 'Book your tickets in advance.'
Sam told her ....
....

3 'I'd like to book two tickets.'
Sarah said ....
....

4 'Can we take our bikes on the train?'
She asked Sam ....
....

5 'You can book your tickets by phone.'
Emma says ....
....

/ 5

2 Re-write the sentences. Use the words in brackets.

6 'I used to be able to play the guitar, but I can't now,' Matt said. (how)
Matt couldn't remember ....
....

7 'When did you stop playing?' Adam asked him. (had)
Adam wanted to know ....
....

8 'Don't buy a new guitar,' Adam told him. (not)
Adam told ....
....

9 'You can borrow my brother's, I think,' Adam said. (that)
Adam said, 'I think ....
.... ,'

10 'I'll ask him tonight,' Adam said. (to)
Adam promised ....
....

/ 5

3 Circle the correct answer.

```
○○○                New Message                ⊏⊐
```

How are you? I hope that you're feeling better. My mum (11) *said / told* me that lots of people in her office have had flu. It sounds horrible!

I'm OK. I've been trying to decide what (12) *to do / I do* next year. I've been reading about all the different courses. One of my brother's friends says that (13) *to enjoy / he's enjoying* his Biochemistry course at Keele, so I asked my tutor if (14) *it was / was it* good. He advised (15) *me to / that I* apply to King's College, London.

I'm really looking forward to seeing you on Sunday. Do you know what time (16) *you'll / will you* arrive? I think Nikhita will be able to come too. Becky spoke to her on Monday and she said she'd got back from her holiday the day (17) *previous / before*. She told Becky (18) *I've / she'd* had a great time. Anyway, I've asked them (19) *that / to* meet us at the restaurant at eight. My mum has offered (20) *taking / to take* us there, so we don't need to get the bus.

/ 10

Total: / 20

✓ Self-check

Wrong answers	Look again at	Try CD-ROM
3, 11, 18	**Unit 68**	Exercise 68
1, 17	**Unit 69**	Exercise 69
5, 13	**Unit 70**	Exercise 70
10, 15, 20	**Unit 71**	Exercise 71
4, 7, 14	**Unit 72**	Exercise 72
2, 8, 19	**Unit 73**	Exercise 73
9, 16	**Unit 74**	Exercise 74
6, 12	**Unit 75**	Exercise 75

Now do **Check 14**

Relative clauses

76 Defining relative clauses

- We use defining relative clauses to give more information about a person, thing, place or time and make it clear which one we are talking about.
- We use these relative pronouns:
  - *who* or *that* for people: **The people who/that** work here are very friendly.
  - *which* or *that* for things: **The bus which/that** goes to Paris leaves from here.
  - *whose* for possession: **The man whose car** was stolen was very upset.
  - *when* or *that* for a time: I remember **the day when/that** I started school.
  - *where* for a place: That's **the house where** she used to live.
  - *why* or *that* for a reason: He explained **the reason why/that** he was so late.
- A relative pronoun can be the subject or object of a relative clause: **The man that lives here** is very nice. (**The man** lives here = subject)   **The man that I met** is very nice. (I met **the man** = object)
  We can leave out the relative pronoun when it is the object of the relative clause: The **man I met** is very nice.
- When a verb is followed by a preposition, we usually put the preposition at the end of the relative clause: Is this the bag (*that*) you were looking **for**?

- We don't use *what* to introduce a relative clause: ~~Here are the shoes what I bought.~~
- We don't use another pronoun (*he, she, it,* etc.) as well as a relative pronoun: ~~The people **who they work here** are very friendly.~~

PRACTICE

76a **Circle the correct answer.**

  0 Do you remember the girl (who) / which / what won the last series of *Pop Idol*?

  1 The programme *who / that / what* makes me laugh the most is *The Simpsons*.

  2 My friend lives near the street *that / whose / where* they filmed *Notting Hill*.

  3 Who's the actress *who / which / whose* husband is a famous director?

  4 She explained the reason *who / which / why* she didn't act any more.

  5 I'll never forget the time *which / where / when* I saw Jude Law in the street!

  6 The film *who / that / what* we saw on Friday wasn't very good.

  7 What's the name of the actor *that / whose / what* plays King Lear?

  8 I've still got that DVD *who / which / what* you lent me.

  9 That was the year *which / when / what* she appeared in her first film.

  10 Is that the boy *who / that / whose* father is a film critic?

76b **Complete the sentences. Use a relative pronoun if necessary. If a relative pronoun is not necessary, write – on the line.**

0 The jeans .... I bought last week are really comfortable.

1 I've been reading the book .... you gave me.

2 A woman .... lives in our building has got a very noisy dog.

3 The girl .... I mentioned to you is sitting by the window.

4 What was that nice song .... you were singing?

5 The man .... was sitting next to me on the bus looked like your brother.

6 This video game is about a city .... is in danger.

76c **Join the sentences. Use relative clauses. Leave out the relative pronouns.**

0 I like the street. We live in it.
I like the street we live in.
....

1 Here's the bus. We've been waiting for it.
....

2 I've got an idea. I want to talk to you about it.
....

3 Did you want to buy that shirt? You were looking at it.
....

4 Who was the woman? Jack was speaking to her.
....

5 I can't remember the name of the company. Sarah works for them.
....

6 Which is the shop? You want to go to it.
....

7 She's got a younger brother. She complains about him.
....

8 Have you got a friend? Can you depend on them?
....

76d **Circle the extra word in these sentences.**

0 The person who (she) told me about the festival was my friend Becky.

1 The tickets what we got were quite cheap.

2 There were people there who they had come from Spain, Finland, Germany – lots of countries.

3 I liked the band which it came on first.

4 Some of the people I met them were good fun.

5 The tent what we borrowed was too small for the three of us.

6 A girl I talked to her recommended a great place to eat.

77 Non-defining relative clauses

- A non-defining relative clause adds extra information and is not essential to identify the person, thing, etc. we are talking about. Compare: *The car **that I've bought** is a Honda.* (This identifies which car.)   *My car**, which is a Honda,** is really great.* (This adds extra information.)

- We use commas to separate a non-defining relative clause from the rest of the sentence: *My sister Anna**, who is a teacher,** lives in Madrid.   I'd like to meet Jessica's sister**, who works in television.***

- We use *who* for people and *which* for things, but we don't use *that*: *My father**, who** is sixty, is going to retire soon.* (Not ~~My father, that is sixty~~)   *Their house**, which** has five bedrooms, is lovely.* (Not ~~Their house, that has five bedrooms~~)

- We use *where* for places, *when* for time and *whose* for possession: *Edinburgh**, where** I live, is a very lively city.   We went there in July**, when** it was very hot. Mr Hall**, whose** son was ill last year, has raised £5,000 for the hospital.*

- We can't leave out the relative pronoun in non-defining relative clauses: *Paul**, who** is French, helped me translate the letter.* (Not ~~Paul, is French, helped me~~)

PRACTICE

77a Complete the article. Use relative pronouns.

Jazz, (0) ......*which*...... is one of the most popular types of music in the world, began in the United States in the early twentieth century. It developed in the south of the country, (1) .... many African Americans lived. It became popular in the 1920s, (2) .... people could hear it on the radio.

Louis Armstrong, (3) .... was a well-known singer and trumpet player, had a great influence on the development of jazz. Another important performer was Duke Ellington, (4) .... band was one of the greatest jazz bands of all time.

Musicians in other countries began to play jazz and to change it, and soon different music styles began to develop around the world. For example, bossa nova, (5) .... began in the late 1950s, is a combination of jazz and samba, the national music of Brazil.

77b Join the sentences. Use non-defining relative clauses. Use the underlined sentences in the relative clauses.

0   Shrewsbury is a small town. <u>It is in the west of England.</u>
    Shrewsbury, which is in the west of England, is a small town. ....

1   The River Severn goes through the town. <u>It is the longest river in Britain.</u>
    ....

2   Charles Darwin was born in Shrewsbury. <u>His statue stands outside the library.</u>
    ....

3   Wilfred Owen also lived in Shrewsbury. He was a famous poet.

....

4   The castle is on a hill above the town. It is also a museum.

....

5   There are a lot of good restaurants. You can enjoy a wide range of food there.

....

6   The Shrewsbury Flower Show attracts a lot of visitors. It is held every year.

....

77c   Complete the sentences. Use the relative clauses in the box. Then add commas where necessary.

> which left at 11 p.m.   which my mother used to sing to me
> which sells very cheap clothes   which they lost 4–0   which you showed me
> who advised him to forget about it   who stole the painting
> ~~who's in my Psychology class~~   who used to be a professional footballer

0   I play tennis with Nina *, who's in my Psychology class* ....

1   They've got a coach ....

2   I got this information from that website ....

3   My favourite song is *What a wonderful world* ....

4   Sam missed the last train ....

5   He discussed it with his father ....

6   What's the name of that shop .... ?

7   He was upset about the match.. .

8   They still haven't found the man ....

78   Other ways of identifying people and things

Instead of using full relative clauses, we can add information about a person, thing, etc. using:

- a prepositional phrase: *The books (~~that are~~) **on the table** are mine.   My brother is the one **with** (= ~~who has~~) **red hair**.   She was talking to a man **in** (= ~~who was wearing~~) **a dark suit**.*

- an *-ing* clause. These have an active meaning: *The man (~~who is~~) **sitting** over there is my uncle.   I saw a woman (~~who was~~) **wearing** a fur coat.*

- a past participle clause. These have a passive meaning: *The food (~~which is~~) **sold** in this shop is all produced locally.   The buildings (~~which were~~) **destroyed** by the earthquake will be rebuilt.*

- a *to*-infinitive clause: *Which is the best place **to** (= ~~where we can~~) **go**?*

PRACTICE

78a **Complete the sentences. Use prepositional phrases.**

0   Tell the man who's sitting at the desk.   Tell the man ....*at the desk*.......... .

1   Jo is the one who's wearing a red shirt.   Jo is the one ....

2   They help people who have brain injuries.   They help people ....

3   The keys that are on the desk are Tim's.   The keys ....

4   The boy who had fair hair won.   The boy ....

5   I ate the grapes that were in the fridge.   I ate the grapes ....

6   The book which is on the left is mine.   The book ....

78b **Join the sentences. Use an *-ing* clause or a past participle clause.**

0   Some police officers have found her phone. They were looking for the girl.
    The police officers ...*looking for the girl have found her phone*.......... .

1   A woman was injured in a car accident. She was cycling home.
    A woman ....

2   A man appeared in court yesterday. He was accused of robbing an elderly woman.
    A man ....

3   The plans have been rejected. They were proposed by a hotel chain.
    The plans ....

4   Fans had to wait hours in a traffic jam. They were travelling to London.
    Fans ....

5   Hundreds of people have died. They were infected by the virus.
    Hundreds of people ....

78c **Complete the e-mail. Use the correct form of the verbs in brackets.**

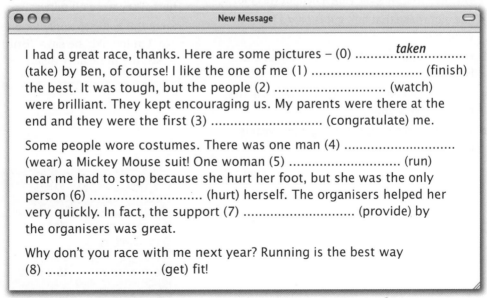

I had a great race, thanks. Here are some pictures – (0) ....*taken*.......... (take) by Ben, of course! I like the one of me (1) .... (finish) the best. It was tough, but the people (2) .... (watch) were brilliant. They kept encouraging us. My parents were there at the end and they were the first (3) .... (congratulate) me.

Some people wore costumes. There was one man (4) .... (wear) a Mickey Mouse suit! One woman (5) .... (run) near me had to stop because she hurt her foot, but she was the only person (6) .... (hurt) herself. The organisers helped her very quickly. In fact, the support (7) .... (provide) by the organisers was great.

Why don't you race with me next year? Running is the best way (8) .... (get) fit!

Check 15 Relative clauses

1 Join the sentences. Use non-defining relative clauses. Use the underlined sentences in the relative clauses.

1 Our flat gets very hot in the summer. <u>It's on the fifth floor.</u>

....

....

2 Emma is Luke's cousin. <u>Her father is an actor.</u>

....

....

3 The restaurant is in King Street. <u>It's very nice.</u>

....

....

4 We met them in 2003. <u>We moved to London then.</u>

....

....

5 Tom is coming to stay. <u>He's my brother's friend.</u>

....

....

/ 5

2 Circle the parts of the relative clauses that can be left out. Circle one or two words in each sentence.

6 The man who was carrying a helmet was Joe.

7 The motorbike that he's got is only a few years old.

8 His bike is the one which is behind that black Fiat Uno.

9 Some of the bikes which are advertised in the paper are very good.

10 The bike that his brother bought last year is fantastic.

/ 5

3 Complete the article. Use one word in each gap.

'I remember the time (11) .... there was a real community here,' Bill says as he looks at the streets of the former coal-mining town (12) .... he lives. 'We all used to work together at the mine.' The mine shut fifteen years ago and all the men (13) .... worked in it had to find new jobs. 'I became a driving instructor,' Bill says.

The mine, (14) .... is three kilometres outside the town, was closed because the government decided that mining was not profitable enough. However, there are now plans to re-open the mine, partly because there is now new technology (15) .... burns coal in a way (16) .... does not harm the environment.

Hundreds of people have applied for jobs in the mine. Why, I ask, when mines are dangerous places (17) .... work? 'The reason (18) .... people want to work in a mine is that it's in their blood. There are lots of people here (19) .... fathers and grandfathers were miners,' Bill says. He proudly shows me an old photo. 'Here's my grandad and his brothers, with his father. My grandad's the one (20) .... the fair hair. They were all miners.'

So is Bill going to apply for a job in the mine? 'No, I'm too old,' he says. 'But it will be great to see the mine alive again.'

/ 10

Total: / 20

✓ Self-check

Wrong answers	Look again at	Try CD-ROM
7, 10, 11, 12, 13, 15, 16, 18, 19	**Unit 76**	Exercise 76
1, 2, 3, 4, 5, 14	**Unit 77**	Exercise 77
6, 8, 9, 17, 20	**Unit 78**	Exercise 78

Now do **Check 15**

Conditionals

79 The zero and first conditionals

- We use the zero conditional to talk about things that are always or generally true as a result or consequence of an action or situation. To form zero conditional sentences, we use *if/when* + present simple + present simple: *If I **don't have** any lunch, I **get** very hungry.   **When** Sarah **phones**, we **talk** for hours.*

- We use the first conditional to talk about possible actions in the future. To form first conditional sentences, we use *if* + present simple + *will/can/could/may/might*: *If it **rains** tomorrow, we**'ll stay** at home.   If you**'re** free later, you **can come** with us. If it**'s** a nice day, we **might go** to the beach.*

⚠ We use the present simple (not *will*) in the *if* clause: *If I **see** Jack, I'll invite him.* (Not *If I'll see Jack, I'll invite him.*)

- We can also use the imperative in first conditional sentences: *If I'm late, **go** without me.*

- The *if* clause can come at the beginning of the sentence or after the main clause. When it comes at the beginning, we put a comma (,) after it: *If I **don't have** any lunch, I get very hungry.   I get very hungry if I **don't have** any lunch.*

▶▶ **For future time clauses, see Unit 89.**

PRACTICE

79a Complete the zero conditional sentences. Use the correct form of the verbs in brackets.

o If Emma ....*sees*............ a dress that she likes, she ....*tries*............ to make it herself. (see, try)

1 We usually .... home together if we both .... at the same time. (walk, finish)

2 .... computer games with Sam when you .... round to his house? (you / usually / play, go)

3 Ben .... music if it .... a fast rhythm. (not like, not have)

4 .... really upset when his team .... ? (he / get, lose)

5 I often .... a bargain in that shop if I .... carefully. (find, look)

6 I .... to bed if I .... tired. (not go, not feel)

7 If you .... red and blue, you .... purple. (mix, get)

8 I usually .... to Jack when I .... advice. (talk, need)

79b Circle the correct answer.

   o If I (have) / 'll have time this evening, I call / ('ll call) you.

  . **1** If you 're / 'll be out, I see / 'll see you tomorrow.

   2 If you don't / won't mind, I don't / won't bring your football into college tomorrow.

   3 We find / 'll find one in the gym if Ben forgets / will forget his.

   4 Where do / will you wait for us if you get / 'll get there early?

   5 Mark doesn't / won't organise another game if we don't / won't go to this one.

   6 If Mark has / will have his car, do / will you ask him to give you a lift home?

79c Complete the first conditional sentences. Use the correct form of the verbs in brackets. Then add commas where necessary.

   o If it ....*doesn't fit*.... you properly, ...*don't buy*.... it. (not fit, not buy)

   1 If you .... anything just .... me. (need, tell)

   2 I .... my shorts if it .... hot. (might / wear, be)

   3 We .... early if you .... tired. (could / leave, feel)

   4 If we .... some fruit we .... a fruit salad. (get, could / make)

   5 She .... if I .... her. (not remember, not remind)

   6 If somebody .... you .... to listen calmly. (criticise, try)

79d Complete the messages from a message board on the Internet. Use the correct form of the verbs in the box.

ask   be (x2)   could / ask   get (x2)   might / not get   not say   refuse

Message 1: posted by Ally

I lent a friend of mine a lot of money a month ago. She hasn't paid me back yet and I'm getting fed up because I need the money. Should I say anything to her? I think that if I (o) ....*ask*.... her, she (1) ....
angry with me or she (2) .... to pay me back.

Message 2: posted by ComputerKid

If you (3) .... anything, things (4) ....
worse. You need to talk to her and find out what's going on. If you
(5) .... worried about her reaction, you
(6) .... her when you're with other people. She
(7) .... angry if there (8) .... other
people there.

80 *unless, provided that, as long as, in case*

- We use *unless* in first conditional sentences to mean 'if not': *I'll meet you tonight **unless** you're busy.* (= I'll meet you tonight if you're not busy.) ***Unless** we leave now, we'll be late.* (= If we don't leave now, we'll be late.)

- We use *provided/providing* (*that*) or a*s long as* to mean 'if' or 'on condition that': *You'll pass the exam **provided** (**that**) you work hard.* (= on condition that you work hard) *I'll pay for the tickets **as long as** they're not too expensive.* (= only if they're not too expensive)

- We use *in case* when we are thinking about something that might happen or something that might be true. Compare these sentences: *I'll buy an umbrella **if** it rains.* (= If it starts to rain, I'll buy one.) *I'm going to buy an umbrella **in case** it rains.* (= I'm going to buy one because it might rain.)

P R A C T I C E

80a Circle the correct answer.

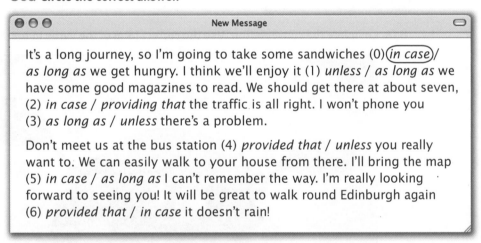

It's a long journey, so I'm going to take some sandwiches (0) *in case* / *as long as* we get hungry. I think we'll enjoy it (1) *unless* / *as long as* we have some good magazines to read. We should get there at about seven, (2) *in case* / *providing that* the traffic is all right. I won't phone you (3) *as long as* / *unless* there's a problem.

Don't meet us at the bus station (4) *provided that* / *unless* you really want to. We can easily walk to your house from there. I'll bring the map (5) *in case* / *as long as* I can't remember the way. I'm really looking forward to seeing you! It will be great to walk round Edinburgh again (6) *provided that* / *in case* it doesn't rain!

80b Complete the second sentence so that it means the same as the first, using the word in bold. Use between two and five words.

0 You'll get ill if you don't get some fresh air every day. **unless**
   You'll get ill ....*unless you get*........ some fresh air every day.

1 If you water your plant every day, it will live for years. **provided**
   Your plant will live for years .... it every day.

2 I'll tell you if you promise not to tell anyone else. **long**
   I'll tell you .... not to tell anyone else.

3 Take the keys because we might be out. **case**
   Take the keys .... out.

4 If they don't invite us, we can't go. **unless**
   We can't go .... us.

5 If you have the receipt, we'll give you your money back. **providing**
   We'll give you your money back .... the receipt.

81 The second conditional

- We use the second conditional to talk about imaginary or impossible situations in the present. To form second conditional sentences, we use *if* + past simple + *would/ could/might*: *If I **had** more money, I'd **be** happy.* (= I don't have much money and I'm not happy.)   *If it **was** warm, we **could eat** outside.* (= It isn't warm and we can't eat outside.)

- We also use the second conditional for unlikely future events or situations. Compare these sentences: *If I **get** the job, I'**ll move** to London.* (This is possible and likely.) *If I **got** the job, I'**d move** to London.* (This is not very likely.)

 We use the past simple (not *would*) in the *if* clause: *If I **had** a car, I'd drive to work.* (Not *If I ~~would have~~ a car, ~~I'd drive to work~~.*)

- We can use *were* instead of *was* in the *if* clause: *If he **were** more powerful, he'd be able to do more.*

- We can use *if I were you* to give advice: *If I **were you**, I'd take the job.*

PRACTICE

81a Complete the conversation. Use the correct form of the verbs in brackets.

A: If somebody (0) ....*gave*.................... (give) you a lot of money, what
(1) .... (you / do)?

B: I'd buy a motorbike and go travelling for a few months.

A: On your own?

B: No, with a friend. I (2) .... (get) lonely if I
(3) .... (go) on my own. I'd ask Rob to come with me.
He likes travelling.

A: He does, and he's good with bikes. If your bikes (4) ....
(break down), he (5) .... (be) able to fix them.

B: That's true. And he's very calm. He (6) .... (not panic) if
we (7) .... (have) a problem.

A: Would you stay in hotels all the time?

B: I don't know. If it (8) .... (not be) cold, it
(9) .... (be) nicer to camp.

A: And cheaper. Your money (10) .... (last) longer if you
camped.

81b **Complete the second sentence so that it means the same as the first. Use the verbs in brackets.**

0 We can't have a party here because our flat's too small. (could)
If our flat ....*was*............ bigger, we ....*could have*............ a party here.

1 I'd like to invite her, but I haven't got her phone number. (would)
If I .... her phone number, I .... her.

2 They can't stay with us because we don't have a spare room. (could)
If we .... a spare room, they .... with us.

3 He'd like to tell them his plans, but it's possible that they'll disagree with them. (might)
If he .... them his plans, they .... with them.

4 We have a lot of exams this year, so we feel stressed. (wouldn't)
If we .... a lot of exams this year, we .... stressed.

5 I'm afraid I don't speak Italian, so I can't join in the conversation. (could)
If I .... Italian, I .... in the conversation.

6 I've thought of going to a festival, but it's possible that I won't like it. (might)
If I .... to a festival, I .... it.

81c **Circle the correct answer.**

0 If I *am* / *were* you, I'd talk to somebody who's doing that course.

1 If I *know* / *knew* somebody on that course, I'd ask them about it.

2 I *'ll* / *'d* help you with your application form if you bring it round next week.

3 Saturday's not a good day. I won't be here if there *'s* / *was* a football match.

4 I *'ll* / *'d* spend a lot of time on it if I were you.

5 You won't get a place if you *apply* / *applied* late, so don't think about it for too long.

6 If you *don't* / *didn't* like the course, you can change to another one.

7 If the college were nearer town, it *will* / *would* be a lot easier to get to.

8 My journey *'ll* / *would* take ages if Tom didn't give me a lift, so I'm very lucky.

82 The third conditional

- We use the third conditional to talk about possible events in the past that didn't happen. To form third conditional sentences, we use *if* + past perfect + *would have* + past participle: *If we'd set out earlier, we **would have arrived** on time.* (= We didn't set out early and we didn't arrive on time.) *If you'd told me about the party, I **would have come**.* (= You didn't tell me about the party and I didn't come.)

- We can also use *could have* or *might have*: *If I'd known you were in town, I **could have met** you.* *If she'd worked harder, she **might have passed** her exam.*

⚠ We use the past perfect (not *would have*) in the *if* clause: *If you'd invited me, I would have come.* (Not *If you would have invited me, I would have come.*)

P R A C T I C E

82a **Complete the third conditional sentences. Use the correct form of the verbs in brackets.**

o If we'd planned it carefully, we ......*wouldn't have had*...... so many problems.
(not have)

1 You .... it if you'd come. (enjoy)

2 I .... you if you'd asked me. (tell)

3 If he hadn't given us a map, we .... the hostel. (not find)

4 He would have come to the party if she .... him. (invite)

5 We wouldn't have minded if you .... your friends. (bring)

6 If we .... our tickets yesterday, we wouldn't have got any.
(not buy)

82b **Complete the second sentence so that it means the same as the first. Use the verbs in brackets.**

o I'm sure we didn't play well because we hadn't trained enough. (would)
If we ......*had trained*...... more, we ...*would have played*... better.

1 I had a chance to score, but I didn't because I missed the ball. (might)
I .... if I .... the ball.

2 Our best player didn't play because he was ill. (could)
If our best player .... ill, he ....

3 I felt tired because I hadn't slept well the night before. (wouldn't)
I .... tired if I .... better the night before.

4 I didn't tell my friends about the match, so they didn't come. (might)
My friends .... if I .... them about the
match.

5 We didn't beat them because they ran too fast. (could)
If they .... so fast, we .... them.

82c **Complete the blog entries. Use the correct form of the verbs in brackets.**

Jade 610:	I had singing lessons from an early age and I sang with my family all the time. If my parents (0) ......*hadn't encouraged*...... (not encourage) me, I (1) .... (not become) a singer.
Amanda344:	When I was fourteen, we moved from London to a small town where there weren't many sports facilities. I had to give up judo and diving. If we (2) .... (stay) in London, I (3) .... (could / continue) these sports.
RachelB:	I had a very good Physics teacher. I think that if I (4) .... (go) to a different school, I (5) .... (might / not decide) to do Physics at university.

83   *I wish*

- To express a wish, to talk about things we would like to change in the present, we use *I wish* + past simple: *I wish I had a car.* (I don't have a car.)
- We often use *I wish* + could: *I wish I could play* the piano.
- We can use *were* instead of *was*: *I wish I was/were* rich!
- To express a wish about the past, we use *I wish* + past perfect: *I wish I'd known about the party.* (I didn't know about it and I'm sorry.)
- *If only* is more emphatic than *I wish*: *If only you didn't live* so far away.   *If only we hadn't wasted* so much time!

 We don't use *I wish* for the future. We use *I'd like* or *I hope*: *I'd like* to work in Spain. (Not ~~I wish I can work in Spain.~~)   *I hope* it won't rain. (Not ~~I wish it won't rain.~~)

P R A C T I C E

83a **Complete the sentences. Use *wish* and the correct form of the verbs in the box.**

> be (x2)   can / buy   ~~can / come~~   can / move
> know   not have (x2)   can / understand

0   I ....*wish I could come*........ with you, but I have to stay at home.

1   I hate big cities. I .... to a quiet little village.

2   I .... the answer to that question, but I don't.

3   My brother .... red hair because he thinks it's ugly.

4   Why do you .... taller? You're taller than a lot of people!

5   I .... here. I really miss her.

6   I .... his lectures, but they're too difficult for me.

7   I .... that dress, but I haven't got enough money.

8   I'm really tired. I .... to go to college today.

83b **Complete the conversation. Use the correct form of the verbs in brackets.**

A: I don't feel well. I wish I (0) ....*didn't have*........ (not have) to go out tonight. If only I (1) .... (not agree) to go!

B: Why don't you phone and say you're not well?

A: I haven't got Scott's phone number. I wish I (2) .... (ask) him for it on Monday. If only I (3) .... (think) of it then!

B: Where are you going?

A: To a restaurant. And I'll have to walk. I wish I (4) .... (not leave) my bike at Jack's last night! If only I (5) .... (have) a car! Anyway, are you going out tonight?

B: No. I've got to start an essay. I've got to hand it in on Wednesday. I wish I (6) .... (start) it earlier, but I hope I'll finish it in time.

Check 16 Conditionals

1 Complete the conversations. Use the correct form of the verbs in brackets.

A: If I'd known you were ill, I (1) .... (phone) you at the weekend. Sorry.

B: That's OK. I was too ill to talk to people!

A: Are you going to college tomorrow?

B: I don't know. I (2) .... (go) if I feel well enough.

_____

A: I always feel better if I (3) .... (do) some exercise. Don't you?

B: Yes, but I'm hopeless at sport, so I don't do enough. If I (4) .... (be) better at sport, I'd do more, I'm sure!

A: I know what you mean. I can't swim very well. I wish I (5) .... (have) swimming lessons when I was younger.

/ 5

2 Circle the correct answer.

6 If you *put / 'd put / would have put* your glass on the table instead of the floor, I wouldn't have knocked it over!

7 I'll finish this tonight if I *work / 'll work / worked* hard on it now.

8 I wish I *know / 'll know / knew* what to do.

9 I'll come with you *as long as / unless / in case* I don't have to stay too long.

10 If you could change one thing about yourself, what *will you change / would you change / would you have changed*?

/ 5

3 Complete the second sentence so that it means the same as the first, using the word in bold. Use between two and five words.

11 We should get there early because there might be a long queue. **case**
We should get there early .... a long queue.

12 I didn't watch the match yesterday afternoon because I went out. **could**
If I'd stayed in yesterday afternoon, I .... the match.

13 It would have been better if I'd brought my mobile phone. **only**
If .... my mobile phone!

14 Don't apply for the course if you don't want to do it. **unless**
Don't apply for the course .... to do it.

15 He'd like to go to the festival, but he doesn't know how to get a ticket. **if**
He'd go to the festival .... how to get a ticket.

/ 5

4 Complete the note. Use the correct form of the verbs in brackets.

I'm sorry I couldn't meet you yesterday. I (16) .... (not go) swimming if I'd known you were coming into town. I hope you had a nice time with Becky. If you (17) .... (see) her tomorrow, say hello from me.

I'm busy learning my lines for the play I'm in. I'm so busy I wish I (18) .... (not agree) to be in it, but never mind. We've done quite a lot of the first part, so I'm learning some of the second part in case we (19) .... (do) that at our next rehearsal. It's not going to be easy. I'm sure it would be easier if I (20) .... (can / understand) my lines, but I don't!

/ 5

Total: / 20

Linking words and structures

84 Adding and listing

- These words have a similar meaning to *and*. Notice their different positions in a sentence:
  - *also: She sings and she **also** plays the piano.*   *They sell food and **also** clothes.*
  - *too: Matt wants to come **too**.*   *I'd like a sandwich and a cup of coffee **too**.*
  - *as well (as): We're going to Rome and Venice **as well**.*   *She speaks German **as well as** French.*
  - *plus: There are three cinemas **plus** a large theatre.*

- *Both ... and, either ... or* and *neither ... nor* add emphasis.
  - *Both ... and* link two similar ideas: ***Both** adults **and** children will enjoy this film. He knows **both** Mary **and** Peter very well.*
  - *either ... or* link two alternatives: *We're going to **either** France **or** Spain this year. We can **either** go to a restaurant **or** eat here.*
  - *neither ... nor* link two similar negative ideas: ***Neither** my mother **nor** my father went to university.*   *The food was **neither** good **nor** cheap.*

- We use *in addition, besides* or *what's more* to add another fact to what has already been mentioned. We use a comma after them: *The café offers good food. **In addition,** it offers computers with free Internet access.*   *It's too cold to go out. **Besides,** I'm not feeling very well.*   *It's a very interesting job. **What's more,** the pay is good.*

- We use *firstly, secondly, finally,* etc. to list the points in an argument: ***Firstly,** the new airport will be expensive. **Secondly,** it will cause pollution. **Finally,** it isn't necessary.*

PRACTICE

84a Circle the correct answer.

0 They sell books *also / too /* (*as well as*) newspapers.

1 I've brought two pairs of jeans *plus / too / also* a pair of shorts.

2 She's clever and *also / as well / too* very pretty.

3 We went to the castle and the museum *also / plus / too*.

4 *Both / Too / Either* the gym and the swimming pool will be closed on Monday.

5 He's brilliant at Maths and he's *too / as / also* very good at Economics.

6 My keys will *or / either / neither* be in my bag or on my desk.

7 Have you got a Renault? We've got one *too / plus / as well as*.

8 He told *neither / both / either* his friends nor his family.

9 Would you like some potatoes *plus / as well / either*?

10 We have classes for *also / both / either* beginners and intermediate students.

84b Complete the articles. Use the words in the boxes.

| finally   ~~firstly~~   secondly   what's more |

The Internet has changed business in several ways. (0) .... *Firstly* .... , businesses can advertise to millions of people. (1) .... , a lot of businesses can sell their products online. Communication is now easier because of e-mail, which is fast and reliable. (2) .... , it is much cheaper than the postal service. (3) .... , the Internet has changed the job market. Many jobs are no longer restricted to a particular place and so large companies can look all over the world for the most efficient and cheapest service.

| as well as   in addition   too |

The Internet has changed the way we buy music (4) .... Instead of buying CDs, many of us download music from websites because it is quick, easy and cheap. (5) .... , it is now easy to get different kinds of audio files from many websites. You can listen to interviews and news reports (6) .... music on your computer or music player.

85 Contrast

These words and phrases have a similar meaning to *but* and link two opposite or contrasting ideas. Notice the use of commas:

- *Although, though, even though* (emphatic), *whereas* and *while* (formal) introduce a clause. This clause can come before or after the main clause: ***Although/Though** the course was difficult**, I enjoyed it. He's hopeless at tennis **even though** he plays every week! **Whereas/While** in the past the journey took four hours**, now it takes just one. The north of the country is cold and wet**, whereas/while** the south is warm and dry.*

- We can also use *though* at the end of a sentence in informal English: *He told everybody he'd got a job. It wasn't true**, though**.*

- *However* can come at the beginning, in the middle or at the end of a sentence: *It's a terrible illness. **However,** doctors can now treat it. It's a very small university. The teaching**, however,** is excellent. That restaurant's very good. It's very expensive**, however**.*

- *In spite of/Despite* + noun/pronoun and *in spite of/despite this* can come at the beginning or in the middle of a sentence: ***In spite of the rain,** we enjoyed ourselves.* (= It was raining, but we enjoyed ourselves.) *She's in a lot of pain, but **in spite of this,** she's always cheerful.*

P R A C T I C E

85a Join the sentences. Use the words in brackets.

0   Sam lives near me. I don't often see him. (although)
    .... *Although Sam lives near me, I don't often* .... see him.

1   I go to college here. Sam goes to college in London. (whereas)
    I go to college here, ...

2   He's older than me. We're good friends. (though)
    .... good friends.

3   He's got a car. He gets the train to London every day. (even though)
    He gets the train ....

4   Sam's very good at Maths. His twin brother is absolutely hopeless! (while)
    .... , his twin brother is
    absolutely hopeless!

5   I like Biology. I'm not very good at it. (although)
    I like .... very good
    at it.

85b Circle the correct answer.

0   Some people say that mobile phones are bad for your health. (However)/ *While*,
    general scientific opinion is that they are not dangerous.

1   Running is a great form of exercise. You shouldn't do too much at first, *despite /*
    though.

2   I think I did well in the exam *although / in spite of* my headache.

3   *Although / However* he eats a lot, he never puts on weight!

4   *Despite / However* the doctor's advice, she played in the match.

5   *In spite of / Even though* that exercise bike was very expensive, he bought it.

6   It's good to eat every three or four hours. Snacks, *however / whereas*, should
    be healthy ones such as fruit.

85c Complete the letter. Use *although*, *however* or *in spite of*.

I am writing to complain about our visit to your restaurant on Sunday.
(0) ...... *Although* .... we arrived early, we were given a table in a cold
corner. We then waited thirty minutes for a waiter (1) ....
there weren't many customers. (2) .... our complaints about
the long wait, we then had to wait another half an hour for our food. When
it came, one of the dishes was wrong. The waiter, (3) .... ,
insisted that we had ordered it, so we had to eat it.

(4) .... this kind of service is acceptable in a cheaper
restaurant, I expect better service in a restaurant like yours.
(5) .... all the good reviews we had read of your restaurant,
our meal was a great disappointment!

86 Reason, cause, purpose and result

- To introduce a reason or cause (to say why something happened), we use *because/ since/as* + clause. The clause can come before or after the main clause. We can also use *for* + clause in formal English, after a main clause. Notice the use of commas: *I went home **because** I was tired.* **As** *he lives near me, I see him quite often. He said nothing, **for** he knew she would not listen.*

- We can also use *because of* or *due to* + noun to introduce a reason or cause: *We didn't enjoy the trip **because of the bad weather**.* **Due to flooding,** *the road is closed.*

- To introduce a purpose (to say what we want to achieve), we use *so* or *so that* + clause: *I put my keys in my pocket **so** (**that**) I wouldn't forget them.*

- To introduce a result or consequence, we use *so* + clause: *I was tired, **so** I went home.*

- *Therefore, as a result* and *for this reason* have a similar meaning to *so*: *Most of the houses were made of wood.* **As a result,** *they burnt quickly.* *There have been a lot of burglaries in the area. Everyone should **therefore** remember to lock their doors. Rats can spread disease. They've always been feared **for this reason**.*

PRACTICE

86a Circle the correct answer.

- **o** Fewer young people watch TV now (because)/ *because of* they spend more time on the Internet.

- **1** There are more TV channels now *due to* / *as* the growth of satellite and cable TV companies.

- **2** This show is very popular with young people *due to* / *since* it's about a group of friends who are at college together.

- **3** No one was surprised when she won the award, *for* / *because of* she had given an amazing performance.

- **4** Lots of people don't go to the cinema *as* / *due to* they prefer renting DVDs.

- **5** Filming was delayed *because of* / *since* bad weather.

86b Join the sentences. Use *so that* and *can* or *could*.

- **o** I lent Sarah some money. She wanted to buy a sandwich.
  I lent Sarah some money so that she could buy a sandwich.

- **1** I want to learn Spanish. Then I'll be able to talk to my Spanish friends.
  ....

- **2** Let's move the table. Then we can put the sofa there.
  ....

- **3** He bought a bike. He wanted to cycle to college.
  ....

- **4** I'll send you the programme. Then you can choose which film you want to see.
  ....

5   We left at eleven. We wanted to catch the last bus home.

    ....

6   She washed her black dress. She wanted to wear it to the party.

    ....

86c Complete the adverts. Use the words in the box.

as a result   because   ~~due to~~   of   so   so that   therefore

Birds are under more pressure than ever before (0) ......*due*...... to climate change. We are (1) .... managing nature reserves around the country in ways that take account of our changing climate.

Some people in their seventies and eighties cannot leave their homes because (2) .... poor health and (3) .... they become isolated and lonely. We provide transport for elderly people (4) .... they can enjoy a better social life.

Many people cannot take their children on holiday (5) .... they are ill or unemployed. (6) ...., their children never see the sea or the countryside. We provide holidays for 500 children a year.

87 Manner: *as if, as though, like*

- We use *as if* or *as though* + clause to say what something seems, looks or feels like, or to describe the way in which someone does something: *It **looks as if** it's going to rain.   That meat **smells as though** it's burnt.   Tom was **behaving as if** nothing had happened.*
- We can use *like* + clause in the same way in informal English: *I **feel like** I haven't had any sleep.   He **looked at me like** I was mad!*

▶▶ **For as and like, see Unit 93.**

PRACTICE

87a Complete the sentences. Use *as if* and the phrases in the box.

~~I can do anything~~   it's going to rain   someone's put perfume on it
they're having a sale   you haven't slept for days   you're enjoying your course

0   I feel very confident! I feel .... *as if I can do anything* ....!

1   You don't look very well. You look ....

2   I'm glad you're happy. You sound ....

3   This pillow smells lovely. It smells ....

4   That shop's open. It looks ....

5   Look at those clouds. It looks ....

87b **Complete the conversation. Use *as though* and the phrases in the box.**

~~he / be~~	he / not hear	he / not trust	he / not want
she / can't	they / not choose	we / know	

Two friends are discussing the contestants in a reality show.

A: Do you like Gary?

B: Not really. He's very bossy. He tells everyone what to do (0) .....*as though he's*..... their dad! And he doesn't listen to other people. Last night he just ignored Luke when he asked him a question. He just acted (1) .... him.

A: I like Luke. He's nice.

B: He is, but he's not very confident. He often asks people for advice (2) .... his own judgement.

A: At least he doesn't complain! A lot of them complain about things (3) .... to be on the show!

B: I know! That's really annoying. But they're very relaxed in front of the cameras, aren't they? I couldn't be like that.

A: They aren't all relaxed. Emma's always doing things (4) .... sit still and Jamie often has his headphones on (5) .... to talk to anyone.

B: It's funny. We talk about them (6) .... them, don't we?

A: Yes!

88 Common linking expressions in speech

- We use linking expressions in speech to add or contrast ideas, or for emphasis. Notice the use of commas.

- To give information a second time in a simpler, more direct way, we use *in other words*: *He didn't give all the facts to the committee.* ***In other words,*** *he lied.*

- To change the subject, we use *by the way, anyway* or *anyhow*: *Oh,* ***by the way,*** *I saw Martin yesterday.* ***Anyway,*** *how are you?*

- To quickly correct or explain something we have just said, we use *I mean*: *I gave it to Sam,* ***I mean*** *Kate.* *It all seems very strange.* ***I mean,*** *what was he doing there at that time of night?*

- To add emphasis or to fill a pause in a conversation, we use *well*: ***Well,*** *I thought it was a good film.* ***Well,*** *I'm not sure.*

- To emphasise that something is true or to disagree politely, we use *actually*: *He looks young, but he's* ***actually*** *65.* ***Actually,*** *I don't agree with you.*

- To express an opinion, we can use some adverbs at the beginning of a sentence, e.g. *luckily, fortunately, unfortunately, interestingly, surprisingly, apparently, obviously, honestly, amazingly*: ***Luckily,*** *no one was hurt.* ***Obviously,*** *it was a really frightening experience for him.*

PRACTICE

88a Circle the correct answer.

o **A:** I'm really annoyed with her! She should have told me!
   B: I know. (Anyway) / *I mean*, did you have a good time at the festival?

1 **A:** I'll see you later.
   B: OK. I'll be back at eight thirty, *actually* / *I mean* seven thirty.

2 **A:** I never go by train as it's too expensive.
   B: *Actually* / *Anyhow*, it's quite cheap if you have a railcard.

3 **A:** It was too long, the story was boring and the dialogue sounded unnatural.
   B: *In other words* / *By the way*, it was awful!

4 **A:** I'm really tired, so I don't want to do much.
   B: That's OK. I'm tired too. Oh, *actually* / *by the way*, Tom phoned last night.

5 **A:** What are you doing tomorrow evening?
   B: *Well* / *By the way*, I'm going to a film, I think.

6 **A:** I don't know where he is.
   B: No, I don't either. *In other words* / *Anyhow*, do you want to have a coffee?

88b Complete the conversations. Use the words in the boxes.

| amazingly   apparently   ~~fortunately~~   interestingly |

A: How was your parade last week?
B: It was great, thanks!
   (o) ....*Fortunately*........ ,
   it didn't rain!
A: Did you finish making your
   costume in time?
B: (1) .... , yes!
   I thought I wasn't going to finish it,
   but I did.
A: What did it look like?
B: It was a yellow bird costume.
   It's a bit hard to describe it!

   (2) .... , there are some photos of us on the website. I haven't
   seen them, but Jenny told me about them.
A: Do you have this parade every summer?
B: Yes. (3) .... , there used to be a parade hundreds of years
   ago, but then it stopped. They started it again about five years ago.

| honestly   obviously   unfortunately |

A: I'm afraid I can't give you a lift tomorrow. (4) .... , there's
   something wrong with my car. I'm really sorry.
B: (5) .... , it doesn't matter. I can get the bus.
A: (6) .... , I'm trying to get it fixed as soon as possible. I'll give
   you a ring as soon as it's fixed.
B: Thanks very much.

Check 17 Linkers

1 Complete the conversation. Use the words in the box. You do not need all of them.

actually anyway apparently as if as well as well as even though

A: I don't know what to do with my old mobile phone.

B: Why don't you take it back to the shop? (1) .... , some shops take them and recycle them. I read about it in the paper.

A: Oh, I don't know. I think I'll just throw it away. They aren't dangerous.

B: (2) .... , they have a lot of poisonous things in them.

A: Do they? I didn't know that. (3) .... , look at this picture on my new phone.

B: Was this in London last weekend? Did you go with Ryan?

A: Yes. Ryan's brother came (4) .... We had a good time.

B: Yes. You look (5) .... you're having fun!

/ 5

2 Complete the sentences. Use one word in each gap.

6 Neither Tom .... Alex came to the match.

7 Smith played well .... spite of his leg injury.

8 I'll have a cheese sandwich – I .... a chicken one.

9 Their bus was late due .... heavy traffic.

10 I'll just leave a note .... that he'll know where we are.

/ 5

3 Circle the correct answer.

New Message

We had a great time on Saturday, thanks. I really enjoyed the film (11) ..... I didn't understand it all.

Would you like to come round next Saturday? We could (12) ..... watch a DVD or just have a pizza. I'm going to invite Nina and Emily (13) ..... . It feels (14) ..... though it's been a really long time since we all got together. None of us had much time in May (15) ..... of our exams, and then (16) ..... Nina and Emily went on holiday, (17) ..... it's weeks since we all saw each other. It looks (18) ..... Kate won't be able to join us – she has to stay at home on Saturday.

I started my summer job on Monday and so far I'm enjoying it (19) ..... having to get up at six! (20) ..... it's quite tiring, it's interesting.

11	A despite	B even though	C as though	D due to
12	A both	B neither	C either	D also
13	A too	B plus	C both	D as well as
14	A as	B like	C even	D if
15	A due	B as	C for	D because
16	A both	B either	C neither	D as
17	A as	B plus	C so	D because
18	A though	B as	C like	D if
19	A although	B despite	C whereas	D however
20	A Since	B Besides	C Therefore	D Although

/ 10

Total: / 20

89 Future time clauses

Notice the tense forms used to refer to the future after linking words such as *after, before, when, while, as soon as, until, once* and *next time*:

- We use the present simple to refer to a future action: *I'll phone him **when I get** home.* (Not ~~when I'll get home~~)   *Keep driving **until you reach** the main road. Would you like a coffee **before you leave**?*

- We use the present continuous to refer to an action that will be in progress in the future: *I'll think about you **while I'm lying** on the beach!* (Not ~~while I'll be lying~~)

- We use the present perfect to refer to an action that will be complete in the future: *Phone me **as soon as you've finished**.* (Not ~~as soon as you will have finished~~) *I'm going out **after I've eaten**.*

- Often the meaning is the same if we use the present simple or the present perfect: *I'll get a job when **I finish/I've finished** college.* But sometimes the meaning is different. Compare: ***When I phone** Tom, I'll tell him.* (= I'll phone Tom and tell him at the same time.)   ***When I've phoned** Tom, I'll phone you.* (= I'll phone Tom first and then I'll phone you.)

▶▶ ***For present simple for future, see Unit 40. For the first conditional, see Unit 79.***

PRACTICE

89a Complete the sentences. Use *will*, the present simple or the present continuous of the verbs in brackets.

- **0** I'll probably find that photo when I ....*tidy*............. my room. (tidy)

- **1** Shall we have a sandwich here before we .... home? (go)

- **2** I won't be able to do anything while I .... after my brother. (look)

- **3** The grass .... again as soon as it rains. (grow)

- **4** I'll read my magazine while I .... for you. (wait)

- **5** I think you .... it once you get used to it. (like)

- **6** She's going to work in the library until it .... (close)

- **7** They'll stay with us until they .... a flat. (find)

- **8** I .... you some of their coffee next time I go to their shop. (get)

89b Re-write the sentences. Use the present perfect.

- **0** I'll have some breakfast and then I'll go into town.
  As soon ...*as I've had some breakfast, I'll go into town.*............. .

- **1** I'll take this skirt back and then I'll look for some shoes.
  After ....

- **2** I'll look round the shops for an hour and then I'll have a coffee with Kate.
  When ....

3 I'll buy a present for Becky and then I'll get the bus home.

After ....

4 I'll phone Becky and then I'll make some dinner.

When ....

5 I'll finish my project and then I'll watch some TV.

When ....

6 I'll arrange to meet my friends and then I'll get changed.

As soon as ....

89c **Circle the correct answer.**

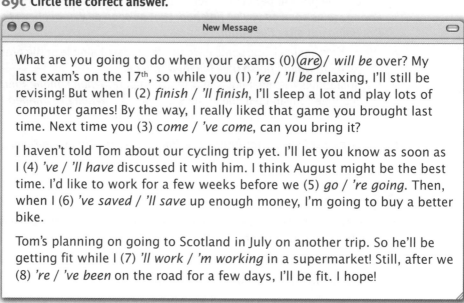

What are you going to do when your exams (0) *are* / *will be* over? My last exam's on the 17ᵗʰ, so while you (1) *'re* / *'ll be* relaxing, I'll still be revising! But when I (2) *finish* / *'ll finish*, I'll sleep a lot and play lots of computer games! By the way, I really liked that game you brought last time. Next time you (3) *come* / *'ve come*, can you bring it?

I haven't told Tom about our cycling trip yet. I'll let you know as soon as I (4) *'ve* / *'ll have* discussed it with him. I think August might be the best time. I'd like to work for a few weeks before we (5) *go* / *'re going*. Then, when I (6) *'ve saved* / *'ll save* up enough money, I'm going to buy a better bike.

Tom's planning on going to Scotland in July on another trip. So he'll be getting fit while I (7) *'ll work* / *'m working* in a supermarket! Still, after we (8) *'re* / *'ve been* on the road for a few days, I'll be fit. I hope!

90 Sequence in narratives

- We use words like *first, then, next, after a while, later, afterwards* and *after that* to show the order in which things happen in a narrative: *He set up his tent and* **then** *lit a fire.* **Later,** *he cooked some food.*

- We can use *suddenly, immediately, just then* and *all at once* to introduce an action that happened suddenly: **Suddenly,** *the door opened.* **Just then,** *Jo arrived.*

- We use *when, while, before, after, as soon as* or *until* to link two actions in a narrative: *The boat sank* **when** *it hit a rock.* **While** *I was waiting for the bus, I saw Ben.* **As soon as** *I'd finished work, I went home.*

- We can also use *before, after* or *while* + *-ing* form: **Before leaving** *the house, he checked that all the doors were locked.* *I phoned Kim* **after talking** *to Mel.*

- We often use *at last* to mean 'after a long time': *He was free* **at last**.

- We use *finally* and *in the end* to introduce the end of a narrative: **In the end,** *everyone got home safely.*

PRACTICE

90a **Circle the correct answer.**

0 Everything changed ...... we left school.
A until   Ⓑ when   C afterwards   D at last

1 ...... , my best friend didn't want to see me.
A After   B When   C While   D Suddenly

2 I felt hurt at first and ...... I felt angry.
A then   B when   C until   D at once

3 I phoned her several times, but ...... I gave up.
A as soon as   B just then   C all at once   D after a while

4 I saw her ...... I was having lunch with my cousin last Sunday.
A next   B after   C while   D later

5 ...... she saw me, she walked away.
A Afterwards   B When   C Then   D Next

6 But ...... , while I was saying goodbye to my cousin, she came up to me and accused me of stealing something.
A later   B after   C as soon as   D when

7 I denied it, of course. ...... , after a long conversation, she believed me.
A As soon as   B All at once   C In the end   D Just then

8 ...... , I told her I didn't want to see her again.
A Last   B After   C When   D After that

90b **Complete the article. Use one word in each space.**

Florence Nightingale made nursing a respectable profession for women. She was born in 1820 into a rich British family. She was in her twenties (0) .... *when* she became interested in health care. Her parents were horrified as rich women did not work at all in those days. However, Nightingale did not change her mind and in the (1) .... , her parents allowed her to train as a nurse for three months in Germany. (2) .... that, she worked in London in a hospital for women.

In 1854, Britain, France and Turkey went to war against Russia. (3) .... reports about the awful conditions for the wounded and sick soldiers appeared in *The Times*, Nightingale was asked to take some nurses to the military hospitals. (4) .... working there, she became famous and money was collected for her work.

She returned to London in 1856. At first, she hid herself away from attention, but (5) .... she established a training school for nurses in London. (6) .... completing their training, the nurses worked in hospitals all over Britain and Nightingale's influence spread. Florence Nightingale continued to work to improve public health for the rest of her life.

Check 18 Time linkers

1 Circle the correct answer.

Michael shut the door and sat down. (1) ..... he was alone! He had thought that Tom would never leave. They had had dinner together and (2) ..... they had had a long conversation about all Tom's problems.

He did the washing-up and (3) ..... he ironed a shirt for the next day. He thought about Tom. 'I wish I hadn't lent him so much money,' he thought. 'As soon as he (4) ..... it, he'll want more. Next time he (5) ..... for a big loan like that, I'll refuse. He won't like it, but I can't keep on helping him.' But then he felt guilty because Tom hadn't been well enough to work for years. 'I'll go and see him when I (6) ..... to London,' he thought to himself and went to bed.

At 1.00 a.m., he was woken by the phone. It was Tom. He sounded frightened. He told Michael that he had fallen off his motorbike on the way home and that he was in hospital. (7) ..... , Michael promised to come. (8) ..... he was getting dressed, he remembered an accident Tom had had at school. He had gone with him to the hospital then. Tom was his younger brother and he had to take care of him.

1	A After	B At last	
	C Afterwards	D Next time	
2	A after	B after that	
	C once	D next time	
3	A while	B until	
	C then	D first	
4	A 'll spend	B 's spending	
	C spent	D 's spent	
5	A asks	B 's asking	
	C 'll ask	D 's asked	
6	A go	B 'll go	
	C 'm going	D 'll be going	
7	A While	B Once	
	C When	D Immediately	
8	A First	B Then	
	C While	D After	

/ 8

2 Circle the correct answer.

9 You'd better talk to him before you *go / 'll go*.

10 I'll have a shower when I *'ll have / 've had* my breakfast.

11 She's going to have a great time while she *'s staying / 'll stay* with Emma.

12 He filled in the form after *read / reading* the instructions carefully.

13 I'll give you all the details once I *'ll book / 've booked* the tickets.

14 We've promised to wait here until they *come / 'll come* back.

15 Before *left / leaving* the house, he hid the key.

/ 7

3 Join the sentences. Use the words in brackets.

16 They got married. Then they moved to London. (as soon as)
They moved ....

17 I want to visit my brother. He's studying in Spain. (while)
I want to ....

18 He kept asking me to help him. I agreed and then he stopped asking. (until)
He kept ....

19 We drove about ten kilometres. Then we could see the sea. (before)
We drove ....

20 We'll go ice-skating again. Do you want to come with us? (next time)
Do you want .... ?

/ 5

Total: / 20

✓ Self-check

Wrong answers	Look again at	Try CD-ROM
4, 5, 6, 9, 10, 11, 13, 14, 17, 20	**Unit 89**	Exercise 89
1, 2, 3, 7, 8, 12, 15, 16, 18, 19	**Unit 90**	Exercise 90

Now do **Check 18**

Prepositions

91 Prepositions of place and movement

● Here are some prepositions of place:
  - *at* refers to a place where someone/something is: *You pay **at** the checkout. This train stops **at** Hull.   Tom's **at** the door.   We live **at** number twenty-four.*
  - *in* refers to the inside of a place, for example a room, town or container: *He's **in** the kitchen.   We live **in** Brighton.   The milk is **in** the fridge.* We also say: *I read it **in** a book/newspaper.*
  - *on* is used when something is touching a surface: *The bread's **on** the table. There's a photo **on** the wall.   She kissed her **on** the cheek.* We also use *on* in these phrases: **on** *the left/right,* **on** *the first/second/top floor,* **on** *the other side of the road*
  - Other prepositions of place include *near, beside, between, among, under, above* and *below*: *The hospital is **near** the station.* (= not far away from)   *He was sitting **beside** me.* (= at my side)   *Our office is **above** the hairdresser's.* (= directly higher than)   *The kitchen is **below** my bedroom.* (= under it)

● Here are some prepositions of movement:
  - *to* and *towards* show movement in the direction of a place: *We drove **to** London. He ran **towards** the door.*
  - *into* and *out* of show movement towards or away from the inside of something: *She jumped **into** the pool.   He climbed **out of** the pool.*
  - *onto* and *off* show movement towards or away from a surface: *The glass fell **onto** the floor.   I took the photo **off** the wall.*
  - Other prepositions of movement include *across, along, over, through, up* and *down*: *She walked **across** the street.* (= from one side to the other)   *He walked **along** the pavement.* (= staying on the pavement)   *She climbed **over** the fence.* (= across the top of)   *He walked out **through** the door.* (= from one side to the other)

● *at* or *in*? *Let's meet **at** the restaurant.* (= inside or outside)   *Let's meet **in** the restaurant.* (= inside)

● *arrive at* or *arrive in*? We arrive *in* a country, city or town, but we arrive *at* a building or other place: *The plane arrived **in** Madrid.   We arrived **at** the airport.*

● *on* or *in*? We travel *on* a train, bus or plane, but *in* a car: *I always read when I'm **on** the train.   The journey takes an hour **in** a car.*

● Compare: *Matt's **in** hospital.* (= He's ill.)   *There are 200 beds **in** the hospital.* (= in the building)   *She goes **to** college.* (= She's a student.)   *We drove **to** the college.* (= to the building)

P R A C T I C E

91a **Complete the sentences. Use prepositions of place.**

0 Can I write ....*on*............ this piece of paper or do you need it for something?

1 I can't find my keys. I thought they were .... my bag.

2 I live .... my college, so I can walk there in five minutes.

3 Who lives .... number fifteen?

4 I've put your magazines .... your bedroom.

5 Have you ever been to the National Gallery .... London?

6 They're waiting for us .... the exit.

7 N comes .... M and O in the English alphabet.

8 Jenny's flat is .... the third floor. I live .... her, ... the second floor.

9 The cinema's .... the other side of town.

10 There was a good article about the music industry .... the newspaper.

91b **Circle the correct answer.**

We walked (0) *into* / *out of* the hostel and turned right. We found a path that went (1) *along* / *through* the bank of a stream. After about 200 metres, the path ended, but we could see it on the other side of the stream. There wasn't a bridge, so we had to walk (2) *over* / *through* the water.

On the other side, the path divided into two. The left-hand path went (3) *into* / *onto* a dark wood and the right-hand one went (4) *across* / *off* a field. We chose the right-hand one because it went (5) *onto* / *towards* a village that we could see in the distance. We followed it for about fifteen minutes and in the end it took us (6) *into* / *out of* the village.

91c **Circle the correct answer.**

0 We had some coffee *on* / *in* the train.

1 We arrived *in* / *at* Leeds at half past six.

2 Last time we went to Leeds, we went *in* / *on* my car, but I haven't got it any more.

3 Nick arrived *in* / *at* the theatre before us.

4 Luke lives near *university* / *the university*.

5 Kate was going to come with us, but her mother had to go into *hospital* / *the hospital*.

6 Nick took her to *hospital* / *the hospital* to visit her mother.

92 Prepositions of time

- ● Here are the main prepositions of time:
  - *at* is used with clock times, periods of time and to refer to somebody's age:
    at *nine*   **at** *lunchtime*   **at** *night*   **at** *the weekend*   **at** *the age of 23*
  - *in* is used:
    - with parts of the day, months, seasons, years and centuries: **in** *the morning*
      in *May*   **in** *the summer*   **in** *2005*   **in** *the 19th century*
    - to talk about things that will happen at the end of a period of time: *I'll be back*
      in *an hour/**in** a week/**in** a few minutes.*
    - to refer to the length of time something takes: *I read the book **in** four hours.*
      *We got back **in** twenty minutes.*
  - *on* is used with days and dates: **on** *Monday*   **on** *12th October*   **on** *Saturday*
    afternoon   **on** *New Year's Day*   **on** *weekdays*
- ● Here are some more prepositions of time:
  - *before*: *Call me **before** ten o'clock.*
  - *after*: *I'll see you **after** the match.*
  - *by* (= not later than): *We must leave **by** six.*
  - *since* (a point in time): *We've been here **since** Thursday.*
  - *for* (a period of time): *We waited **for** an hour.*
  - *during* (= all through or at some point in a period of time): *I shared a flat **during***
    my stay in London.   *I fell asleep **during** the play.*
  - *until/till* (a point in time): *We'll work **until** six o'clock and then we'll go home.*
  - *from … (a time) to/until/till … (a time)*: *The library is open **from** nine **to** five.*
  - *past* (a point in time): *It's **past** midnight!*
  - *through* (a period of time): *They worked **through** the night.*

   ● Compare *during* and *for*: *We rented a cottage **for** the summer.* (tells us how
  long)   *He fell ill **during** the summer.* (tells us when: at some point in time)
  *We had wonderful weather **during** the summer.* (= all through the summer)

  ● We don't use prepositions before *every, last, next* or *this*: *We meet **every***
  ***Saturday**.* (Not *~~on every Saturday~~*)

PRACTICE

92a **Complete the conversation. Use *at, in* or *on*.**

> **A:** We went to see some friends (0) ....*on*........
> New Year's Day. We went for a long walk with
> them (1) .... the afternoon. It was
> really nice. We don't often see them because
> they usually work (2) .... weekends,
> and we're usually busy (3) ....
> weekdays. Anyway, we had a good time and we
> got back (4) .... about six. When did
> you get back from your aunt's?
>
> **B:** (5) .... Tuesday.

92b Complete the article. Use *at, in* or *on*.

Wolfgang Amadeus Mozart

Wolfgang Amadeus Mozart was born (0) ....*on*........ 27th January 1756 in Salzburg, Austria. His father was a musician and he began teaching him to play the keyboard and violin when he was very young. Wolfgang was a fast learner: he learnt his first piece (1) .... half an hour!

Mozart began to compose his own music (2) .... the age of five. When he was six, he began touring Europe with his family. (3) .... the 18th century, there were many different rulers in Europe and musicians used to visit them all. The young Mozart astonished everyone with his musical gifts.

(4) .... 1781, Mozart settled in Vienna and (5) .... August 1782 he married Constanze Weber. They had six children, but four died as babies. Mozart himself died (6) .... 5th December 1791, but he left behind more than 600 compositions.

92c Circle the correct answer.

0   I get up early ⊖/ *on* / *in* every day and go running.

1   I have a shower – / *before* / *after* my run and then I go to college.

2   I often go swimming – / *in* / *at* lunchtime.

3   The sports centre should be open now. It's *past* / *from* / *by* eight o'clock.

4   Do you want to play tennis with me – / *at* / *on* this weekend?

5   I haven't played tennis *for* / *after* / *since* last summer.

6   I'll have more free time – / *in* / *by* a few weeks.

7   I've got to be fit – / *for* / *by* April because I want to run the marathon then.

8   I'm going to train hard *during* / *until* / *by* the marathon and then I'll relax.

92d Complete the e-mail. Use *during* or *for*.

● ● ●	New Message	⊖

I'm enjoying this year of my course a lot. (0) ....*During*...... the first two years, we had to cover a lot of different areas, but this year we're allowed to specialise. Last year I worked for a company that made computer games (1) .... six weeks and I've decided to specialise in that. I'd like to work for a company (2) .... a few years and then start my own business. We've learnt quite a lot about business management (3) .... the course, so I think I could do it.

When are you coming to London? It would be really nice to see you! Some relatives are coming to stay (4) .... a week in March and I won't be free (5) .... their visit, but I'll be free the rest of the time.

Tell me when you're coming and we can arrange something.

93 *as, like*

- We use *as* when we describe someone's job or the main purpose/function of something: *She works **as** a teacher.*   **As** *the captain, he has a lot of responsibility.* (= because he is the captain)   *He used his shirt **as** a bandage.*

- *Like* means:
  - 'similar to': *His car is **like** mine.*   *She looks **like** her brother.*
  - 'for example': *Rubbish, **like** glass and paper, can be recycled.*

- ⚠️ We say *the same **as*** (Not ~~the same like~~): *Your car's **the same as** mine.*

- We also use *what + be/look/sound/smell/taste + like* to ask for a description of someone or something: **What's** *Tom **like**?*   **What does** *curry **taste like**?*

PRACTICE

93a Circle the correct answer.

o You look *as* / (like) your mother.

1 At the moment, he's working *as* / *like* an assistant in a bookshop.

2 Could I use this paper *as* / *like* wrapping paper?

3 Shall we get some fruit, *as* / *like* strawberries or cherries?

4 I'd like to get a jacket *as* / *like* the one I saw in your catalogue.

5 Her jeans are the same *as* / *like* yours.

93b Complete the quiz questions. Use *as* or *like*.

o Who is known ......*as*...... the king of reggae music?

1 What did the first steel band players use .... drums?

2 Where do types of music .... mambo and rumba come from?

3 Which country is on the same island .... the Dominican Republic?

4 Limes are very popular in Caribbean cooking. What other fruit are they .... ?

5 Who starred .... the pirate Jack Sparrow in *Pirates of the Caribbean*?

Answers:
0 Bob Marley 1 Dustbins 2 Cuba
3 Haiti 4 Lemons 5 Johnny Depp

93c Complete the questions. Use *What + be/look/smell/taste/sound like*.

o A: ....*What's*.... your campsite ....*like*.... ? B: It's quite good.

1 A: .... your meal .... ? B: It tastes horrible!

2 A: .... that band .... ? B: They sounded strange!

3 A: .... her friend .... ? B: She was tall and thin.

4 A: .... that soap .... ? B: It smells nice.

5 A: .... his cousins .... ? B: They're very quiet.

94 Prepositional phrases

Here are some common prepositional phrases:

at	at first, at home/work/school/college, at last, at once, at present, at times, at **the** moment
by	by accident/chance, by car/bus/train, by cheque/credit card, by heart, by mistake
for	for sale, for hire, for rent
from	from memory, from now on, from time to time
in	in advance, in bed, in cash, in danger, in general, in time, in use, in **a** hurry, in **a** mess, in **the** end
on	on business, on fire, on foot, on holiday, on purpose, on TV, on time, on **a** diet, on **the** phone, on **the** way, on **the** whole
out of	out of breath, out of control, out of date, out of order
under	under control, under discussion

- We say *in cash* but *by cheque/credit card: Would you like to pay **in cash** or **by cheque**?*
- We say *on purpose* but *by accident/chance: He was late **on purpose**. I met Anna **by chance**.*
- Compare *on time* and *in time: The train arrived **on time**.* (= at the correct time) *We got to the station **in time** to catch our train.* (= early enough)

PRACTICE

94a Complete the sentences. Use prepositions.

0 Nina's ...... *on* ...... holiday with her sister. She'll be back on Saturday.

1 The house next to ours is .... sale. Our neighbours are moving to London in September.

2 I must tidy my room today. It's .... an awful mess!

3 You can only get there .... foot, I'm afraid.

4 This photocopier is .... order, so you'll have to use the one on the second floor.

5 I know this poem because I had to learn it .... heart when I was at school.

6 He didn't like his job much .... first, but now he says he loves it.

7 I've decided that .... now on I'm not going to watch so much television.

8 It was really frightening! I'd never been .... danger before.

9 I bought the wrong size .... mistake, so I'll have to take them back.

10 Our street can be noisy, but .... the whole it's very peaceful.

94b Complete the conversations. Use prepositions and the words in the box.

accident   a hurry   cash   credit card   purpose   ~~the way~~   time (x2)

A: Shall we stop for a coffee (0) .... *on the way* .... to the coach station?
B: No, I don't want to be late. The coaches always leave (1) ....
If we're two or three minutes late, we'll miss ours.
A: OK.

_____

A: Do you think Joe dropped Ben's camera in the water (2) .... ?
B: No. I think it happened (3) .... Joe slipped on some wet
rocks and dropped the camera when he fell.

_____

A: You looked as if you were (4) .... when I saw you yesterday.
You were walking really fast.
B: Yes. I wanted to get home (5) .... to have a shower before I
went out again.

_____

A: Can I pay (6) .... ?
B: No, I don't think they take cards. You have to pay (7) ....

94c Circle the correct answer.

A: How did you get there? Did you go (0) ...... train?
B: No, my sister took me in the car. It took ages because there was a lorry (1) ......
fire on the motorway.
A: Oh, I saw that (2) ...... TV. It looked awful! They said that it took the firefighters
a long time to get it (3) ...... control. Did you see it?
B: No. When we drove past it, the fire was out. It looked horrible, though. After
that, we got lost, so we were very glad to get there (4) ...... last!
A: And did you enjoy seeing your cousins again?
B: I did, thanks. We had a great time. Unfortunately, my uncle wasn't well on
Saturday and had to stay (5) ...... bed. He got up (6) ...... time to time, but he
seemed very tired and (7) ...... breath. He seemed better on Sunday, though.
A: That's good. And are you going to see them again soon?
B: Not for a few weeks. I'm quite busy (8) ...... the moment.

0	A in	B on	C by	D from
1	A in	B on	C under	D from
2	A on	B by	C from	D at
3	A in	B out of	C at	D under
4	A in	B on	C at	D for
5	A in	B on	C at	D under
6	A at	B on	C for	D from
7	A on	B from	C under	D out of
8	A on	B at	C by	D from

Check 19 Prepositions

1 Choose and complete the sentences.

1 (to school, to the school)
His parents went .... and talked about his behaviour with the head teacher.

2 (as, like)
This CD sounds the same .... their last one.

3 (by, on)
I'm really sorry. I didn't do it ....
purpose.

4 (in, on)
I got up .... time to have breakfast with them before they left.

5 (at, in)
Let's go now. I don't want to arrive .... the restaurant late.

/ 5

2 Circle the correct answer.

> ### WOULD YOU LIKE TO WORK (6) ...... A TOUR GUIDE?
>
> We are a tour company offering visitors short trips around London. Our customers are people who come here (7) ...... business and want to visit famous sights (8) ...... Big Ben, the Tower of London and Buckingham Palace. We give them private tours (9) ...... our luxurious cars and make sure that they see as much of London as they wish (10) ...... their visit. We are looking for people who are enthusiastic, good communicators and confident drivers.

6 A as	B like	C by	D from
7 A at	B on	C in	D to
8 A as	B like	C are like	D to
9 A on	B by	C in	D at
10 A in	B for	C at	D during

/ 5

3 Complete the sentences. Use the words in the box. You do not need all of them.

> along at before by onto out of towards

11 As soon as we saw the sea, we ran .... it.

12 You can pay me .... cheque if you like.

13 I always feel nervous .... a performance, but when I'm on stage, I feel fine.

14 We need a new train timetable as this one's .... date.

15 I noticed several empty classrooms as I walked .... the corridor.

/ 5

4 Complete the conversation. Use a preposition where necessary. If a preposition is not necessary, write – on the line.

A: Are you going to do anything (16) ....
New Year?

B: Yes. My uncle, aunt and cousins are coming round (17) .... the evening. They come (18) .... every year. We usually have a meal together. I'm going to try not to eat too much this year! I've decided to go (19) .... a diet.

A: Really? You don't need to lose weight!

B: Well, I'm going to try and lose four kilos (20) .... a month.

A: That sounds quite a lot!

/ 5

Total: / 20

✓ Self-check

Wrong answers	Look again at	Try CD-ROM
1, 5, 9, 11, 15	**Unit 91**	Exercise 91
10, 13, 16, 17, 18, 20	**Unit 92**	Exercise 92
2, 6, 8	**Unit 93**	Exercise 93
3, 4, 7, 12, 14, 19	**Unit 94**	Exercise 94

Now do **Check 19**

Words that go together

95 Adjective/Noun + preposition

- We use a preposition after some adjectives and nouns.

- Some common prepositions used after adjectives are: **of**: *afraid/ashamed* **of** *something* **at**: *good/bad/brilliant* **at** *something* **about**: *happy/upset* **about** *something* **with**: *bored/pleased* **with** *something*

- Some common prepositions used after nouns are: **of**: *the beginning* **of** *something* **for**: *the reason* **for** *something* **with**: *a conversation* **with** *someone* **about**: *a discussion* **about** *something* **to**: *a reaction* **to** *something* **in**: *an increase/ decrease* **in** *something*

- Sometimes more than one preposition is possible, with a change in meaning: *I was **angry about** the broken window.* *She was **angry with** Mike.* *Lisa and her husband were having an **argument about** the children.* *Lisa had an **argument with** Bill.*

⚠ After a preposition, we use the *-ing* form of a verb: *I'm **worried about failing** my exam.* *He isn't very **good at spelling**.*

▶▶ **See Appendix 13: Adjective + preposition and Appendix 14: Noun + preposition, page 173.**

PRACTICE

95a Complete the conversation. Use prepositions.

A: Why were you angry (0) ....*with*.... Kate last night?

B: Oh – she kept saying silly things. I got fed up (1) .... her!

A: I've noticed a change (2) .... her lately. I think she's upset (3) .... something.

B: Yes. And she doesn't seem enthusiastic (4) .... her course any more. I don't know why. She's brilliant (5) .... Art.

95b Circle the correct answer.

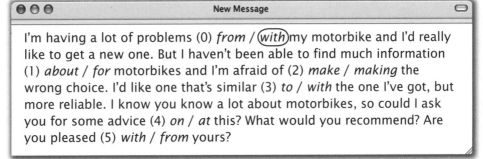

New Message

I'm having a lot of problems (0) *from /* (with) my motorbike and I'd really like to get a new one. But I haven't been able to find much information (1) *about / for* motorbikes and I'm afraid of (2) *make / making* the wrong choice. I'd like one that's similar (3) *to / with* the one I've got, but more reliable. I know you know a lot about motorbikes, so could I ask you for some advice (4) *on / at* this? What would you recommend? Are you pleased (5) *with / from* yours?

96 Verb + preposition

- We use a preposition after some verbs. Some common prepositions that we often use after verbs are: *about, for, from, on, to* and *with*.
- The pattern is verb (+ object) + preposition + noun/pronoun/-*ing* form: *That car **belongs to him**. She **complained about the food**. He **accused me of stealing**.*
- Sometimes more than one preposition is possible after the same verb, with a change in meaning: *I **agree with** you. We **agreed on** a plan. I **apologised to** Mike. I **apologised for** being late.*
- Some combinations of verb + preposition have an idiomatic meaning: *I **take after** my mother.* (= I'm like my mother.) *I'll **see to** the food.* (= I'll take care of the food.)

▶▶ **See Appendix 15: Verb + preposition, page 173.**

PRACTICE

96a Circle the correct answer.

The EASTBROOK PARK SCHEME has won the GREEN LIGHT AWARD for their work in the north of England. They have changed an old industrial site (0) *in /* (*into*) a park with paths, cycleways, trees and a lake. 'We wanted to provide people and animals (1) *with / from* a green space,' Tom Hughes, the organiser of the scheme, said. 'We couldn't have done it without the support of hundreds of people. We would like to thank them (2) *to / for* their help. They really care (3) *about / at* their environment and they worked hard to improve it. Their hard work has resulted (4) *in / for* this beautiful park! We hope that everyone in the community will benefit (5) *to / from* it.'

96b Complete the sentences. Use the correct form of the verbs in the box and an object where necessary.

| ask (somebody) about   break into   deal with   feel like |
| introduce (somebody) to   think about   ~~think of~~ |

0 I can't .... *think of* .... a present for Louise's birthday. Have you got any ideas?

1 They .... the school and stole several computers.

2 .... you .... coming swimming with me or do you want to stay at home?

3 I don't know the answer. I'll have to .... it for a few days.

4 It was a difficult situation, but she .... it very well.

5 I hope you can come. I'd like to .... my friend Ben.

6 If they .... your work experience, tell them about your job last summer.

97 Phrasal verbs

- A phrasal verb is a combination of verb + adverb (*in, out, up,* etc.). The combination often has a new, idiomatic meaning.
- Intransitive phrasal verbs have no object: *We arranged a party, but no one* **turned up**. *They're worried that war will* **break out**.
- Transitive phrasal verbs have an object. If the object is:
  - a noun, it can come before or after the adverb: *We'll* **sort out the problem**. *We'll* **sort the problem out**.
  - a pronoun, it comes before (not after) the adverb: *We'll* **sort it out**. (Not ~~*We'll sort out it.*~~)

▶▶ **See Appendix 16: Common phrasal verbs, page 174.**

PRACTICE

97a **Complete the conversation. Use the correct form of the phrasal verbs in the box.**

| break down   carry on   get back   get up   ~~go out~~   lie down   stay in |

A: Do you want to (o) .... *go out* .... tonight? Shall we go to the cinema?

B: I think I'd prefer to (1) .... I feel quite tired. The car
(2) .... on the way home last night, so I (3) ....
very late and then I had to (4) .... early this morning.

A: Oh. Well, I'll (5) .... watching my DVD if we're not going out.

B: OK. I'm going to (6) .... now and have a rest.

97b **Re-write the sentences. Use the correct form of the verbs in brackets.**

o Could you find the answer to it? (work)
Could you ....*work it out*.. ?

1 Did you invent it? (make)
Did you .... ?

2 We had to cancel the performance. (call)
We had to ....

3 Shall I put these old pens in the bin? (throw)
Shall I .... ?

4 Why didn't they include her? (leave)
Why did they .... ?

5 I haven't completed my form yet. (fill)
I haven't ....

6 Who started talking about it? (bring)
Who .... ?

7 Michael arrived at seven thirty. (turn)
Michael ....

8 I put her name on a piece of paper. (write)
I ....

98 Phrasal-prepositional verbs

- A phrasal-prepositional verb is a combination of verb + adverb + preposition:
  I'm **looking forward to** the meal.   We **came up with** some good ideas.   I must **get back to** work.   I can't **put up with** this noise any longer!
- The object always comes after the adverb and preposition: Do you **get on with Sam**?
  Do you **get on with him**?

▶▶ *See Appendix 17: Common phrasal-prepositional verbs, page 174.*

P R A C T I C E

98a Complete the sentences. Use adverbs or prepositions.

0 When I saw him in the street, I went up ....*to*....... him and asked him for his autograph.

1 They were walking so fast that we couldn't catch up .... them.

2 He handed the folder over .... us and explained what was in it.

3 Kirsty fell out .... Sarah last term.

4 They finally came .... with a name for their band after weeks of discussion.

5 I'm trying to cut .... on all my unnecessary spending.

98b Complete the conversation. Use the correct form of the phrasal-prepositional verbs in the box.

| cut down on   get back to   get on with   get out of |
| ~~look forward to~~   put up with   run out of |

A: When's your play?
B: Next week! I (0) ....'m.... really ....*looking forward to*.... it. It's going to be good!
A: Did you make your costume yourself?
B: No, I didn't. Luckily, I managed to (1) .... that! Amy made it. It's not very comfortable, but I'll have to (2) .... it. It's too short as well as we (3) .... material! And it's a bit tight. I must have put on weight.
A: You'll have to (4) .... cakes for a couple of weeks.
B: I know!
A: What are the other people in the play like? Are they nice?
B: Yes, I (5) .... them very well. We have a lot of fun. Anyway, I'd better (6) .... college. I have to finish an essay.

Check 20 Words that go together

1 Circle the correct answer.

1 Would you like to look ...... this magazine or have you already read it?
   A for   B to   C at   D to

2 I'm worried ...... Emma. She hasn't called me this week.
   A about   B at   C for   D in

3 We set ...... early this morning, but we still arrived late.
   A on   B up   C off   D in

4 What was Tom's reaction ...... the news?
   A with   B on   C at   D to

5 Kevin apologised ...... being late.
   A at   B for   C to   D of

/ 5

2 Complete the second sentence so that it means the same as the first, using the word in bold. Use between two and five words.

6 Carol arrived late, as usual. **turned**
   Carol .... late, as usual.

7 Are you excited about your holiday? **looking**
   Are you .... your holiday?

8 I didn't want to do the washing-up, but I couldn't avoid it. **get**
   I didn't want to do the washing-up, but I couldn't .... it.

9 I told him to drive more slowly because he was making me nervous. **slow**
   I told him to .... because he was making me nervous.

10 It's not an easy situation, but we've learnt to accept it. **put**
   It's not an easy situation, but we've learnt to .... it.

/ 5

3 Complete the message from a message board on the Internet. Use the words in the box. You do not need all of them.

about at away down on out up with

I've fallen out (11) .... my best friend and I feel unhappy. She's been very depressed recently and last weekend I just ran (12) .... of patience and told her to stop complaining (13) .... everything. We both got angry and quarrelled. I've calmed (14) .... now, but I'm too afraid to ring her (15) ....

/ 5

4 Complete the conversation. Use prepositions or adverbs.

A: Have you seen this advertisement (16) .... the CitySpace Leisure Centre? It sounds really good.

B: Does it? What's the difference (17) .... it and our leisure centre?

A: It's got a big pool, some climbing walls, a mini golf course, a big skate park and lots of shops.

B: Actually, I think Matthew went there last week. He was talking (18) .... Sam (19) .... it. He said it was really crowded.

A: Well, I'd like to go. I'd like to try their skate park.

B: Me too. I'm hopeless (20) .... skating, though!

/ 5

Total: / 20

✓ Self-check

Wrong answers	Look again at	Try CD-ROM
2, 4, 16, 17, 20	**Unit 95**	Exercise 95
1, 5, 13, 18, 19	**Unit 96**	Exercise 96
3, 6, 9, 14, 15	**Unit 97**	Exercise 97
7, 8, 10, 11, 12	**Unit 98**	Exercise 98

Now do **Check 20**

Word formation

99 Compound adjectives

We can form compound adjectives with:

adjective/adverb + past participle	a **good-natured** man **old-fashioned** clothes a **well-known** artist a **badly-behaved** child the **best-dressed** woman
adjective/adverb + *-ing* form	a **best-selling** book a **fast-moving** story a **good-looking** man a **long-running** argument
adjective + noun	a **low-fat** diet a **modern-day** problem a **second-hand** car **small-scale** changes **high-tech** equipment

P R A C T I C E

99a Complete the sentences. Use the words in the box.

> best   fast   low   modern   ~~newly~~   ready

0 This beautiful photo album is the perfect gift for a ......*newly*......-married couple.

1 Our ....-fat sauces have plenty of flavour but not calories!

2 Get three of our ....-selling CDs for the price of two!

3 For a new view of ....-day relationships, watch this funny, intelligent film.

4 A new, ...-moving adventure story from Frederick Forsyth.

5 Try our new ....-made meals!

99b Circle the correct answer.

0 The badly-...... people were taken to hospital immediately.
   A injured   **B** affected   **C** behaved   **D** managed

1 This exhibition includes some of Monet's well-...... paintings.
   A dressed   **B** behaved   **C** known   **D** paid

2 Do you know anywhere I can buy a second-...... computer?
   A hand   **B** hands   **C** handed   **D** handing

3 Obviously, you have to be very good-...... to be a model.
   A dressed   **B** built   **C** moving   **D** looking

4 Small-...... radio stations can give people a voice in their community.
   A area   **B** scale   **C** shape   **D** style

5 He's always been extremely stylish and has been in the top ten of the best-......
   actors for years.
   A dress   **B** dressed   **C** look   **D** looked

6 Hundreds of new companies have been formed in this fast-...... industry.
   A running   **B** stepping   **C** increasing   **D** growing

100 Prefixes

● We use these prefixes to make words negative:

un- + **adjective/verb/noun**	**un**happy **un**lock **un**certainty
dis- + **adjective/verb/noun**	**dis**organised **dis**agree **dis**honesty
il- (+ *-l*) + **adjective/noun**	**il**legal **il**literacy
im- (+ *-m/-p*) + **adjective/noun**	**im**mature **im**perfection
in- + **adjective/noun:**	**in**accurate **in**convenience
ir- (+ *-r*) + **adjective/noun**	**ir**regular **ir**relevance

● These are prefixes with other meanings:

mis- (= badly/wrongly) + **verb/noun**	**mis**understand **mis**management
re- (= again) + **verb/noun**	**re**build **re**union
over- (= too much) + **verb/adjective**	**over**achieve **over**paid
under- (= not enough) + **verb/adjective**	**under**achieve **under**paid

PRACTICE

100a Complete the sentences. Use negative prefixes.

0 A lot of the information in this article is ....*in*accurate.

1 Some journalists like finding out all kinds of ....relevant details about famous people, like what they eat for breakfast.

2 A journalist was jailed for using ....legal methods to obtain personal information about members of the government.

3 The two politicians agree in public, but journalists say that in private they ....agree with each other about everything.

4 Some famous actors never give interviews because they think they will always be ....understood.

5 He never hides his ....patience with journalists.

100b Complete the sentences. Use the correct form of the words in capitals.

0 A place that has too many people in it is ....*overcrowded*............ . CROWDED

1 If you .... a door, you open it with a key. LOCK

2 Somebody who is .... behaves without thinking about the results of their actions. RESPONSIBLE

3 .... is the state of not knowing how to read or write. LITERACY

4 If you .... at school or work, you don't do as well as you could. ACHIEVE

5 If you .... something you are in charge of, you deal with it badly. MANAGE

101 Forming adjectives

● We often add these suffixes to verbs and nouns to form adjectives:

-able/-ible	enjoy**able** comfort**able** accept**able** access**ible**
-al	natur**al** profession**al** tradition**al** environment**al**
-ent/-ant	depend**ent** differ**ent** pleas**ant** resist**ant**
-ful	care**ful** hope**ful** pain**ful** stress**ful** use**ful**
-less	care**less** hope**less** fear**less** pain**less** use**less**
-ic/-ical	artist**ic** scientif**ic** biolog**ical** psycholog**ical**
-ish	child**ish** fool**ish** self**ish** styl**ish**
-ive	attrac**tive** crea**tive** progress**ive** produc**tive**
-ous	danger**ous** fam**ous** myster**ious** luxur**ious**
-y	health**y** scar**y** sport**y** dirt**y** cloud**y** luck**y**

● Adjectives ending in *-ed* describe how someone feels. Adjectives ending in *-ing* describe what something is like. Compare: *I was **interested** in his ideas.   His ideas were **interesting**.*

 Notice the changes in spelling: *forgive → forgiv**able**   beauty → beaut**iful** mystery → myster**ious**   hung**er** → hung**ry**   science → scien**tific***

P R A C T I C E

101a Complete the sentences. Use the correct form of the words in brackets.

   0 I felt very ....*angry*............ , but I didn't say anything. (anger)

   1 My glasses are .... at the moment – one of the lenses is broken. (use)

   2 His plans for next year sound really .... (excite)

   3 We had a really .... game. (enjoy)

   4 They make clothes that are .... , cheap and comfortable. (style)

   5 We were all .... when we heard the news. (amaze)

101b Complete the article. Use the correct form of the words in capitals.

Many societies have developed their own (0) ....*medical*............ systems.	MEDICINE
Some (1) .... systems, such as the Chinese, are still	TRADITION
widely used. In the Middle Ages, (2) .... knowledge was	SCIENCE
mixed with (3) .... belief. People did not know much	RELIGION
about the human body and surgery was very (4)	PAIN
and (5) .... In the 19th century, medicine in Europe	DANGER
changed enormously and became more (6) .... as people	EFFECT
began to understand what caused (7) .... diseases.	INFECT

102   Forming nouns

● We often add these suffixes to verbs and adjectives to form nouns:

-ance/-ence	perform**ance** import**ance** independ**ence** pat**ience**
-ion	introduc**tion** imagin**ation** compet**ition** depres**sion** divi**sion**
-ment	agree**ment** employ**ment** encourage**ment** improve**ment**
-ness	happ**iness** ill**ness** kind**ness** mean**ness** nervous**ness**
-y	loyal**ty** sensitiv**ity** responsib**ility** psychiat**ry**
-th	warm**th** leng**th** dep**th**

● Nouns with these suffixes refer to a person:

-ant/-ent	assist**ant** stud**ent**
-er/-or	sing**er** paint**er** writ**er** act**or** sculpt**or**
-ist	art**ist** novel**ist** scient**ist** tour**ist**
-ian	music**ian** comed**ian**

⚠ Notice the changes in spelling: *reduce → reduc**tion**   mean → mean**ness***
*happy → happ**iness**   responsible → responsib**ility**   deep → dep**th***

P R A C T I C E

102a Complete the quiz. Use the correct form of the words in the box.

> o ~~intelligent~~   1 kind   2 warm   3 generous   4 mean
> 5 insensitive   6 impatient   7 irresponsible

Which two qualities in others ...

... do you like the most?		... do you dislike the most?	
● (0) ......*intelligence*...... ☐		● (4) .... ☐	
● (1) .... ☐		● (5) .... ☐	
● (2) .... ☐		● (6) .... ☐	
● (3) .... ☐		● (7) .... ☐	

102b Complete the conversation. Use the correct form of the words in brackets.

A: She's a very good (o) ....*pianist*.......... (piano). She won a piano
(1) .... (compete) last year. I saw her (2) ....
(perform). It was fantastic! She's a (3) .... (study) at the London
College of Music now.

B: Really? How wonderful! Is her family musical?

A: Her father's a (4) .... (music). He's always given her a lot of help
and (5) .... (encourage).

Check 21 Word formation

1 Circle the correct answer.

I went on a short art course at the weekend. It was very (1) *interested / interesting*.

We had two teachers: a painter and a (2) *sculpter / sculptor*. They were both very (3) *helpful / helpless* and showed us some good techniques. My drawings looked less (4) *childy / childish* than they usually do! I'd like to go again. It was a good way of relaxing after a (5) *stressed / stressful* week and I learnt a lot.

/ 5

2 Complete the letter. Use prefixes.

I'm enjoying my summer job although I think I'm (6) ....paid! I work really hard and I don't earn very much. I didn't think that I'd get the job as I'm totally (7) ....experienced, but I did. Everyone's very nice although the manager's quite (8) ....organised and she doesn't explain things very well, so there are a lot of (9) ....understandings. The hours are a bit (10) ....regular – I usually work in the evenings until about half past eleven.

/ 5

3 Complete the sentences. Use one word from each box in each gap.

fast long old short well

fashioned known moving distance term

11 She wears quite .... clothes, so she looks older than she is.

12 Our neighbour is a(n) .... scientist who has written several books.

13 I think selling your bike is only a(n) .... solution to your problem.

14 I don't make many .... phone calls.

15 It was an entertaining, ... story, but it was like hundreds of others.

/ 5

4 Complete the article. Use the correct form of the word in brackets.

SAMUEL LANGHORNE CLEMENS was an American (16) .... (novel) who lived in the 19th century. He wrote the two great novels *The Adventures of Tom Sawyer* and *The Adventures of Huckleberry Finn*. Before he started writing, he worked as a steamboat pilot on the Mississippi. He then found (17) .... (employ) as a reporter for a small newspaper and gave himself the pen name Mark Twain. 'Mark twain' was something boatmen on the Mississippi said when they were measuring the (18) .... (deep) of the water.

Clemens led a (19) .... (produce) life: he wrote many stories, articles and travel books. Unfortunately, he also suffered from deep (20) .... (depress) when two of his daughters and his wife died. However, he continued to write until his death in 1910.

/ 5

Total: / 20

Self-check

Wrong answers	Look again at	Try CD-ROM
11, 12, 13, 14, 15	Unit 99	Exercise 99
6, 7, 8, 9, 10	Unit 100	Exercise 100
1, 3, 4, 5, 18	Unit 101	Exercise 101
2, 16, 17, 19, 20	Unit 102	Exercise 102

Now do **Check 21**

Appendices

1 Spelling rules for plural nouns

Noun	Rule	Examples
most nouns	add -s	car → cars table → tables
nouns ending in consonant + -y	change -y to -i and add -s	baby → babies family → families
nouns ending in vowel + -y	add -s	day → days key → keys
nouns ending in -ch, -sh, -ss, -s or -x	add -es	match → matches dish → dishes boss → bosses bus → buses fox → foxes
nouns ending in -o	add -s or -es	photo → photos video → videos potato → potatoes tomato → tomatoes
nouns ending in -f or -fe	change -f to -v and add -s	leaf → leaves life → lives

2 Spelling rules for adverbs

To make an adverb, we often add -ly to an adjective.

Adjective	Rule	Examples
most adjectives	add -ly	quick → quickly careful → carefully
adjectives ending in -y	change -y to -i and add -ly	happy → happily easy → easily
adjectives ending in -le	take away the -e and add -y	simple → simply horrible → horribly
adjectives ending in -ic	add -ally *	tragic → tragically romantic → romantically
adjectives ending in -ll	add -y	full → fully dull → dully

* But to form the adverb of *public*, we ad -ly: *public → publicly*

3 Spelling rules for comparative and superlative adjectives

Adjective	Rule	Examples
most adjectives	add -er or -est	quick → quicker → quickest short → shorter → shortest
adjectives ending in -e	add -r or -st	nice → nicer → nicest wide → wider → widest
adjectives ending in -y	change -y to -i and add -er or -est	heavy → heavier → heaviest lucky → luckier → luckiest
adjectives ending in one vowel + consonant	double the final consonant* and add -er or -est	big → bigger → biggest thin → thinner → thinnest

* But we don't double -w: *slow → slower → slowest*

4 Spelling rules for present simple verbs (*he, she, it*)

Verb	Rule	Examples
most verbs	add -s	eat → eats work → works
verbs ending in consonant + -y	change -y to -i and add -es	cry → cries study → studies
verbs ending in vowel + -y	add -s	play → plays enjoy → enjoys
verbs ending in -ch, -sh, -ss or -x	add -es	touch → touches finish → finishes miss → misses mix → mixes
verbs ending in -o	add -es	go → goes do → does

5 Spelling rules for verbs + -ing

Verb	Rule	Examples
most verbs	add -ing	sleep → sleep**ing** help → help**ing**
verbs ending in -e	take away the -e and add -ing	give → giv**ing** make → mak**ing**
verbs ending in -ee	add -ing	see → see**ing** agree → agree**ing**
verbs ending in -ie	change -ie to -y and add -ing	lie → **ly**ing tie → **ty**ing die → **dy**ing
verbs ending in one vowel + consonant	double the final consonant* and add -ing	stop → sto**pping** sit → si**tting**
verbs ending in two vowels + consonant	add -ing	read → read**ing** cook → cook**ing**

* But we do not double the final consonant if the last part of the word is not stressed:
  begin → beginning BUT *open → opening*
  And we do not double -w or -x: *snow → snowing, mix → mixing*

6 Spelling rules for verbs + -ed

Verb	Rule	Examples
most verbs	add -ed	work → work**ed** help → help**ed**
verbs ending in -e or -ee	add -d	live → live**d** agree → agree**d**
verbs ending in consonant + -y	change -y to -i and add -ed	try → tr**ied** study → stud**ied**
verbs ending in vowel + -y	add -ed	play → play**ed** enjoy → enjoy**ed**
verbs ending in one vowel + consonant	double the final consonant * and add -ed	stop → sto**pped** plan → pla**nned**
verbs ending in two vowels + consonant	add -ed	rain → rain**ed** book → book**ed**

* But we do not double the final consonant if the last part of the word is not stressed:
  prefer → preferred BUT *answer → answered*

7 Verb forms
Present simple

Affirmative	I/you/we/they **eat**	he/she/it **eats**
Negative	I/you/we/they **don't eat**	he/she/it **doesn't eat**
Question	**Do** I/you/we/they **eat**?	**Does** he/she/it **eat**?

Present continuous

Affirmative	**I'm** eat**ing**	you/we/they**'re** eat**ing**	he/she/it**'s** eat**ing**
Negative	**I'm not** eat**ing**	you/we/they **aren't** eat**ing**	he/she/it **isn't** eat**ing**
Question	**Am** I eat**ing**?	**Are** you/we/they eat**ing**?	**Is** he/she/it eat**ing**?

Past simple

Affirmative	I/you/he/she/it/we/they **ate**
Negative	I/you/he/she/it/we/they **didn't eat**
Question	**Did** I/you/he/she/it/we/they **eat**?

Past continuous

Affirmative	I/he/she/it **was** eat**ing**	you/we/they **were** eat**ing**
Negative	I/he/she/it **wasn't** eat**ing**	you/we/they **weren't** eat**ing**
Question	**Was** I/he/she/it eat**ing**?	**Were** you/we/they eat**ing**?

Present perfect

Affirmative	I/you/we/they**'ve eaten**	he/she/it**'s eaten**
Negative	I/you/we/they **haven't eaten**	he/she/it **hasn't eaten**
Question	**Have** I/you/we/they **eaten?**	**Has** he/she/it **eaten?**

Present perfect continuous

Affirmative	I/you/we/they**'ve been** eat**ing**	he/she/it**'s been** eat**ing**
Negative	I/you/we/they **haven't been** eat**ing**	he/she/it **hasn't been** eat**ing**
Question	**Have** I/you/we/they **been** eat**ing?**	**Has** he/she/it **been** eat**ing?**

Past perfect

Affirmative	I/you/he/she/it/we/they**'d eaten**
Negative	I/you/he/she/it/we/they **hadn't eaten**
Question	**Had** I/you/he/she/it/we/they **eaten?**

be going to

Affirmative	I**'m going to** eat	he/she/it**'s going to** eat	you/we/they**'re going to** eat
Negative	I**'m not going to** eat	he/she/it **isn't going to** eat	you/we/they **aren't going to** eat
Question	**Am** I **going to** eat?	**Is** he/she/it **going to** eat?	**Are** you/we/they **going to** eat?

will

Affirmative	I/you/he/she/it/we/they**'ll** eat
Negative	I/you/he/she/it/we/they **won't** eat
Question	**Will** I/you/he/she/it/we/they eat?

Future continuous

Affirmative	I/you/he/she/it/we/they**'ll be** eat**ing**
Negative	I/you/he/she/it/we/they **won't be** eat**ing**
Question	**Will** I/you/he/she/it/we/they **be** eat**ing?**

Future perfect

Affirmative	I/you/he/she/it/we/they **will have eaten**
Negative	I/you/he/she/it/we/they **won't have eaten**
Question	**Will** I/you/he/she/it/we/they **have eaten?**

Future in the past

Affirmative	I/he/she/it **was going to** eat	you/we/they **were going to** eat
Negative	I/he/she/it **wasn't going to** eat	you/we/they **weren't going to** eat
Question	**Was** I/he/she/it **going to** eat?	**Were** you/we/they **going to** eat?

8 Irregular verbs

Infinitive	Past simple	Past participle
be	was/were	been
beat	beat	beaten
become	became	become
begin	began	begun
bend	bent	bent
bet	bet	bet
bite	bit	bitten
bleed	bled	bled
blow	blew	blown
break	broke	broken
bring	brought	brought
broadcast	broadcast	broadcast
build	built	built
burn	burned/burnt	burned/burnt

Infinitive	Past simple	Past participle
burst	burst	burst
buy	bought	bought
catch	caught	caught
choose	chose	chosen
come	came	come
cost	cost	cost
cut	cut	cut
deal	dealt	dealt
dig	dug	dug
do	did	done
draw	drew	drawn
dream	dreamed/dreamt	dreamed/dreamt
drink	drank	drunk
drive	drove	driven

Infinitive	Past simple	Past participle
eat	ate	eaten
fall	fell	fallen
feed	fed	fed
feel	felt	felt
fight	fought	fought
find	found	found
fly	flew	flown
forbid	forbade	forbidden
forget	forgot	forgotten
forgive	forgave	forgiven
freeze	froze	frozen
get	got	got
give	gave	given
go	went	gone
grow	grew	grown
hang	hung	hung
have	had	had
hear	heard	heard
hide	hid	hidden
hit	hit	hit
hold	held	held
hurt	hurt	hurt
keep	kept	kept
kneel	knelt	knelt
keep	kept	kept
kneel	knelt	knelt
know	knew	known
lay	laid	laid
lead	led	led
lean	leaned/leant	leaned/leant
learn	learned/learnt	learned/learnt
leave	left	left
lend	lent	lent
let	let	let
lie	lay	lain
light	lit	lit
lose	lost	lost
make	made	made
mean	meant	meant
meet	met	met
pay	paid	paid
put	put	put
read	read	read
ride	rode	ridden
ring	rang	rung
rise	rose	risen

Infinitive	Past simple	Past participle
run	ran	run
say	said	said
see	saw	seen
seek	sought	sought
sell	sold	sold
send	sent	sent
set	set	set
sew	sewed	sewed/sewn
shake	shook	shaken
shine	shone	shone
shoot	shot	shot
show	showed	shown
shrink	shrank	shrunk
shut	shut	shut
sing	sang	sung
sink	sank	sunk
sit	sat	sat
sleep	slept	slept
slide	slid	slid
smell	smelled/smelt	smelled/smelt
speak	spoke	spoken
spell	spelled/spelt	spelled/spelt
spend	spent	spent
spill	spilled/spilt	spilled/spilt
spread	spread	spread
stand	stood	stood
steal	stole	stolen
stick	stuck	stuck
sting	stung	stung
stink	stank	stunk
strike	struck	struck
swear	swore	sworn
sweep	swept	swept
swim	swam	swum
take	took	taken
teach	taught	taught
tear	tore	torn
tell	told	told
think	thought	thought
throw	threw	thrown
understand	understood	understood
wake	woke	woken
wear	wore	worn
win	won	won
write	wrote	written

9 Verbs followed by -ing form

admit   can't help   consider   dislike   feel like   hate   mention   practise   risk
adore   can't stand   delay   enjoy   finish   imagine   mind   propose   suggest
avoid   carry on   deny   fancy   give up   keep   miss   recommend

10 Verbs followed by to-infinitive

agree   can't afford   expect   learn   offer   promise   would like
arrange   can't wait   help   manage   plan   refuse   would love
ask   decide   hope   need   prepare   want   would prefer

11 Verbs followed by *-ing* form or *to*-infinitive

(a) With no change in meaning

begin	intend	prefer
continue	love	start

(b) With a change in meaning

forget	remember	try
like	stop	

12 Verbs followed by object + *to*-infinitive

(a) Verbs that need an object before the *to*-infinitive

advise	cause	force	invite	persuade	teach	warn
allow	encourage	get	order	remind	tell	

(b) Verbs that can have an object before the *to*-infinitive

ask   expect   help   need   want   would like   would love   would prefer

13 Adjective + preposition

afraid of
amazed at/by
angry about (something)
angry with (someone)
annoyed about (something)
annoyed with (someone)
ashamed of
aware of
bad at (something)
bored with
brilliant at
careful with
crazy about
different from
enthusiastic about
excited about

famous for
fed up with
frightened of
full of
good at (something)
happy with/about
hopeless at
interested in
jealous of
keen on
kind to (someone)
kind of (someone to do something)
married to
nice to (someone)
nice of (someone to do something)
pleased with/about

polite to
proud of
ready for
responsible for
rude to
similar to
sorry about/for
sure about/of
surprised at/by
terrible at
tired of
upset about (something)
upset with (someone)
worried about

14 Noun + preposition

advertisement for
advice on/about
answer to
argument about (something)
argument with (someone)
beginning of
cause of
change in
comment on

conversation between (two people)
conversation with (someone)
decrease in
difference between
discussion about (something)
discussion between (two people)
discussion with (someone)
increase in
information on/about

interest in
lack of
need for
permission for (something)
permission from (someone)
problem with
reaction to
reason for
reply to

15 Verb + preposition

accuse (someone) of (something/doing something)
agree on/with (something)
agree with (someone) about (something)
apologise to (someone) for (something/doing something)
approve of (something/someone)
argue with (someone) about (something)
ask (someone) about (something)
ask (someone) for (something)
believe in (something/someone)
belong to (someone/an organisation, club, etc.)
benefit from (something)
break into (a building)
care about (something/someone)
change (something) into (something)
communicate with (someone)

complain about (something/someone)
consist of (something)
deal with (something)
depend on (something/someone)
disagree with (something)
disagree with (someone) about (something)
dream about (something/doing something)
feel like (something/doing something)
forget about (something/someone)
forgive (someone) for (something/doing something)
hear about (something/someone)
insist on (something/doing something)
introduce (someone) to (someone)
know (something) about (something/someone)
laugh at (something/someone)

listen to (something/someone)
look after (something/someone)
look at (something/someone)
look for (something/someone)
look like (something/someone)
pay for (something/someone)
prefer (something/someone) to (something/someone)
provide (someone) with (something)
react to (something)
reply to (something/someone)
result in (something)

see to (something)
succeed in (doing something)
suffer from (an illness)
take after (someone)
talk to (someone) about (something)
tell (someone) about (something)
thank (someone) for (something/doing something)
think about (something/someone)
think of (something/doing something)
wait for (something/someone)
worry about (something/someone)

16 Common phrasal verbs

break down = if a car or machine breaks down, it stops working
break out = if a disease, fire or war breaks out, it starts to happen
bring up = to start talking about something
call off = to cancel something
calm down = to become calm and less angry
carry on = to continue doing something
check in = to go to the desk at a hotel, airport, etc. and say that you have arrived
come back = to return
come round = to visit someone
drive off = if a car drives off, it leaves
fill in = to write all the necessary information on an official document
find out = to discover information about something
get back = to return
get off = to leave a bus, train, plane, etc.
get on = to walk onto a bus, train, plane, etc.
get up = to wake up and get out of bed
give up = to stop doing something
go away = to leave a place or person
go back = to return
go on = to happen
go out = to leave your house to do something you enjoy
grow up = to develop from being a child to being an adult
hurry up = to do something more quickly
keep up = to continue doing something
leave out = to not include someone or something in a group, list or activity
lie down = when you lie down, your body is flat on a bed, on the floor, etc.
look out = used to warn someone of danger

look up = to find information in a book, on a computer, etc.
make up = to invent something
put on = to put clothes on your body
ring up = to telephone someone
run away = to escape by running
set off = to leave and start going somewhere
sit down = to lower yourself down so that you are sitting
slow down = to become slower or make something slower
sort out = if you sort out a problem, you deal with it
stand up = to get up so that you are standing
stay in = to stay in your home and not go out
stay up = to not go to bed
take off = when a plane takes off, it leaves the ground
take off = to remove something
take up = to begin doing a job or activity
throw away = to get rid of something that you do not want
try on = to put on a piece of clothing to find out if it fits or if you like it
turn down = to make a machine produce less heat, sound, etc.
turn off = to make a machine, light, etc. stop working
turn on = to make a machine, light, etc. start working
turn up = to arrive
turn up = to make a machine produce more heat, sound, etc.
wake up = to stop sleeping, or to make someone stop sleeping
wash up = to wash the plates, dishes, etc. after a meal
work out = to find the answer to a question or problem
write down = to write something on a piece of paper

17 Common phrasal-prepositional verbs

catch up with = to come up from behind someone or something and reach the same point
come up with = to think of an idea, plan, reply, etc.
cut down on = to reduce the amount of something you eat, do, use, etc.
fall out with = to have a quarrel with someone
get back to = to start doing something again after not doing it for some time
get on with = to have a friendly relationship with someone
get out of = to avoid doing something you ought to do

go up to = to walk towards someone or something until you are next to them
hand (something) over to = to give something to someone
look forward to = to be excited and happy about something that is going to happen
put up with = to accept an unpleasant situation without complaining
run out of = to use all of something so that there is none left

Index

The numbers in this index are unit numbers (not page numbers).

Answer key

In your answers, you can use the full or short forms of verbs, e.g. *She is coming or She's coming*. Both forms are generally correct. There are only a few occasions when it is not possible to use the short form of a verb.

Unit 1

1a

1 series, women, men 2 Wolves, deer, sheep 3 people, means 4 butterflies, species 5 photos, aircraft 6 toys, children

1b

1 My sunglasses are very good.
2 All her belongings are in that bag.
3 Tonight's audience is very small.
4 This pair of jeans is my favourite.
5 The news is very worrying.
6 The electrical goods here are quite cheap.
7 Physics is a fascinating subject.
8 Are these scissors sharp?

1c

1 work 2 want/wants 3 is 4 do/does 5 play/plays 6 are 7 don't/doesn't pay 8 has

1d

1 does this 2 They're 3 hurt 4 is 5 They were 6 it 7 it 8 They weren't

Unit 2

2a

coin	C	bread	U	furniture	U
money	U	electricity	U	cupboard	C
suitcase	C	plastic	U	magazine	C
luggage	U	machine	C	article	C
advice	U	progress	U	news	U
career	C	homework	U	weather	U
office	C	college	C	accident	C
information	U	project	C	storm	C
piece	C	lecture	C	music	U

2b

1 a 2 – 3 a 4 a 5 – 6 an 7 a 8 – 9 – 10 –

2c

1 piece 2 carton 3 slices 4 piece 5 can 6 grams 7 kilos 8 cup 9 metres 10 piece

2d

1 room 2 glass 3 an ice cream 4 ice cream 5 a paper 6 money 7 a strange 8 an empty

Unit 3

3a

1 some 2 some 3 some 4 any 5 any 6 no 7 any 8 some 9 no 10 any/some 11 some 12 no

3b

1 a lot of 2 much 3 much 4 many 5 many 6 lots of 7 much 8 a lot of

3c

1 a few 2 few 3 a little 4 little 5 little 6 a few 7 a few

3d

1 enough 2 too many 3 plenty of 4 several 5 enough 6 a bit of 7 a lot of

Unit 4

4a

1 most of 2 some of 3 Most 4 None of 5 Not all 6 No

4b

1 Most of 2 None of 3 Some of 4 All 5 Some of 6 Most of

Unit 5

5a

1 every 2 Each 3 each 4 Each/Every 5 Each/Every

5b

1 every 2 every 3 every 4 each 5 each

Unit 6

6a

1 Neither 2 either 3 neither 4 either 5 Both 6 both 7 Either 8 Neither

6b

1 Neither of 2 either 3 both of 4 both (of) 5 either of 6 both 7 neither of

Check 1

1

1 Some of 2 has 3 few 4 are 5 each 6 most of 7 some 8 Either

2

9 a coffee 10 coffee 11 piece 12 Either 13 both

3

14 of 15 all 16 few 17 are 18 much 19 a 20 every

Unit 7

7a

1 Fiona's 2 Dan's 3 men's 4 The black horse's 5 My sisters' 6 that singer's 7 my parents' 8 children's 9 the dancers' 10 our neighbours' 11 your friend's 12 The dogs'

7b

1 the dentist's 2 the chemist's 3 the butcher's 4 a very good baker's 5 Emma's 6 Matt and Luke's

7c

1 I left a T-shirt of mine at your house.
2 I think he's a cousin of Nina's.
3 It's an idea of his.
4 She's a friend of Mark's.
5 We went to a gig of theirs.
6 I've read a poem of his.

7d

1 side of the main building 2 college cafeteria 3 end of the course 4 back of an envelope 5 phone numbers

Unit 8

8a
1 himself 2 myself 3 yourselves 4 herself 5 themselves
6 itself

8b
1 herself 2 themselves 3 each other 4 her 5 herself
6 one another

Unit 9

9a
1 our own 2 her own 3 on your own 4 my own 5 on his own
6 on their own 7 on her own 8 their own 9 his own
10 on our own

9b
1 his own 2 by himself 3 my own 4 our own
5 by themselves 6 their own

Unit 10

10a
1 No one 2 was 3 was 4 something 5 anybody 6 is, their
7 anywhere 8 's 9 something 10 nowhere

10b
1 Everyone 2 nothing 3 something 4 Someone 5 anything
6 anywhere 7 Everything 8 anything

10c
1 They were 2 nobody 3 works 4 anybody 5 nowhere
6 somewhere

Unit 11

11a
1 one 2 ones 3 one 4 ones 5 ones 6 one

11b
1 another 2 other 3 other 4 other 5 others 6 other
7 another 8 another

11c
1 ones 2 other 3 another 4 other 5 other 6 one 7 another
8 others

Check 2

1
1 another 2 myself 3 winners' 4 themselves 5 women's
6 mine 7 their own

2
8 ones 9 of 10 yourself/yourselves 11 on 12 by

3
13 D 14 D 15 C 16 B 17 C 18 A 19 A 20 B

Unit 12

12a
1 a 2 an 3 a 4 the 5 a 6 the, the 7 a 8 a, the

12b
1 a 2 a 3 one 4 one 5 a 6 one

12c
1 the 2 the 3 one 4 the 5 a 6 the 7 a 8 a 9 the 10 a
11 one 12 the 13 a 14 the 15 the

Unit 13

13a
1 Stress 2 the poor 3 new technology 4 The British 5 Dark
chocolate

13b
1 the guitar 2 The King Cobra 3 the aeroplane 4 Honesty
5 science 6 nature 7 A 8 Children

13c
1 – 2 the 3 an 4 a 5 the 6 –

Unit 14

14a
1 a 2 the 3 a 4 the 5 the 6 a

14b
1 Asia 2 California, the United States 3 Mount Fuji, Japan
4 Mandarin, China 5 Malaria, Africa 6 The Sahara,
the Atlantic, the Nile 7 Lake Superior, North America
8 Ice hockey, lacrosse, Canada 9 Edinburgh, Scotland
10 The Sydney Opera House, Australia

14c
1 – 2 – 3 the 4 – 5 the 6 a 7 – 8 –

Check 3

1
1 motorbikes 2 the United States 3 fashion 4 bronchitis
5 the telephone

2
6 Dublin 7 the West Court 8 Cork 9 the theatre 10 The Irish

3
11 A 12 the 13 a 14 the 15 the 16 a 17 the 18 the 19 a
20 the

Unit 15

15a
1 Everybody seems relaxed.
2 There are some nice buildings.
3 The former palace is enormous.
4 The food tastes fantastic.
5 The people are kind and friendly/friendly and kind.
6 The streets are clean and quiet/quiet and clean.
7 The main street is busy.
8 We're having a great time.

15b
1 some rare old American comics 2 a black plastic digital
watch 3 a long black woollen coat 4 a small practical nylon
rucksack 5 a lovely handmade African necklace 6 two big
colourful Indian rugs

15c
1 crowded 2 sick 3 clean 4 only 5 outdoor 6 good

Unit 16

16a
1 patiently   2 quickly   3 angrily   4 worried   5 politely
6 nervous   7 slowly   8 confident

16b
1 long   2 in a lovely way   3 lazily   4 in a silly way   5 fast
6 in a friendly way   7 sleepily   8 sympathetically

16c
1 painful, hardly   2 late, quickly   3 expensive, free   4 lately,
busy   5 happy, freely   6 hard, famous   7 angry, honest
8 badly, horrible

Unit 17

17a
1 She's working hard.
2 Our exams start on Monday.
3 She organises her time well.
4 She's never failed an exam.
5 I sometimes have lunch with her.
6 We had a nice chat yesterday.
7 We went for a walk by the river.
8 It was very relaxing there.

17b
1 Our relatives often stay with us at New Year.
2 I sometimes visit my grandparents in the summer.
3 I occasionally go camping for a few days.
4 I always have a lovely time in Wales.
5 I usually meet interesting people there.

17c
1 I had arranged to meet my friends at six at the bowling alley.
2 I ran quickly through the park.
3 I got to the bowling alley at half past six.
4 My friends were waiting patiently at the entrance.
5 I played badly most of the evening.
6 I kept thinking about the things I had to do at home later
   that evening.

Unit 18

18a
1 less interested   2 more popular   3 less concerned   4 more
quickly   5 better

18b
1 most dangerous   2 the most fluently   3 the least enjoyable
4 the hardest   5 the least enthusiastically

18c
1 the least sporty   2 more carefully than   3 the second best
4 the least calmly   5 less cautious than   6 the most
immaturely

Unit 19

19a
1 slightly   2 much   3 a lot   4 far   5 a bit   6 much

19b
1 a   2 by   3 the   4 lot   5 a

Unit 20

20a
1 really hungry   2 quite well   3 quite good   4 fairly quickly
5 very fit   6 very carefully

20b
1 absolutely   2 very   3 fairly   4 really   5 absolutely   6 a bit

Check 4

1
1 We've never eaten there.
2 They serve wonderful traditional French food.
3 She always works hard.
4 Are you going to the theatre tonight?
5 Tom's got a fantastic new electric guitar.

2
6 loudly   7 hardly   8 hard   9 happy   10 quite

3
11 A   12 C   13 A   14 C   15 B   16 D   17 C   18 D   19 B   20 D

Unit 21

21a
1 the most   2 less   3 more   4 the least   5 the most   6 more
7 less   8 the least

21b
1 fewer   2 less   3 more   4 more   5 less

Unit 22

22a
1 as important as   2 as sensitive as   3 as far as   4 as hard as
5 as well as   6 wasn't as enjoyable   7 as good as   8 doesn't
drive as fast

22b
1 as many sweets as   2 as many photos as   3 as much success
as   4 as many people as   5 as much money as   6 as much
coffee as

22c
1 more   2 to   3 the   4 many   5 from   6 as

Unit 23

23a
1 very   2 regularly enough   3 too   4 too quickly   5 very
6 big enough

23b
1 too short to see   2 was too tired to play   3 walk slowly
enough for   4 too heavy for him to   5 well enough to be
6 too quietly for me to

23c
1 too   2 for   3 enough   4 for   5 to

Unit 24

24a
1 so   2 such a   3 such   4 such   5 so   6 such a

24b
1 so much noise that   2 so strong that   3 such a beautiful day
that   4 so brightly that   5 such good food that   6 so many
insects that   7 so boring that   8 such a good book that

Unit 25

25a
1 hotter and hotter   2 worse and worse   3 less and less
4 fewer and fewer   5 more and more quickly

25b
1 the nicer it tastes   2 the more expensive they are
3 the more slowly we drive   4 the more mistakes you'll make
5 the more energetic you feel

25c
1 The bigger the better!
2 The harder the better!
3 The stronger the better!
4 The cheaper the better!
5 The sooner the better!

Check 5

1
1 More and more   2 less and less   3 more or less   4 the least
5 the fewest

2
6 such a   7 so   8 less   9 the nicer   10 too complicated

3
11 too shy to ask   12 as good as   13 so expensive that
14 as much television as   15 big enough for them to

4
16 a   17 as   18 to   19 the   20 for

Unit 26

26a
1 isn't working   2 're sitting   3 don't speak   4 reads
5 's always talking   6 always start   7 's making   8 Does it get

26b
1 loses   2 use   3 never eat   4 'm living   5 'm helping   6 lives
7 works   8 're becoming   9 are moving   10 are opening

Unit 27

27a
1 don't agree   2 do, cost   3 are, crying   4 prefer   5 are waiting
6 'm not enjoying

27b
1 'm tasting   2 Do you see   3 'm thinking   4 tastes   5 smells
6 thinks   7 has   8 's smelling

27c
1 'm seeing   2 Do you feel/Are you feeling   3 think
4 's listening   5 sounds   6 look/'re looking   7 'm thinking
8 needs

Unit 28

28a
1 went   2 took   3 cycled   4 saw   5 didn't stay   6 didn't finish,
was   7 felt, reached   8 didn't know

28b
1 crashed   2 had   3 didn't have   4 started   5 lost   6 didn't
play   7 admitted   8 didn't perform

Unit 29

29a
1 were planning   2 was taking, were drawing   3 didn't believe
4 was getting   5 didn't like   6 weren't doing   7 were waiting
8 didn't want   9 sounded   10 was listening

29b
1 was Laura going   2 Were you and Mark practising   3 did you
feel   4 Were people dancing   5 did you do   6 did you hide

29c
1 saw   2 were watching   3 got   4 was happening   5 was lying
6 was bleeding   7 were standing   8 was holding   9 was crying
10 shouted   11 stopped   12 stood   13 noticed   14 realised
15 were making

Unit 30

30a
1 would/used to leave   2 didn't use to have   3 Did you use to
live   4 would/used to spend   5 would/used to tell   6 didn't
use to be   7 used to love   8 would/used to play

30b
1 get   2 get   3 I'm not   4 I'm   5 get   6 get

30c
1 to   2 would   3 used   4 would   5 'm   6 used   7 to   8 got

Check 6

1
1 's having   2 Did you live   3 parks   4 were doing   5 's getting

2
6 didn't answer   7 were waiting   8 lasts   9 Do, see   10 sends

3
11 left   12 got   13 was working   14 became   15 want

4
16 used to tell   17 would make   18 got used to   19 used to
going   20 didn't use to like

Unit 31

31a
1 's grown   2 's done   3 has she sold   4 have joined   5 haven't
brought   6 have you decided   7 haven't given   8 have they
finished   9 hasn't called   10 've put

31b
1 recently   2 already   3 just   4 yet   5 recently   6 yet   7 just
8 already

31c
1 has won   2 beat   3 have returned   4 agreed   5 has given
6 received

31d
1 've decorated   2 hasn't changed   3 has improved
4 've learnt   5 bought   6 've hired   7 had   8 've got

Unit 32

32a
1 Has Sophie ever talked, 's never mentioned   2 Have you ever played, 've always thought   3 Have they ever performed, 've never had   4 Have you ever tried, 've always been   5 Has he ever shouted, 's always been   6 Have you ever sent, 've never done

32b
1 the first time they've   2 've never been   3 time she's ever tried   4 've never made this before   5 the first time you've

32c
1 I've ever had   2 I've ever seen   3 I've ever worked   4 I've ever met   5 I've ever had

32d
1 gone   2 've only been, didn't enjoy   3 been   4 've been, saw 5 hasn't always lived, moved   6 've met, was

Unit 33

33a
1 I haven't watched TV for ages.
2 I haven't tidied my room for weeks.
3 I haven't spoken to Emma since Friday.
4 I haven't checked my e-mails for ten days.
5 I haven't seen Nikki since last month.
6 I haven't heard from her since she left.

33b
1 's lived here for   2 've worn glasses since   3 's been upstairs for   4 've known them since   5 've worked here for   6 've been married since

33c
1 've written   2 came   3 Did you have   4 've had
5 've watched

33d
1 've known   2 for   3 was   4 've done   5 since   6 had

Unit 34

34a
1 've been standing   2 's been jogging   3 's been sitting 4 's been working   5 's been reading   6 've been talking

34b
1 've been driving   2 've been sleeping   3 Has Emily been singing   4 have you been doing   5 've been reading   6 hasn't been doing

34c
1 's worked/'s been working   2 's had   3 've been walking 4 's been learning   5 've lived/'ve been living   6 've spilled/ spilt   7 has it been raining   8 've made   9 's designed 10 have you been standing

Unit 35

35a
1 Did anybody help   2 did   3 Have you ever ridden   4 took 5 've added   6 haven't been   7 grew up   8 've been

35b
1 sleep   2 feel   3 've had   4 haven't done   5 haven't seen 6 phone

35c
1 has had   2 works   3 employ   4 bought   5 manages   6 came 7 've been   8 don't teach   9 collect   10 've worked   11 got 12 've enjoyed

Check 7

1
1 've burnt   2 yet   3 's worked   4 's had   5 've lived

2
6 Have you heard   7 told   8 forgot   9 've been   10 went

3
11 's been raining for   12 've never driven   13 've lived in Stockport since   14 have been working since   15 've known Rob for

4
16 got   17 haven't had   18 've been   19 has been staying 20 bought

Unit 36

36a
1 hadn't taken   2 'd arranged   3 'd saved   4 hadn't slept 5 had you ordered   6 'd forgotten

36b
1 'd never won   2 'd ever run   3 had already advised 4 'd already recovered   5 'd never written

Unit 37

37a
1 'd repaired/repaired, sold   2 came, 'd taken/took
3 'd tidied/tidied, went   4 'd put/put, had   5 'd left, arrived 6 'd talked/talked, felt

37b
1 met, 'd left   2 saw, 'd had   3 left, 'd spent   4 failed, was 5 arrived, had destroyed   6 started, 'd eaten   7 looked, found

37c
1 'd read/read   2 tore   3 came   4 'd formed   5 'd left
6 phoned   7 'd signed/signed   8 took   9 asked   10 smiled

Unit 38

38a
1 hadn't prepared   2 was having   3 found   4 was
5 had dropped   6 were   7 sent   8 got   9 'd forgotten 10 was walking

38b
1 were returning   2 hit   3 'd checked/checked   4 'd chosen/ chose   5 wasn't snowing   6 were walking   7 started
8 carried   9 were falling   10 stopped   11 managed   12 saw 13 had landed   14 dug   15 got

Check 8

1

1 got, 'd found   2 arrived, had already left   3 went out, 'd had/had   4 'd finished/finished, felt   5 'd read/read, went   6 had taken off, got

2

7 hadn't practised   8 'd already seen   9 gave   10 'd never been   11 took   12 moved

3

13 A   14 B   15 A   16 C   17 D   18 A   19 D   20 A

Unit 39

39a

1 won't mind   2 won't come   3 's going to get   4 will be   5 'm going to have   6 will notice   7 's going to be   8 'll have

39b

1 'll   2 'll   3 'm going to   4 won't   5 'm going to

39c

1 'll be   2 are you going to live   3 'll rent   4 's going to move   5 'll give   6 'll call

Unit 40

40a

1 're going   2 leaves   3 change   4 gets   5 're camping   6 aren't competing   7 isn't coming   8 ends

40b

1 are going   2 're meeting   3 starts   4 finishes   5 are taking   6 begins

40c

1 leaves   2 gets   3 'll see   4 'm looking   5 'll bring   6 is   7 'm helping   8 'll give

Unit 41

41a

1 will you be watching   2 'll be practising   3 'll be trying   4 won't be paying   5 'll be shouting   6 'll be working

41b

1 will help   2 'll be having   3 won't go   4 'll be thinking   5 'll revise   6 won't be doing

Unit 42

42a

1 won't have made, arrive   2 'll have moved   3 Will you have started, see   4 'll have gone   5 won't have left   6 perform, 'll have rehearsed

42b

1 will experience   2 will need   3 will have improved   4 will have disappeared   5 will move   6 will have landed

Unit 43

43a

1 was going to go   2 weren't going to share   3 was going to earn   4 were going to be   5 wasn't going to stay   6 were going to set up

43b

1 were going to cost   2 wasn't going to get   3 was going to meet   4 wasn't going to come   5 wasn't going to say   6 was going to be

Check 9

1

1 'll feel   2 'm not going to do   3 Are you going to come   4 will let   5 'll pick

2

6 'll be playing   7 will have gone   8 was going to hit   9 will you be getting   10 won't have eaten

3

11 are coming   12 're performing   13 were going to give   14 'll have sold   15 're going   16 'm going to book   17 leave   18 won't be   19 'll be rehearsing   20 was going to start

Unit 44

44a

1 can   2 will be able to   3 can/'ll be able to   4 could   5 will be able to/can   6 could

44b

1 both   2 both   3 both   4 ~~could~~   5 ~~could~~   6 both

44c

1 managed   2 'll   3 were   4 could   5 can   6 be

Unit 45

45a

1 might   2 must   3 might   4 might   5 must   6 might

45b

1 can't   2 must   3 may not   4 can't   5 could   6 must   7 might   8 might not

45c

1 could be   2 might come   3 may not see   4 might know   5 must have

45d

1 may/might/could   2 may/might/could   3 must   4 may not/might not   5 can't

Unit 46

46a

1 might not have locked   2 must have spent   3 must have worked   4 might not have got   5 might have written   6 must have been

46b

1 might not   2 may not   3 can't   4 might not   5 can't   6 can't

46c

1 can't have taken   2 might not have seen   3 could/might/must have forgotten   4 must have been   5 might not have been   6 can't have been

Unit 47

47a
1 can't 2 may 3 can't 4 're allowed to 5 'll be allowed to
6 couldn't 7 couldn't 8 weren't allowed to 9 can 10 weren't allowed to

47b
1 ~~could~~ 2 both 3 both 4 both 5 both 6 ~~could~~ 7 ~~could~~
8 ~~could~~

47c
1 sorry 2 allowed 3 can/may 4 to 5 Can/May 6 course

Unit 48

48a
1 have to 2 have to 3 has to 4 must 5 have to 6 must

48b
1 Did, have to 2 Do, have to 3 had to 4 've got to
5 've got to/'ll have to 6 'll have to

48c
1 had to 2 mustn't 3 had to 4 don't have to 5 have to
6 must 7 must 8 don't have to

Unit 49

49a
1 need to 2 needn't 3 needs to 4 need to 5 needn't
6 needn't

49b
1 don't need 2 needn't have got up 3 didn't need to go
4 didn't need to get 5 need to 6 needn't have bought

Unit 50

50a
1 ought 2 ought not 3 should 4 shouldn't 5 ought not
6 should

50b
1 'd better start 2 have to try 3 must not tell 4 had better call 5 better not go 6 must ask 7 'd better apologise
8 have to see

50c
1 should tell 2 should have talked 3 shouldn't have gone
4 shouldn't do 5 shouldn't have applied 6 should explain

Unit 51

51a
1 Will you do 2 Would you mind posting 3 Would you take/ Would you mind taking 4 Could you put 5 Can you pick

51b
1 Shall 2 'll/can/could 3 Shall 4 Why 5 Let 6 'll/can/could
7 can/could 8 Let

Check 10

1
1 must 2 was allowed to 3 needn't have taken 4 were able to 5 can't

2
6 must 7 might 8 needn't 9 mustn't 10 ought

3
11 don't have to get 12 weren't able to get 13 aren't allowed to park 14 you mind taking 15 'd better go

4
16 Shall 17 to 18 Why 19 must 20 should

Unit 52

52a
1 It is a big venue.
2 We stood at the front.
3 The band were brilliant.
4 The music made me happy.
5 The singer had a great voice.
6 Dan called her a natural performer.
7 I took some pictures with my phone.
8 They look great.

52b

	Subject	Verb	Object	(Object) Complement	Adverbial
0	*Dan and I*	*saw*	*a band*		*at the Dome.*
1	It	is		a big venue.	
2	We	stood			at the front.
3	The band	were		brilliant.	
4	The music	made	me	happy.	
5	The singer	had	a great voice.		
6	Dan	called	her	a natural performer.	
7	I	took	some pictures		with my phone.
8	They	look		great.	

52c
1 Don't leave 2 What 3 do not 4 your bag is 5 this is
6 lovely 7 it sounds 8 Tell

Unit 53

53a
1 to 2 for 3 for 4 for 5 to 6 for

53b
1 one to Lucy 2 one for her 3 some for her 4 them for her
5 it to Zoe 6 them to anyone 7 one for me 8 mine to a friend

53c
1 I'm cooking Ben some sausages.
2 Have you sold Jamie your bike?
3 Could you pass this note to Matt?
4 She's saving those chocolates for Kim.
5 Tom offered an old lady his seat.
6 I've found some information for you.

Unit 54

54a
1 Will they bring   2 Do you live   3 Should I tell   4 Have you been working   5 Did Jack come   6 Do we have   7 Did she send 8 Does he play (tennis)

54b
1 Where did you make   2 How long did you spend   3 How do you feel   4 What are you going to do   5 Who are you going to work with   6 Whose performances do you admire

54c
1 What   2 Which   3 Which   4 What   5 What   6 Which

54d
1 What   2 How   3 How   4 Which   5 often   6 Are

Unit 55

55a
1 Who took the money/it?
2 What fell off?
3 What can you see?
4 Who's meeting us/you?
5 What's happening?
6 Who should we tell?
7 What did he buy?
8 Who helped him?

55b
1 people came   2 money is missing   3 camera had he borrowed   4 bag/one costs £100   5 milk have we got   6 friend might join us   7 shirt/one would you like to buy   8 tickets can we get

Unit 56

56a
1 Haven't you finished yet?   2 No   3 Didn't your sister go to Highfield School?   4 Yes   5 Didn't you call Tom last night? 6 No

56b
1 Why hadn't you dressed   2 Why couldn't you answer 3 Why weren't you able to think   4 Why won't you apply 5 Why don't you want

Unit 57

57a
1 hadn't we   2 won't it   3 isn't it   4 did there   5 shall we 6 should we   7 have you   8 didn't you

57b
1 have   2 won't   3 can   4 will   5 need   6 shouldn't

57c
1 very hot, isn't it →   2 older than your cousin, aren't I →
3 starts at eight, doesn't it →   4 is a doctor, isn't she →
5 doesn't work in a bank, does she →

Unit 58

58a
1 Didn't   2 Was   3 Did   4 Will   5 Hasn't   6 Isn't

58b
1 Didn't you?   2 Have you?   3 Can't you?   4 Is he?   5 Are they? 6 Don't they?

58c
1 B   2 C   3 D   4 A   5 A   6 C

Unit 59

59a
1 so did they   2 Kirsty has too   3 neither was I   4 so will the museum   5 my brother hadn't either   6 nor did Nick   7 we do too   8 neither will Rachel

59b
1 me/I do   2 I don't   3 did I   4 was I   5 Me/I have   6 do I

59c
1 think   2 so   3 not   4 so   5 don't   6 hope

Check 11

1
1 It's become a very popular café.
2 Who wants some ice cream?
3 She cooked us a great meal.
4 What should we bring tomorrow?
5 Don't leave your dirty plate on the table.

2
6 Will   7 Haven't you   8 so   9 belongs   10 didn't   11 What 12 Does

3
13 did   14 What   15 were   16 for   17 so   18 has   19 neither/ nor   20 to

Unit 60

60a
1 thinking   2 not being   3 to move   4 to work/working 5 riding   6 making/to make   7 to help   8 not to get   9 to take 10 staying

60b
1 to have   2 cooking   3 to eat   4 to leave   5 to plan

60c
1 to do   2 to save   3 sitting   4 being   5 to become   6 to sing 7 writing/to write   8 playing

Unit 61

61a
1 to arrive   2 playing   3 adding   4 raining   5 to work   6 to take

61b
1 falling   2 to move   3 to look   4 riding   5 feeling   6 to show

61c
1 remember to book   2 forgot to tell   3 stopped having 4 forget scoring   5 try clicking   6 remember crying

Unit 62

62a
1 her to play   2 me to give   3 him to buy   4 me to phone 5 us to visit   6 her to come

62b

1 – 2 you 3 – 4 you 5 them 6 –

62c

1 made him sign 2 expected her to be 3 let her borrow 4 someone to advise 5 made everyone feel 6 lets anyone use 7 invited them to meet 8 reminded me to take

62d

1 to change 2 them to go 3 them to behave 4 to get away 5 teenagers to respect 6 them to talk 7 behave 8 watch

Unit 63

63a

1 for removing 2 to catch 3 for making 4 to recover 5 to read 6 for cleaning 7 to impress 8 for mending

63b

1 For 2 What 3 for 4 to 5 for 6 What 7 For 8 order 9 for 10 for

Unit 64

64a

1 went shopping 2 went sightseeing 3 went swimming 4 went cycling 5 went sailing 6 go hiking

64b

1 spent four hours watching 2 no good trying 3 no use feeling 4 not worth buying 5 a waste of time calling

Unit 65

65a

1 Sam was silly not to apply for it.
2 I was right to listen to Jack.
3 I was grateful to get his advice.
4 I was lucky to have some very good tutors.
5 I was sorry not to get an A in the exam.
6 I was stupid not to work hard enough.

65b

1 stupid of me not to bring 2 difficult for us to get 3 wrong of him not to help 4 impossible for ordinary people to understand 5 kind of them to invite 6 safe for children to use

Check 12

1

1 not to see 2 to look 3 borrow 4 printing 5 to use

2

6 us 7 no 8 for 9 – 10 of

3

11 afford to hire 12 stopped working 13 fancy watching 14 no use asking 15 spends hours walking

4

16 to become 17 thinking 18 working 19 me to arrange 20 to give

Unit 66

66a

1 has spent 2 are being carried out 3 disappeared 4 haven't paid 5 is going to be knocked down 6 be informed 7 will attend 8 has not been found

66b

1 was written by 2 are sold 3 is being planned 4 will be sorted out 5 can be arranged 6 wasn't taken by 7 hadn't been chosen 8 enough being done

66c

1 C 2 D 3 A 4 C 5 B 6 D

Unit 67

67a

1 have them removed 2 've had the air-conditioning checked 3 had some tables delivered 4 'm having some new equipment installed 5 had the walls painted 6 have another room added

67b

1 don't get them cleaned 2 had my application turned down 3 get that tap fixed 4 had my money stolen 5 did you get your bike repaired 6 had their electricity cut off

Check 13

1

1 was scored 2 rose 3 be examined 4 died 5 are expected

2

6 Have, had it cut 7 had/got it done 8 've just had the windows replaced 9 're having/getting some new cupboards fitted 10 're having/getting/'re going to have/'re going to get the sitting room decorated

3

11 've been given 12 printed 13 used 14 my bike fixed 15 be asked

4

16 have been proposed by 17 had their cameras stolen 18 get the computer repaired 19 was directed by 20 should have your eyes tested

Unit 68

68a

1 said (that) she hadn't been feeling well all day 2 said (that) he'd found some great trainers 3 said (that) he hadn't been looking for them 4 said (that) he was going to wear them to college 5 said (that) she hadn't seen David 6 said (that) she'd called him 7 said (that) he was staying at home 8 said (that) he didn't feel like going out 9 said (that) she was late 10 said (that) she had to be there at eight

68b

1 He said (that) they were going to have a game of football.
2 Stephen said (that) he might come too.
3 Paul said (that) they'd be in their usual place.
4 Stephen said (that) he couldn't stay long because his friends were coming at six.

5 He said (that) they were taking him to the skate park in
Burnley.
6 He said (that) he'd never been there before.
7 Paul said (that) he'd like to go to the skate park in
Manchester.
8 Stephen said (that) they could go together.

68c
1 was   2 said   3 her   4 had   5 told   6 had   7 would   8 her
9 had   10 could

Unit 69
69a
1 that   2 there, before   3 before   4 Monday   5 following
6 then   7 that   8 previous

69b
1 that afternoon   2 the day before/the previous day   3 before,
there   4 that night   5 then, the following week/the week after

Unit 70
70a
1 (that) he's exhausted   2 (that) he'll be back at six   3 (that)
the film is wonderful   4 (that) she didn't borrow Kate's
earrings   5 (that) they've never been to the theatre   6 (that)
they're going to be away next month

70b
1 bought   2 have   3 need   4 're   5 doesn't/didn't want
6 doesn't/didn't like

Unit 71
71a
1 refused to pay   2 denied starting/that he'd started
3 warned us not to go   4 accused Emma of taking
5 apologised for shouting   6 invited me to play   7 offered to
wrap   8 advised him to do

71b
1 complained that her computer is/was   2 explained that the
bus is/was   3 reminded Adam that we were   4 admitted that
he didn't/doesn't   5 promised that he would call/to call
6 denied giving/that she'd given

Unit 72
72a
1 if/whether I was/'m looking for somewhere cheap
2 if/whether his flat was/is near the city centre   3 if/whether
he could/can get there easily   4 if/whether his flat had/has
a washing machine   5 if/whether it had been very hard to
find his room   6 if/whether he'd looked at a lot of flats   7 if/
whether I'd looked on the Internet   8 if/whether I'd like to stay
with him for a few days

72b
1 us when we were going to visit them   2 to know why
everybody was looking at me   3 me what sports I did/do at
college   4 to know what her brother had decided to do
5 them how they 'd got to the beach   6 us how long we'd been
there   7 to know who wouldn't be here the following week/

the week after   8 him how much he'd paid for his ticket   9 her
how often her cousins stayed/stay with her   10 to know where
Kate was

72c
1 if/whether I lived   2 how I spent   3 how often I went
4 if/whether I went   5 how many films I saw   6 what kind of
films I liked   7 if/whether I did   8 if/whether I had

Unit 73
73a
1 to save a seat for her   2 to bring our essays on Monday
3 to stay at home for the rest of the week   4 not to tell Sarah
5 to stop fighting   6 not to be late   7 to lend him some money
8 not to be afraid of the other team   9 to pay a fine of £2,000
10 to turn the computer off

73b
1 to stay, not to   2 told, to   3 asked, to get   4 told, that I'd
5 asked, to move   6 asked, if

Unit 74
74a
1 I hope that he likes it there.
2 I know that he's still looking for a flat.
3 I think that he's sold his car.
4 I imagine that he's made new friends.
5 I realise that his career's important to him.
6 I understand that he's been very busy.

74b
1 how much it costs   2 if/whether they're going to do a tour
soon   3 where they're going to play   4 if/whether they'll be at
any of the festivals next summer   5 why their drummer left
6 if/whether they've found a new drummer yet   7 (that)
they're as good as they used to be   8 when their next CD's
coming out

74c
1 were   2 they are   3 were   4 brought   5 what

Unit 75
75a
1 how to use a drill   2 how to hold it   3 how to cut it   4 where
to put the glue   5 what colour to paint it   6 how much paint
to buy

75b
1 whether to camp   2 where to sign   3 whether to join   4 what
to bring   5 how to make   6 what time to get up   7 how to get
8 which places to visit

Check 14
1
1 they wanted to go to Oakham the following Sunday/the
Sunday after/want to go to Oakham next Sunday   2 to book
her tickets in advance   3 (that) she'd like to book two tickets
4 if/whether they can/could take their bikes on the train
5 (that) you can book your tickets by phone

2

6 how to play the guitar 7 when he had stopped playing
8 him not to buy a new guitar 9 that you can borrow my
brother's 10 to ask him that night/tonight

3

11 told 12 to do 13 he's enjoying 14 it was 15 me to
16 you'll 17 before 18 she'd 19 to 20 to take

Unit 76

76a

1 that 2 where 3 whose 4 why 5 when 6 that 7 that
8 which 9 when 10 whose

76b

1 – 2 who/that 3 – 4 – 5 who/that 6 which/that

76c

1 Here's the bus we've been waiting for.
2 I've got an idea I want to talk to you about.
3 Did you want to buy that shirt you were looking at?
4 Who was the woman Jack was speaking to?
5 I can't remember the name of the company Sarah works for.
6 Which is the shop you want to go to?
7 She's got a younger brother she complains about.
8 Have you got a friend you can depend on?

76d

1 what 2 they 3 it 4 them 5 what 6 her

Unit 77

77a

1 where 2 when 3 who 4 whose 5 which

77b

1 The River Severn, which is the longest river in Britain, goes
   through the town.
2 Charles Darwin, whose statue stands outside the library,
   was born in Shrewsbury.
3 Wilfred Owen, who was a famous poet, also lived in
   Shrewsbury.
4 The castle, which is also a museum, is on a hill above the
   town.
5 There are a lot of good restaurants, where you can enjoy a
   wide range of food.
6 The Shewsbury Flower Show, which is held every year,
   attracts a lot of visitors.

77c

1 They've got a coach who used to be a professional
   footballer.
2 I got this information from that website which you showed
   me.
3 My favourite song is *What a wonderful world*, which my
   mother used to sing to me.
4 Sam missed the last train, which left at 11 p.m.
5 He discussed it with his father, who advised him to forget
   about it.
6 What's the name of that shop which sells very cheap
   clothes?
7 He was upset about the match, which they lost 4–0.
8 They still haven't found the man who stole the painting.

Unit 78

78a

1 in/with a red shirt 2 with brain injuries 3 on the desk are
Tim's 4 with fair hair won 5 in the fridge 6 on the left is
mine

78b

1 cycling home was injured in a car accident 2 accused of
robbing an elderly woman appeared in court yesterday
3 proposed by a hotel chain have been rejected 4 travelling
to London had to wait hours in a traffic jam 5 infected by the
virus have died

78c

1 finishing 2 watching 3 to congratulate 4 wearing
5 running 6 to hurt 7 provided 8 to get

Check 15

1

1 Our flat, which is on the fifth floor, gets very hot in the
   summer.
2 Emma, whose father is an actor, is Luke's cousin.
3 The restaurant, which is very nice, is in King Street.
4 We met them in 2003, when we moved to London.
5 Tom, who's my brother's friend, is coming to stay.

2

6 who was 7 that 8 which is 9 which are 10 that

3

11 when 12 where 13 who/that 14 which 15 which/that
16 which/that 17 to 18 why/that 19 whose 20 with

Unit 79

79a

1 walk, finish 2 Do you usually play, go 3 doesn't like,
doesn't have 4 Does he get, lose/loses 5 find, look
6 don't go, don't feel 7 mix, get 8 talk, need

79b

1 're, 'll see 2 don't, won't 3 'll find, forgets 4 will, get
5 won't, don't 6 has, will

79c

1 If you need anything, just tell me.
2 I might wear my shorts if it's hot.
3 We could leave early if you feel tired.
4 If we get some fruit, we could make a fruit salad.
5 She won't remember if I don't remind her.
6 If somebody criticises you, try to listen calmly.

79d

1 'll get 2 'll refuse 3 don't say 4 will get 5 're 6 could ask
7 might not get 8 are

Unit 80

80a

1 as long as 2 providing that 3 unless 4 unless 5 in case
6 provided that

80b
1 provided (that) you water   2 as long as you promise
3 in case we're   4 unless they invite   5 providing (that) you
have

Unit 81
81a
1 would you do   2 'd get   3 went   4 broke down   5 'd be
6 wouldn't panic   7 had   8 wasn't/weren't   9 would be
10 would last

81b
1 had, would invite   2 had, could stay   3 told, might disagree
4 didn't have, wouldn't feel   5 spoke, could join   6 went,
might not like

81c
1 knew   2 'll   3 's   4 'd   5 apply   6 don't   7 would   8 would

Unit 82
82a
1 would have enjoyed   2 would have told   3 wouldn't have
found   4 'd invited   5 'd brought   6 hadn't bought

82b
1 might have scored, hadn't missed   2 hadn't been, could have
played   3 wouldn't have felt, had slept   4 might have come,
had told   5 hadn't run, could have beaten

82c
1 wouldn't have become   2 'd stayed   3 could have continued
4 'd gone   5 might not have decided

Unit 83
83a
1 wish I could move   2 wish I knew   3 wishes he didn't
have   4 wish you were   5 wish she was/were   6 wish I could
understand   7 wish I could buy   8 wish I didn't have

83b
1 hadn't agreed   2 'd asked   3 'd thought   4 hadn't left   5 had
6 'd started

Check 16
1
1 'd have phoned   2 'll/may/might go   3 do   4 was/were
5 'd had

2
6 'd put   7 work   8 knew   9 as long as   10 would you change

3
11 in case there's   12 could have watched   13 only I'd brought
14 unless you want   15 if he knew

4
16 wouldn't have gone   17 see   18 hadn't agreed   19 do
20 could understand

Unit 84
84a
1 plus   2 also   3 too   4 Both   5 also   6 either   7 too   8 neither
9 as well   10 both

84b
1 Secondly   2 What's more   3 Finally   4 too   5 In addition
6 as well as

Unit 85
85a
1 whereas Sam goes to college in London   2 Though he's older
than me, we're   3 to London every day even though he's got
a car   4 While Sam's very good at Maths   5 Biology although
I'm not

85b
1 though   2 in spite of   3 Although   4 Despite   5 Even though
6 however

85c
1 although   2 In spite of   3 however   4 Although   5 In spite of

Unit 86
86a
1 due to   2 since   3 for   4 as   5 because of

86b
1 I want to learn Spanish so that I can talk to my Spanish
   friends.
2 Let's move the table so that we can put the sofa there.
3 He bought a bike so that he could cycle to college.
4 I'll send you the programme so that you can choose which
   film you want to see.
5 We left at eleven so that we could catch the last bus home.
6 She washed her black dress so that she could wear it to the
   party.

86c
1 therefore   2 of   3 so   4 so that   5 because   6 As a result

Unit 87
87a
1 as if you haven't slept for days   2 as if you're enjoying your
course   3 as if someone's put perfume on it   4 as if they're
having a sale   5 as if it's going to rain

87b
1 as though he hadn't heard   2 as though he doesn't trust
3 as though they hadn't chosen   4 as though she can't
5 as though he doesn't want   6 as though we know

Unit 88
88a
1 I mean   2 Actually   3 In other words   4 by the way   5 Well
6 Anyhow

88b
1 Amazingly   2 Apparently   3 Interestingly   4 Unfortunately
5 Honestly   6 Obviously

Check 17

1

1 Apparently   2 Actually   3 Anyway   4 as well   5 as if

2

6 nor   7 in   8 mean   9 to   10 so

3

11 B   12 C   13 A   14 A   15 D   16 A   17 C   18 C   19 B   20 D

Unit 89

89a

1 go   2 'm looking   3 will grow   4 'm waiting   5 'll like
6 closes   7 find   8 'll get

89b

1 I've taken this skirt back, I'll look for some shoes   2 I've
looked round the shops for an hour, I'll have a coffee with
Kate   3 I've bought a present for Becky, I'll get the bus home
4 I've phoned Becky, I'll make some dinner   5 I've finished my
project, I'll watch some TV   6 I've arranged to meet my friends,
I'll get changed

89c

1 're   2 finish   3 come   4 've   5 go   6 've saved   7 'm working
8 've been

Unit 90

90a

1 D   2 A   3 D   4 C   5 B   6 A   7 C   8 D

90b

1 end   2 After   3 When   4 While   5 later/then   6 After

Check 18

1

1 B   2 B   3 C   4 D   5 A   6 A   7 D   8 C

2

9 go   10 've had   11 's staying   12 reading   13 've booked
14 come   15 leaving

3

16 to London as soon as they got/'d got married   17 visit my
brother while he's studying in Spain   18 asking me to help him
until I agreed/'d agreed   19 about ten kilometres before we
could see the sea   20 to come with us next time we go
ice-skating

Unit 91

91a

1 in   2 near   3 at   4 in   5 in   6 at/near/in front of   7 between
8 on, under/below, on   9 on   10 in

91b

1 along   2 through   3 into   4 across   5 towards   6 into

91c

1 in   2 in   3 at   4 the university   5 hospital   6 the hospital

Unit 92

92a

1 in   2 at   3 on   4 at   5 On

92b

1 in   2 at   3 In   4 In   5 in   6 on

92c

1 after   2 at   3 past   4 –   5 since   6 in   7 by   8 until

92d

1 for   2 for   3 during   4 for   5 during

Unit 93

93a

1 as   2 as   3 like   4 like   5 as

93b

1 as   2 like   3 as   4 like   5 as

93c

1 What does, taste like   2 What did, sound like   3 What did,
look like   4 What does, smell like   5 What are, like

Unit 94

94a

1 for   2 in   3 on   4 out of   5 by   6 at   7 from   8 in   9 by   10 on

94b

1 on time   2 on purpose   3 by accident   4 in a hurry   5 in time
6 by credit card   7 in cash

94c

1 B   2 A   3 D   4 C   5 A   6 D   7 D   8 B

Check 19

1

1 to the school   2 as   3 on   4 in   5 at

2

6 A   7 B   8 B   9 C   10 D

3

11 towards   12 by   13 before   14 out of   15 along

4

16 at   17 in/for   18 –   19 on   20 in

Unit 95

95a

1 with   2 in   3 about   4 about   5 at

95b

1 about   2 making   3 to   4 on   5 with

Unit 96

96a

1 with   2 for   3 about   4 in   5 from

96b

1 broke into   2 Do, feel like   3 think about   4 dealt with
5 introduce you to   6 ask you about

Unit 97
97a
1 stay in 2 broke down 3 got back 4 get up 5 carry on
6 lie down
97b
1 make it up 2 call the performance off/call off the
performance 3 throw these old pens away/throw away these
old pens 4 leave her out 5 filled in my form yet/filled my
form in yet 6 brought it up 7 turned up at 7.30 8 wrote her
name down/wrote down her name (on a piece of paper)

Unit 98
98a
1 with 2 to 3 with 4 up 5 down
98b
1 get out of 2 put up with 3 ran out of 4 cut down on
5 get on with 6 get back to

Check 20
1
1 C 2 A 3 C 4 D 5 B
2
6 turned up 7 looking forward to 8 get out of doing 9 slow
down 10 put up with
3
11 with 12 out 13 about 14 down 15 up
4
16 for 17 between 18 to 19 about 20 at

Unit 99
99a
1 low 2 best 3 modern 4 fast 5 ready
99b
1 C 2 A 3 D 4 B 5 B 6 D

Unit 100
100a
1 ir 2 il 3 dis 4 mis 5 im
100b
1 unlock 2 irresponsible 3 Illiteracy 4 underachieve
5 mismanage

Unit 101
101a
1 useless 2 exciting 3 enjoyable 4 stylish 5 amazed
101b
1 traditional 2 scientific 3 religious 4 painful 5 dangerous
6 effective 7 infectious

Unit 102
102a
1 kindness 2 warmth 3 generosity 4 meanness
5 insensitivity 6 impatience 7 irresponsibility
102b
1 competition 2 performance 3 student 4 musician
5 encouragement

Check 21
1
1 interesting 2 sculptor 3 helpful 4 childish 5 stressful
2
6 under 7 in 8 dis 9 mis 10 ir
3
11 old-fashioned 12 well-known 13 short-term
14 long-distance 15 fast-moving
4
16 novelist 17 employment 18 productive 19 depression
20 death